SEX, LOVE, & ROMANCE IN THE MASS MEDIA

Analysis & Criticism
of Unrealistic Portrayals & Their Influence

Dr. Mary-Lou Galician
Walter Cronkite School of Journalism & Mass Communication
Arizona State University

2004

LAWRENCE ERLBAUM ASSOCIATES, PUBLISHERS
Mahwah, New Jersey   London

Desktop Publisher & Designer: *Janet Soper*

The focus of this publication is, as the title clearly states, media analysis and criticism. It is designed to provide accurate and authoritative information in regard to the subject matter covered. It is presented with the understanding that the author is not engaging in rendering psychological, medical, or other related professional services. If you need expert assistance or counseling, you should seek the services of a competent professional.

Library of Congress Cataloging-in-Publication Data
Galician, Mary-Lou.
Sex. Love & romance in the mass media : analysis & criticism
of unrealistic portrayals & their influence / Mary-Lou Galician.
p. cm.
Includes bibliographical references and index.
ISBN 0-8058-4832-0 (pbk. : alk. paper)
1. Man-woman relationships. 2. Love in mass media. 3. Sex in mass media.
I. Title: Sex, love, and romance in the mass media.   II. Title.
HQ801.G273   2004
306.7—dc22
2003058419
CIP
Books published by Lawrence Erlbaum Associates are printed on acid-free paper,
and their bindings are chosen for strength and durability.

Printed in the United States of America
10 9 8 7 6 5 4 3 2 1

SEX, LOVE, & ROMANCE IN THE MASS MEDIA

LEA's COMMUNICATION SERIES
Jennings Bryant/Dolf Zillmann, General Editors

Selected titles in Mass Communication (Alan Rubin, Advisory Editor) include:

Alexander/Owers/Carveth/Hollifield/Greco • Media Economics: Theory and Practice, Third Edition

Bryant/Bryant • Television and the American Family, Second Edition

Harris • A Cognitive Psychology of Mass Communication, Third Edition

Kundanis • Children, Teens, Families, and Mass Media: The Millennial Generation

Moore • Mass Communication Law and Ethics, Second Edition

Palmer/Young • The Faces of Televisual Media: Teaching, Violence, Selling to Children, Second Edition

Perse • Media Effects and Society

Van Evra • Television and Child Development, Second Edition

For a complete list of titles in LEA's Communication Series, please contact Lawrence Erlbaum Associates, Publishers

FOR
students, educators, and media literacy advocates
who asked for a textbook like this.

STOP!

Before you begin

to read this book,

take

Dr. FUN's

Mass Media Love Quiz©

on the next page.

DR. FUN'S MASS MEDIA LOVE QUIZ©

Created by Dr. Mary-Lou Galician

Answer TRUE (T) or FALSE (F) to each statement to indicate your own personal belief:

___ 1. Your perfect partner is cosmically predestined, so nothing/nobody can ultimately separate you.

___ 2. There's such a thing as "love at first sight."

___ 3. Your true soul mate should KNOW what you're thinking or feeling without your having to tell.

___ 4. If your partner is truly meant for you, sex is easy and wonderful.

___ 5. To attract and keep a man, a woman should look like a model or a centerfold.

___ 6. The man should NOT be shorter, weaker, younger, poorer, or less successful than the woman.

___ 7. The love of a good and faithful true woman can change a man from a "beast" into a "prince."

___ 8. Bickering and fighting a lot mean that a man and a woman really love each other passionately.

___ 9. All you really need is love, so it doesn't matter if you and your lover have very different values.

___10. The right mate "completes you" — filling your needs and making your dreams come true.

___11. In real life, actors and actresses are often very much like the romantic characters they portray.

___12. Since mass media portrayals of romance aren't "real," they don't really affect you.

ABOUT YOUR ANSWERS[1]

handwritten: Conclusion / Solution

All 12 statements in my *Dr. FUN's Mass Media Love Quiz* are myths and stereotypes perpetuated by the mass media, so I hope you answered "FALSE" to all of them. The *Quiz* is based on my research of what I call "The Romanticization of Love in the Mass Media" — examining what we learn about sex, love, and romance from the mass media and how these portrayals affect us. It's an issue that I am most passionate about — not only professionally but also personally. And it's an issue that affects everyone — men and women, young children and seniors, singles and couples.

If you answered "TRUE" to some of the myths in the *Quiz*, don't worry: You're like most people who take it. The problem is that while most of us "know" the "right" responses to the *Quiz* items, we still "believe" (or want to believe!) the unrealistic ones our popular culture presents to us. Consciously or subconsciously, we want some of them to be true.

From the time we're very young, we're barraged with fairy-tale depictions and hard-to-break stereotypes of sex, love, and romance in the popular culture — movies and television, books and magazines, radio and recorded music, advertising, and even the news. Mass media are very powerful socialization agents that rely on simplification, distortions of reality, and dramatic symbols and stereotypes to communicate their messages, so we shouldn't feel too bad if we wind up with some unrealistic expectations.

Unfortunately, "false-love" images and scripts of coupleship put pressure on *both* women and men to measure up to media-myth "P.C." — *Playboy* Centerfolds or Prince Charmings. Some media-constructed unrealistic expectations can lead to depression and other dysfunctions, and several can be downright dangerous.

So, What Can We Do?

We've got to "*dis*-illusion" ourselves. I know that's not easy. I myself was a casualty of the mass media's deluge of delusions, and that's why I began my work to resist our inadvertent adoption of these damaging images and our unwitting concession to them.

It's important to consider how mass media portrayals at the least reinforce (if not create) unrealistic expectations that most of us (if we're honest) can't dismiss completely. It's smart to become aware of our unhealthy views. Then we must learn how to analyze and critique them and how to reframe them more constructively.

The 12 mass media myths about love in the *Quiz* have 12 related counteracting *Dr. Galician's Prescriptions™ for Getting Real About Romance* (see Chapter 3), based on my research and personal experience as well as the scholarly literature and the advice of other specialists, including my husband, Dr. David Natharius, a gender communication expert.

Should We Avoid Sex, Love, & Romance in the Mass Media Entirely?

We can still enjoy the metaphoric meanings and the "escape" that unrealistic romantic media portrayals offer us, but it's not wise to use them — or media celebrities — as models in our real lives. It's much healthier and smarter to make yourself the hero or heroine of your own true love story.

My Ultimate Advice: "Get Real!"

This book will teach you how.

My life changed dramatically and delightfully once I became aware of the mass media myths in *Dr. FUN's Mass Media Love Quiz* and developed *Dr. Galician's Prescriptions™ for Getting Real About Romance*. When I was finally and for the first time "romantically realistic," I met and married David, with whom I enjoy a genuinely *realistic romance*! In fact, we created and conduct *Realistic Romance™* seminars and workshops to share our research and experience with singles and couples as well as with parents. (I strongly advise parents to begin "media literacy" training of even very young children from the time they become media consumers.) Hundreds of students have taken my Sex, Love, & Romance in the Mass Media course. And, although I'm now known as the nation's "Realistic Romance Guru," my life has ironically turned into a *happily-ever-after* story. These guidelines have worked for me — and I know they can work for *YOU*.

---

[1]Adapted from *Dr. Galician's Prescriptions™ for Getting Real About Romance: How Mass Media Myths About Love Can Hurt You.*

ABOUT THE AUTHOR

DR. MARY-LOU GALICIAN (*The Original "Dr. FUN"!*) is an award-winning researcher, educator, and performer with more than 25 years of mass media experience. She's Head of the Media Analysis & Criticism Concentration in the Walter Cronkite School of Journalism & Mass Communication at Arizona State University in Tempe, where thousands of students have learned how to be media literate in her popular classes.

Photo by Chrys Gakopoulos

An entertainer, media personality, and published writer since childhood, she attended the famous Professional Children's School in New York City. She has held positions as a newspaper columnist, book editor, nighttime television talk-show host/producer, and special events anchor, as well as national executive posts in advertising, marketing, and public relations. She earned her doctorate at Memphis State University (now University of Memphis). The Outstanding Americans Foundation honored her as Woman of the Year, and her biography is published in *Who's Who in America, Who's Who in the World,* and *Who's Who in Entertainment.*

"Dr. FUN" is the creator and presenter of *FUN-dynamics!® — The FUN-damentals of DYNAMIC Living,* a musical motivation program that helps people generate energy and enthusiasm, balance success and happiness, and beat burn-out, the blues, and the bad news, so they can get "F – U – N" — her acronym for "Fired Up Now!"

Dr. Galician served as the founding national Vice Head and Program Chair of the Entertainment Studies Interest Group (ESIG) of the Association for Education in Journalism and Mass Communication (AEJMC), for which she created and moderated *Washington Goes Hollywood: The New Role of Entertainment Media in Politics,* televised nationally by C-SPAN and archived at the Freedom Foundation's Newseum. She created and headed Media Forums for the National Communication Association (NCA), and she also served on the national Board of Directors of Women in Communications, Inc. (WICI). She directed the research project, *Good News and Bad News on Television: The American Dream and the Media Nightmare.* She was guest editor of a special edition of the *Journal of Promotion Management* devoted to product placement in the mass media, and she is the editor of *Cue the Soda Can: Product Placement in the Mass Media* (Best Books).

From her extensive research of what she calls "The Romanticization of Love in the Mass Media," she created *Dr. FUN's Mass Media Love Quiz* and *Dr. Galician's Prescriptions™ for Getting Real About Romance,* which she has shared via national television, radio, newspapers, and magazines as well as at scholarly conferences and on her websites. Each year on February 14, she announces her *Dr. FUN's Stupid Cupid & Realistic Romance™ Awards* for media portrayals of sex, love, and romance, and she herself has been called the nation's "Realistic Romance Guru." Hundreds of students have already taken her new course — Sex, Love, & Romance in the Mass Media, for which she wrote this textbook. Her tradebook for the general public, *Dr. Galician's Prescriptions™ for Getting Real About Romance: How Mass Media Myths About Love Can Hurt You,* will be available soon.

Dr. Galician is happily married to Dr. David Natharius, a professor emeritus of communication, humanities, and visual media. Together, they conduct *Realistic Romance™* seminars and workshops.

DR. GALICIAN WOULD ENJOY HEARING FROM YOU.
Email her at DrFUN@asu.edu or DrFUN@RealisticRomance.com.
You can also write to her at the Cronkite School:
PO Box 871305, Tempe, AZ 85287-1305.

FOR MORE INFORMATION VISIT HER WEBSITES:
http://www.asu.edu/cronkite/faculty/galician/drfun/
or
www.RealisticRomance.com.

CONTENTS AT A GLANCE

CONTENTS

CHAPTER 2. IDEALS & ILLUSIONS (UNREALISTIC MODELS)
Myths & Stereotypes of Love & Coupleship 33

CHAPTER 3. DIAGNOSES & *DIS*-ILLUSIONS (REALISTIC MODELS)
Designs for Rational Love & Coupleship 53

CHAPTER 4. MASS MEDIA NARRATIVE CONSTRUCTIONS
Mass Media Storytelling Approaches, Techniques, & Devices 67

CHAPTER 5. THE INFLUENCE OF THE MASS MEDIA
Research & Theories of Mass Media Effects on Individuals & Society 81

CHAPTER 6. STRATEGIES & SKILLS OF MEDIA LITERACY
Tools for Media Analysis & Criticism 99

PART II
Applications of Analysis & Criticism
of Sex, Love, & Romance in the Mass Media 115

CHAPTER 7. *DR. FUN'S MASS MEDIA LOVE QUIZ* MYTH #1
Your perfect partner is cosmically predestined, so nothing/nobody can ultimately separate you. 119

CHAPTER 8. *DR. FUN'S MASS MEDIA LOVE QUIZ* MYTH #2
There's such a thing as "love at first sight." 127

CHAPTER 9. *DR. FUN'S MASS MEDIA LOVE QUIZ* MYTH #3
Your true soul mate should KNOW what you're thinking or feeling (without your having to tell). 135

PREFACE

Why I Wrote This Book for You

I wrote this book because in 2002 I created and began teaching a new course — Sex, Love, & Romance in the Mass Media — for the Media Analysis & Criticism concentration that I head at Arizona State University's Walter Cronkite School of Journalism & Mass Communication.

For years, students in my Mass Media & Society class at ASU have completed a learning module about mass media stereotypes that incorporates my research of what I've termed "The Romanticization of Love in the Mass Media," centered around the 12 mass media love myths and stereotypes in *Dr. FUN's Mass Media Love Quiz*. Year after year, these students tell me that this module is very effective and very important for them both as media consumers and as young people in relationships. It has been eye-opening for many students who are planning careers *in* the mass media. And, over the years, a number of graduate students have asked me to direct their master's thesis research designed around my studies.

The *Quiz* has also been published in a featured byline essay I was invited to write for McGraw-Hill's best-selling textbook *Mass Media/Mass Culture* by James Wilson and Stan Wilson, and I've presented it at national conferences and on national television, so professors around the country have used the *Quiz* with their classes and have rated it highly as a valuable tool in media analysis and criticism.

Every time I do a presentation about The Romanticization of Love in the Mass Media, people ask if I've written a book they can buy — so I wrote ***Dr. Galician's Prescriptions™ for Getting Real About Romance: How Mass Media Myths About Love Can Hurt You***, a "self-help" book to show people how to de-mythify mass media stereotypes that cultivate unrealistic expectations and dissatisfaction with their own real-life romantic relationships as well as how to become romantically realistic *and* realistically romantic. Although it's geared to adults and adolescents, it also offers parents and teachers tips for "media literacy" training of children from the time that they become media consumers.

But that book is a *tradebook* for the general public rather than a textbook for students.

For the university course, I needed a book with a more academic approach, covering both **foundational theories and practical applications** of analysis and criticism of mass media portrayals of sex, love, and romance. Having reviewed the literature of this field very thoroughly, I discovered no one had written either a textbook or a tradebook that covered analysis and criticism of these portrayals in *all the mass media*. A few books cover images of women, and a few even cover images of men — but if *couples* are covered it's only in a few of the mass media, and usually it's only in *one* medium: movies, or romance novels, or television soap operas, for example.

I realized *I* had to write the textbook for my new course — and for students, educators, and media literacy advocates who had been asking for it. This book is dedicated to you.

ACKNOWLEDGMENTS

Whenever I research, write, present, or teach about what I've termed "The Romanticization of Love in the Mass Media," I'm always keenly aware and deeply appreciative of the many others who have helped me with this "mission" over the past several years, especially —

- My late beloved and magnificent mother, Evelyn-Nancy Galician — my first and foremost teacher of Love and a true artist and a courageous realist whose magnificent spirit constantly surrounds and supports me;

- "Former romantic partner" whose insightful comment triggered my adoption of this line of study in a moment of epiphany (see Introduction);

- "Lewis Carroll" [Charles Dodgson] for "my" *Alice* and Stephen Sondheim for *Into the Woods* (either of which inspirational classics I wish *I* had written!);

- Scholars and gurus whose work I respect and whose ideas are foundational to my own, especially Dr. Albert Ellis, Dr. Harville Hendrix, Dr. Stan Katz and his coauthor Aimee Liu, Dr. Arnold Lazarus, Dr. Pepper Schwartz, Dr. Judith Sills, and Dr. Robert Sternberg;

- Colleagues at ASU and other universities and institutions who graciously provided their time and talent to help me launch my research, especially Effie Baker, Dr. Norman Epstein, Dr. Carol Heady, Dr. Mary Laner (whose in-depth, expert commentary on an earlier version of this manuscript was invaluable), Dr. Gary Warren Melton, Kathy Nagel, Dr. Joan Shapiro, and Dr. Thelma Shinn — and the financial support of Dean's Incentive Grants from ASU's College of Public Programs;

- Graduate Assistants Chris Anderson, Karla Gower, Donna Goyette, Amber Hutchins, Susan Kilgard, Niels Marslev, Lacey Phelps, and Adriana Robles; and Master of Mass Communication research mentees Sandra Adler, Rebecca Crotts, Karen Emery, Denise Estfan, Abbie Fink, Andrea Gerdes, Jen Hays, Christina Hecht, Susan Kilgard, Jyothi Sampat, Jennifer Shimkus — all of whom were delightful associates and hard workers with special insights;

- Research participants around the country and the world who volunteered their personal reports and perceptions (young and old; men and women; couples and singles), especially experts Dr. Elaine Katzman, Dr. William Mermis, and Dr. Nancy Signorielli — and special thanks to Karol Householder at ASU's Institutional Review Board/Human Subjects Committee for her always gracious assistance in assuring the highest ethical standards and to Mary Fran Draisker for her fastidious and faithful transcription of my interviews;

- Audiences at my formal academic presentations (AEJMC, NCA, OSCLG, PCA, and WSCA), my lectures for schools and for the general public, and my *Realistic Romance*™ Seminars and Workshops who enthusiastically responded to me and to my "mission"; web friends who discovered my work and my site and asked for more — and those dear people who spotted me in airports after seeing me on TV and encouraged me to get a book ready for them *and* for their sons and daughters;

- Students in my Sex, Love, & Romance in the Mass Media class as well as those in my Mass Media & Society class and Research Methodology for Mass Communication class — who always stimulate me with their great ideas and interpretations;

- Special advocates who were instrumental in my own realistic romance and marriage — especially Dr. Carol Valentine, who invited me to moderate my first formal research panel on this subject at my first national Organization for the Study of Communication, Language, and Gender conference (where I first met my husband, Dr. David Natharius!) and all our OSCLG "fairy godmothers"; Greg Ceman of British Airways, whose generous donation of their First Class Lounge for our wedding and our upgrade on their flight did indeed "give our love wings"; The Reverend William Forrest, who is a model of the wholesome realist with inspiring ideals; Sue Kern, consummate public relations professional, who managed the media who covered our "Whirlwind Wedding"; and the 30 participants on the Cultural & Performing Arts Travel Study David and I led, who joined us on our honeymoon in London and Paris;

- Mass media writers and broadcast hosts who interviewed me and cited my work (especially the very talented Sherry Arpaio, Amanda Kingsbury, and Jamie Rose); the savvy producer of ABC-TV's *Mike & Maty Show,* for which I created my original 8-item *Dr. FUN's Mass Media Love Quiz;* the producers and crew of LIFETIME Cable Television's *New Attitudes Show,* who came from Los Angeles to my home in Phoenix to interview me;

- The wonderful Wilson brothers (Dr. Stan and Jim) and their excellent editor Valerie Raymond, formerly of McGraw-Hill, who published earlier versions of my 10-item and current 12-item *Dr. FUN's Mass Media Love Quiz* in my byline essay (in their best-selling *Mass Media/Mass Culture* textbook), which evolved into this textbook as well as into my tradebook, *Dr. Galician's Prescriptions™ for Getting Real About Romance: How Mass Media Myths About Love Can Hurt You;*

- Barbara Ricketts (Lifestyle Management Associates of Santa Clarita, CA) — phenomenal professional organizer and dear friend who miraculously helped me clear sufficient space on my home office workstation — and in my mind — and find a "home" for my piles of research data and other paperwork;

- Julie Knapp (Higher Ground Training & Development of Chandler, AZ) — software training guru and special friend who taught me how to make the most of my computer *and* made it so much FUN;

- Stan Wakefield — gallant agent who championed this project;

- Linda Bathgate — gracious and knowledgeable Erlbaum communication editor who shared my passion and beliefs about this project and whose excellent suggestions are always accompanied by the sunniest smiles;

- Dr. Alan Rubin — mass communication legend and Erlbaum series editor whose inspiration and advice were invaluable;

- Publisher's reviewers — whose insights were stellar, leading me to include additional aspects that enhanced the book;

- Janet Soper — publication designer and web wizard who makes reality of my visions, editor extraordinaire who shares a mental shorthand with me, and dear friend who never fails to "be there";

- Dr. David Natharius — (last but *most!*) "Dr.-*Mr.*-Dr. FUN," touchstone of the authenticity of my work and my life; my "Arts *and* Science Project"; my true soul mate and genuine partner; my marvelous mass media maven and incredibly creative coproducer of the video versions of my *Quiz;* outstanding chef who tirelessly prepared our superb suppers while I was writing this book around the clock; and the Love of my life with whom I laugh 'til the tears roll down my cheeks, with whom I joyfully "walk my talk," and with whom romance is healthily *realistic* and reality is gloriously *romantic*!

SEX, LOVE, & ROMANCE IN THE MASS MEDIA

INTRODUCTION

"The Romanticization of Love in the Mass Media"

Losing an illusion makes you wiser than finding a truth.
— Ludwig Borne, 19th-century German political writer

Because I've been a professional journalist and mass communicator since I was a child, I've also been a researcher nearly all my life — well before I left the media business and got my doctorate and began teaching media analysis & criticism and research methodology. Perhaps the word that captures all these job titles is *investigator*. Whenever I consider the reports of mass media communicators or the research findings of scholars or the advice of self-help experts, I want to know their background. I want to know their personal experience and bias as well as their professional credentials and expertise.

My question always is: "Who *is* this person who's trying to change my thoughts, feelings, and actions?"

As a media literacy advocate, I believe it's vital that mass media consumers know and evaluate not only the credentials and content but also the viewpoints and assumptions of mass media creators (including textbook authors) whose messages they utilize. That's why I make it a point to disclose that information to my students, colleagues, audiences, and readers — even if it's more than they might want at the time. I hope the following details about me, my research, and my philosophy will help you to place this book in perspective.

WHY I BEGAN MY FORMAL RESEARCH OF SEX, LOVE, & ROMANCE IN THE MASS MEDIA

I began my formal study and public presentation of what I have termed "**The Romanticization of Love in the Mass Media**" in 1992 (just a year before I met my husband) because of my own personal romantic failures. Although I was considered smart and successful in other aspects of my life and enjoyed the companionship of a great many wonderful friends, I must tell you that for most of my life I myself was romantically *un*realistic (and *really un*successful in romance).

In a life-changing moment, this point was driven home to me. Yet another of my disastrous romantic relationships had just ended. I was in my mid-40s but still clueless and unhappy. During a late-night soul-searching phone conversation (I'm glad it wasn't face-to-face!), a former romantic partner — who had become a pal after we'd dated briefly — hesitantly informed me:

> Mary-Lou, your problem is that you're looking for a knight-in-shining-armor, but no man in his right mind would ever think of YOU as a damsel-in-distress!

I was both flattered and furious, but his comment turned on a lightbulb for me! I realized that *he was right*:

- even though I'd had an incredibly strong, heroic, and successful mother as a realistic role model ...,

- even though I had held a variety of exciting high-level mass media positions and had been a respected university professor for many years ...,

- even though I had a great life filled with lots of good friends ...,

I had nevertheless been waiting for a Prince Charming straight out of a Walt Disney movie to come and rescue me (Don't ask, "From what?") so I could live "happily-ever-after — THE END!" *(Cue the violins and let the music swell. Fade out and roll credits.)*

What Was Missing from the Research Literature

Looking for answers, I talked to friends and experts, and I read countless books and research articles about romantic relationships. I was intrigued by how frequently the problem of "unrealistic romantic expectations" was mentioned, and I was particularly struck by how often the *blame* for these unrealistic expectations was ascribed to my own field of expertise — the mass media. Yet even in the most serious writings, practically *none* of these accusers had conducted or even cited any research to support their indictments.

Well, this subject of study was right down my alley: For 20 years, through my popular "Mass Media & Society" class in the Walter Cronkite School of Journalism & Mass Communication at Arizona State University, I've taught thousands of students across the entire university how to be "media literate" — how to be wise, aware consumers of mass media. And, for years, through my musical motivation program *FUN-dynamics!*® — *The FUN-damentals of DYNAMIC Living,* I've shown people nationwide how to be the successful *and* happy "super-stars" of their own true lives.

I knew then (passionately) that from the ashes of my own romantic failures could rise a research-based remedy for myself and for others. And I vowed to devote myself to this quest. (You can see that I was still pretty romantic, but I was about to embark on the journey to reality.)

I figured that if I held such unrealistic beliefs — despite my very *un*stereotypical role model of a mother and my own unusual life — then other people might have the same or even more trouble. And because of the dearth of data about this topic, I started my own scholarly study to find answers to my own questions and to help others. Many of my graduate students and undergraduate honors students have joined me in conducting my ongoing research. Thousands of participants have provided me with invaluable information.

In 1995 I directed several large surveys with hundreds of male and female Baby Boomers and Generation Xers to learn how mass media portrayals affect our expectations and satisfactions of romantic love. From the thousands of research programs at my university in the Fall of 1995, ABC-TV selected mine to feature on their national morning television talk show — on location from our campus. To more easily communicate my scholarly studies to a national television audience and to help viewers assess their "romantic realism," I created my ***Dr. FUN's Mass Media Love Quiz***. It was an instant hit!

The following year, with my *Quiz* as the core, I expanded my research to in-depth personal interviews with males and females from 3 years of age to 103 years old as well as with media producers, relationship experts, and marital therapists. Students in my classes and colleagues around the country have shared their personal stories[1] with me, as have members of the public.

I've learned a lot!

What My Research Found

Bottom-line: Higher usage of certain mass media is related to unrealistic expectations about coupleship, and these unrealistic expectations are also related to dissatisfaction in real-life romantic relationships. Specific mass media are associated with a greater level of unrealistic expectation and related dissatisfaction.

I'll share the details of my research findings with you in Chapter 5 as well as at the relevant points in each of the 12 chapters of Part II of this book, but here's **a key factor** that I learned about myself that I have found applies to a great many other people: I now realize that no matter what I "knew" in my higher mind about love and romance, my "primitive brain" was conditioned by those Walt Disney full-length feature cartoons — *Snow White* and *Cinderella* — that I saw on a huge movie screen as a little girl and read over and over again in my impressively illustrated *Little Golden Books* editions. (We didn't have VCRs or DVDs back then.)

Even though it's the woman's story and she's the "star," she's either unconscious during most of it or stuck in the kitchen talking to mice until the very end of her story when she has to be rescued — by a prince she doesn't even know — so she can live *happily-ever-after*. And the poor prince: He's no better off. Look what's expected of *him* in every story. (Of course, he only has to rescue damsels who are beautiful and virtuous.)

This pathetic phenomenon is not something that happens only to females. It affects males, too. In *The Celluloid Closet*, movie star (and father of Jamie Lee Curtis) Tony Curtis acknowledged:

> The movies were part of my life. Movies are part of everyone's life. That's where we learn about life. Watching Cary Grant taught me how to behave with a woman.

Like Tony and me, most people learn a lot about coupleship from the mass media, starting in childhood when we watch TV, go to movies, listen to recorded music, and read comic books. However, the mass media rarely present models of healthy, realistic romance and love.

The problem is that our unrealistic expectations about romance can make us very dissatisfied with the *reality* of our lives, including our partners — even if they really *are* princes and princesses: Just look at the tragic "love story" of poor Prince Charles and Lady Diana.

Here's what you can do: Resolve to analyze the mythic and stereotyped portrayals of the mass media, resist their seductive and hazardous influence, and begin living a *real* love story — your own.

---

[1]You'll read some of these in Part II of this textbook.

And, of course, if you are planning a career in the mass media, you can create healthier portrayals of sex, love, and romance.

This book will show you how.

WHAT THIS BOOK OFFERS YOU

This textbook, whose focus is media analysis and criticism, is centered around the 12 major myths and stereotypes of *Dr. FUN's Mass Media Love Quiz* and the 12 corresponding *Dr. Galician's Prescriptions™* that encapsulate healthy strategies to counteract the myths and stereotypes (see Chapter 3).

The Purpose of This Book

The primary purpose of this book is to help you identify, illustrate, deconstruct, evaluate, and reframe the mass media's mythic and stereotypic portrayals of sex, love, and romance. It will also help you to use your own formal critical evaluations to clarify your own values and — as a media consumer or mass communication creator — to share your insights with others.

Thus, the **learning objectives** of this book (and most courses for which it's used) encompass all three major educational domains: **cognitive** (thoughts or perceptions), **affective** (emotions or values), and **behavioral** (actions).

The Plan of This Book

Part I of this book, which begins with an overview of **key foundational terms and concepts** (Chapter 1), covers the basics of what I call **the five foundations** of analysis and criticism of unrealistic portrayals of sex, love, and romance in the mass media and their influence on individuals and society:

- **myths and stereotypes of love and coupleship** that have given rise to unrealistic models based on ideals and illusions (Chapter 2);
- **models of realistic and constructive love and coupleship** recommended in the social psychology literature and endorsed by cognitive-behavioral coupleship therapists (Chapter 3);
- **mass media story-telling approaches, techniques, and devices** that frame narrative constructions of sex, love, and romance in both print and electronic forms of entertaining, informative, and persuasive messages (Chapter 4);
- **research and theories of mass media effects** on individuals and society (Chapter 5);
- **strategies and skills of media literacy** that constitute the tools for media analysis and criticism (Chapter 6).

Part II centers on **applications** of these foundations. Each of these 12 chapters focuses on one of the 12 major mass-mediated myths and stereotypes synthesized as *Dr. FUN's Mass Media Love Quiz*. To conduct your analyses and criticisms of unrealistic portrayals of sex, love, and romance in the mass media, you'll follow **Dr. Galician's Seven-Step *Dis*-illusioning Directions** *(Detection-Description-Deconstruction-Diagnosis-Design-Debriefing-Dissemination)*. These seven steps help you to discover if and how the mass media *manifest* these myths and stereotypes, to determine what you think and feel about the portrayals, and to design more realistic ones.

Guiding the criticisms and reconstructions of the 12 myths are corresponding strategies for healthy, realistic coupleship (rarely presented by the mass media) — advice from the social psychology and therapeutic literature synthesized as the 12 *Dr. Galician's Prescriptions™ for Getting Real About Romance.* (There's a *Prescription™* for each myth in the *Quiz.*) We'll examine these mass media manifestations in the content not only of entertainment but also of news and advertising across a wide variety of media: novels, magazines, newspapers, comics, movies and animated features, television, radio, and popular music.

The Epilogue offers some final thoughts about the influence of unrealistic portrayals of sex, love, and romance in the mass media and advocates your continuing analysis and criticism of them — personally, publicly, and professionally.

The book has wide "scholar's margins" so you can make notes as you go along.

The Philosophy of This Book

As I explained earlier, I believe authors have an ethical obligation to disclose their philosophy to their readers, so I offer you mine *before* you begin studying this book.

My Methodological Perspective

My **methodological perspective**, which is multidisciplinary, embraces a variety of traditions along the so-called quantitative-qualitative continuum. Although some of the researchers, analysts, and critics I cite in this book speak from the feminist tradition and from the cultural/critical studies tradition, and although some of their ideas inform some of my work (which could be regarded as mythic analysis and sociocultural critique), I myself am neither a feminist scholar nor a cultural critic. I was trained as a literary analyst, as a journalist and mass communicator, and as a social scientist. My work, which centers on mass media effects research and media literacy education, reflects my training and experience.

While I can certainly be considered a *feminist*[2] with total allegiance to the aim of sexual equity and peer coupleships (which I believe are in the best interest of *both* sexes), I nevertheless prefer to describe myself as a ***personist*** — a term I coined to express my passionate aim and continual effort to extend equal respect, dignity, and opportunity to *all persons* without regard to their sex. It is my belief that unrealistic portrayals of sex, love, and romance adversely affect males to the same degree as they affect females. I do not tolerate "male-bashing." Males who attend my programs and participate in my courses and classroom modules on The Romanticization of Love in the Mass Media are as interested in this topic as the females.

Because this book reflects my research and teaching expertise, it focuses on **heterosexual relationships** in Western (primarily American) culture. However, it is not meant to exclude same-sex or non-Western culture close relationships, to which its applicability might extend.

---

[2]Be aware that this term has a great variety of meanings and represents a broad diversity of beliefs and behaviors — despite the stereotypic views often perpetuated by the mass media.

My Precepts

Clearly, my book — like my teaching — advocates my public and personal philosophy about the potential damage of unrealistic (mythic and stereotyped) portrayals of sex, love, and romance in the mass media as well as my convictions about the importance of media literacy in general and media analysis and criticism in particular. Because I believe these viewpoints will make your life healthier and happier, I will strongly encourage you to adopt them. Here they are:

- **Our mass media are powerful influencers of society and individuals.** While we're not all influenced by everything all the time, even those of us who like to believe that we're beyond media influence can't escape it. We certainly don't have to be slaves to this influence. Keep in mind that the first step toward freedom is awareness of domination (see Mass Media Myth #12).

- **Ignorance is *never* "bliss."** Being clueless about how the mass media work and influence us and believing in fantasies about sex, love, and romance limit our options and, therefore, our freedom to choose what's best for ourselves. It's ignorant to imagine that knowledge and skill will diminish your appreciation for and enjoyment of the mass media or of love. In both domains, however, what you don't know *will* hurt you, so being uninformed is both foolish and dangerous. As a mass communicator and as an educator, I believe nothing is as important as opening our minds and our hearts to becoming the best that we can be. And that means taking personal responsibility for personal growth.

- **Media literacy is a vital strategy and skill for everyone** — from very young children to the most senior adults. Used wisely, mass media can offer us enlightenment and enhancement. I certainly don't recommend doing without them. However, we should strive for higher and higher levels of media literacy to *empower ourselves to resist undue and unthinking media influence* — intentional or not — that can be damaging to us as individuals and as a society. We have many more options when we are active rather than passive consumers of the mass media, maintaining awareness and control of our thoughts, feelings, and behaviors rather than being misled and manipulated. *(Please note that media literacy education is internationally endorsed by a wide variety of parent, educational, medical, and religious groups.)*

- **We can be critical *and* constructive — and *still* enjoy the mass media.** We can use the tools of media literacy to become critical mass media consumers *without* sacrificing the many benefits the mass media bring us, including our pure enjoyment of them. In fact, once we've developed our media literacy skills, we can appreciate the good things the media have to offer us even more than ever. Like most advocates of media literacy, I also strongly believe that constructive *action* must be part of our media analysis and criticism; therefore, my own methodology for analysis and criticism of unrealistic portrayals of sex, love, and romance in the mass media — the Seven-Step *Dis*-illusioning Directions — includes both a *debriefing* step to clarify your own values and a *dissemination* step to take action based on your thoughts and feelings.

- **Women are *not* "from Venus"; men are *not* "from Mars."** We're all from the *same* planet, which we inhabit together. We're more alike than different. We don't have an *"Opposite* Sex"; we have an *"Other* Sex." (There's some merit to the "Vive la difference!" perspective, particularly as a way of enlarging ourselves through diversity; however, when we view *others* as *opposites,* we set up a clearly oppositional scenario that leads anywhere *except* to true love by any definition.) The most healthy and happy love relationships are those that enable and encourage individuals of both sexes to reach their full potential without sexual stereotyping or prejudice. And that's best for both sexes (see Mass Media Myth #6).

- **Sex and romance alone never constitute real love.** Physical attraction is important, and romance (if *realistic*) can be delightful, but successful coupleships require genuine intimacy, which goes beyond the purely physical (see Mass Media Myth #4). Moreover, real love takes real time (see Mass Media Myth #2) and shared *values* (see Mass Media Myth #9). "Opposites" can be attractive and exciting, but their long-term success rate in real life is dismally low. Furthermore, constant conflict is *not* an indicator of the passion healthy people associate with love (see Mass Media Myth #8). Love is about peace, not war.

- **You are responsible for and to yourself.** No one else — of your own sex or of the other sex — can read your mind (see Mass Media Myth #3) or make your dreams come true (see Mass Media Myth #10). Part of being sensitive to your partner's thoughts, feelings, and behaviors is investing the time to develop an intimate understanding of your loved one's patterns. The key to that intimacy is honest communication built on trust, which takes time and courage (see Mass Media Myth #2). And while it's great to have a loving partner to walk alongside you as you *realize* your goals, only *you* can make yourself happy (or sad). There's no magic pathway, and there's no "one-and-only" who will make your life perfect for you (see Mass Media Myth #1). (But isn't that exciting: You have *many* appropriate matches from which to select!) A completer, fixer, or rescuer often turns into a controller and abuser. That's just as true if *you* are the one trying to be the fixer. We can't change others, no matter how good we think the change might be for them (see Mass Media Myth #7).

- **Using media models as standards of beauty is as irrational as using actors and actresses as ideals of perfection.** Using people as objects to satisfy our own fantasies and inadequacies is as far from real love as anyone can get. It's anything from foolish to obsessive to use popular culture icons we've never met on a personal basis as our ideals or role models (see Mass Media Myth #11). And it's dehumanizing and disastrous to use unnatural body images from the media as standards for yourself or others (see Mass Media Myth #5).

- **"Being *realistic*" does *not* mean forsaking your ideals, romance, or FUN.** While unrealistic portrayals of sex, love, and romance can be extremely harmful, some of these depictions can also be uplifting and worthwhile — *if* we use them as *metaphors* rather than as models. Just as media literacy can help you enjoy the media more rather than less, "getting real about romance" can actually help you clarify your values and set your *achievable standards* higher rather than lower. Likewise, we needn't simply reject all fantasy and art in our lives or in our love. That would make for a very dull existence indeed! The world needs creative imagination and talented artists to help soften the harshness or routine we encounter in life and inspire us to greatness and goodness. We all need the *occasional* healthy escape from reality that media fictions can supply. The key is to understand the wider implications of idealized media portrayals and to make conscious and educated determinations about how they fit into our larger perspectives and how they relate to our actual behaviors. For example, my *own* personal "archetypal heroine" is a fairy tale figure: **Alice in Wonderland**, who — though a child — rescues *herself* by seeing past the illusions. As described in my Disney *Little Golden Book* edition:

> "So!" cried the Queen. "So, she won't play! Off with her head then!" But Alice was tired of Wonderland now, and all its nonsensical ways. "Pooh!" she said. "I'm not frightened of you. You're nothing but a pack of cards!" (Carroll, 1951, n.p.)

The original version, written and published in 1865 by Lewis Carroll (the pen name of Charles Dodgson, an Oxford University mathematics professor and clergyman), includes this significant physical description, which we can read metaphorically as being about far more than Alice's mere physical growth:

> "Who cares for you"? said Alice (she had grown to her full size by this time). (Carroll, 1865/1982, p. 78)

The *Little Golden Book* has a wonderful Disney illustration of a defiant Alice standing in front of a very long line of "playing-card" soldiers armed with lances. She is sticking out her right foot smartly and firmly against the first-in-line. The rest of the cards are crashing upon each other domino-style. The text concludes with this useful explanation:

> And with that she ran back through that l.and of dreams, back to the river bank where she had fallen asleep. "Hm," she said, as she rubbed her eyes. "I'm glad to be back where things are what they seem. I've had quite enough of Wonderland." (Carroll, 1951, n.p.)

The original text offers more subtext about the playing-card soldiers' response to Alice's courageous effort:

> At this the whole pack rose up into the air, and came flying down upon her; she gave a little scream, half of fright and half of anger, and tried to beat them off, and found herself lying on the bank, with her head in the lap of her sister, who was gently brushing away some dead leaves that had fluttered down from the trees upon her face. "Wake up, Alice dear!" said her sister. "Why, what a long sleep you've had!" (Carroll, 1865/1982, p. 78)

For me, those leaves are a vivid symbol of Alice's "*leav*-ing" Wonderland.

I want *you* to leave Wonderland, too. I'm not promoting the total destruction of the mythic or the fantastical or the sublime. What I'm advocating is **dis-illusionment** — waking up like Alice from the stupefying sleep of deceptions and disasters caused by false perceptions or beliefs. I'm telling you that we *must* maintain our standards and ideals of *healthy* beliefs and behaviors. That's why I offer you the 12 *Dr. Galician's Prescriptions™ for*

Getting Real About Romance as "antidotes" to the myths and stereotypes in *Dr. FUN's Mass Media Love Quiz.* Best of all, I can assure you that — while we should strive to embody realistic models in our real lives — *we don't have to give up the ROMANCE or the FUN.*

"Dr. FUN" at the Alice Shop in Oxford, England

The Alice Shop is just across the street from the Oxford University campus where Charles Dodgson wrote *Alice's Adventures in Wonderland.* Dodgson, an Oxford University mathematics professor and clergyman, used "Lewis Carroll" as his pen name.

Photo by Dr. David Natharius

SOURCES CITED

Carroll, L. [Charles Dodgson]. (1982). *Alice's adventures in Wonderland.* In E. Guiliano (Ed.), *Lewis Carroll: The complete illustrated works* (pp. 1–80). New York: Gramercy Books (Random House). (Original work published in 1865)

Carroll, L. [Charles Dodgson]. (1951). *Walt Disney's Alice in Wonderland meets the White Rabbit: A Little Golden Book* [Retold by J. Werner; adapted by A. Dempster from the motion picture based on the story by Lewis Carroll]. New York: Simon & Schuster.

Epstein, R., & Friedman, J. (Producers & Directors). (2001). *The celluloid closet* [DVD]. Culver City, CA: Columbia TriStar Home Entertainment.

PART I

Foundations of Analysis & Criticism of Sex, Love, & Romance in the Mass Media

The beginning is the chiefest part of any work.
— Plato, *The Republic*

Romantic love and mass media share a long association. The Mesopotamian *Epic of Gilgamesh* — one of the world's oldest narratives of friendship and sex, love, and romance (compiled orally as long ago as 5,000 years in the third or second millennium B.C.E.) — comprised 12 clay tablets of 300 lines of verse each when they were later written down in cuneiform for the royal library in 600 B.C.E. Nineveh (Mason, 1970; McLeish, 1996).

The very word *romance* dates from 12th century "courtly love" *romans* (French for "stories"), first disseminated to the masses by troubadours — precursors, in a sense, of modern mass media recording artists — and later by the very first mass medium's early chapbooks and romance novels (Stone, 1988).

"If no one had learned to read," offered Barreca (1993), quoting an unnamed "French philosopher" in her own book, *Perfect Husbands & Other Fairy Tales: Demystifying Marriage, Men, and Romance,* "very few people would be in love" (pp. 146–147).

Love is complex and complicated. Passionate love — "romance" — has become a precondition for most coupled relationships (Lauer & Lauer, 1994). Unfortunately, "romance," by definition, is the opposite of reality, and one liability of romance is that it creates unrealistic expectations that can lead to a considerable amount of "misery, disappointment, and disillusionment" in coupleships (Crosby, 1991, p. 20). The divorce rate in the United States is now half the marriage rate (National Center for Health Statistics, 2001). The personal and societal costs are enormous.

Many social critics, relationship therapists, and popular books about coupleship have accused the mass media of brainwashing consumers with portrayals of romanticized love that is unattainable as a goal and unhealthy as a model and, thereby, contributing to the construction of these unrealistic expectations (Dyer, 1976; Fromm, 1956; Johnson, 1983; Norwood, 1985; Peele, 1975; Russianoff, 1981; Shapiro & Kroeger, 1991; Shostrom & Kavanaugh, 1971). For example, Katz and Liu (1988) warned:

> A large part of the problem is the glorification of false love through the media, which hold out insubstantial but glamorous relations as a never-ending lure. ...

[T]he relationships portrayed by the media are a symbol of status rather than of emotional health or personal well-being. (p. 329)

WHY STUDY MASS MEDIA PORTRAYALS OF SEX, LOVE, & ROMANCE?

It's important to gain the knowledge and skills to resist the power of mass media portrayals that promote unrealistic expectations of sex, love, and romance. As they did for me, these unrealistic portrayals can have serious negative consequences for so many of us — males and females, young and old, singles and couples. It's particularly important to take some of that power back and be more in charge of our beliefs and behaviors. We don't have to give up the mass media we enjoy, but we need to resist being seduced by them.

In *Part I,* we build a foundation of some of the basics underlying the subject as a first step in constituting a repertoire of tools and strategies we can use.

WHAT ARE THE FIVE FOUNDATIONS?

We'll examine **five foundations** for analysis and criticism of unrealistic portrayals of sex, love, and romance in the mass media. Each foundation is covered in a separate chapter.

- Chapter 2 surveys the **major myths and stereotypes** that undergird the unrealistic models dominating today's mass media portrayals of sex, love, and romance.

- Chapter 3 describes **realistic models of love** — based on scientific research — proposed by social psychologists and endorsed by relationship therapists (but rarely seen in the mass media!).

- You'll find a host of reasons why these more healthy rational relationships are rarely depicted when you examine Chapter 4's checklist of **mass media story-telling approaches, techniques, and devices.**

- Chapter 5 highlights **key research and theories of the effects of mass media** on individuals and society and concludes with key findings of studies of mass-mediated sex, love, and romance.

- Chapter 6, a bridge to the applications of media analysis and criticism in Part II, details some of the **strategies and skills of media literacy** — the ability to "read" print and electronic mass media messages *(texts)* with keen awareness of their impact on us as individuals and as a society — and specifies the seven-step approach to analysis and criticism we'll use.

SOURCES CITED

Barreca, R. (1993). *Perfect husbands & other fairy tales: Demystifying marriage, men, and romance.* New York: Harmony Books.

Crosby, J. F. (1991). *Illusion and disillusion: The self in love and marriage* (4th ed.). Belmont, CA: Wadsworth.

Dyer, W. W. (1976). *Your erroneous zones.* New York: Avon Books.

Fromm, E. (1956). *The art of loving.* New York: Bantam Books

Johnson, R. A. (1983). *WE: Understanding the psychology of romantic love.* San Francisco: Harper & Row.

Katz, S. J., & Liu, A. E. (1988). *False love and other romantic illusions.* New York: Pocket Books.

Lauer, R. H., & Lauer, J. C. (1994). *Marriage and family: The quest for intimacy* (2nd ed.). Madison, WI: William C. Brown.

Mason, H. (1970). *Gilgamesh: A verse narrative.* New York: Mentor Books.

McLeish, K. (1996). *Myth: Myths and legends of the world explored.* New York: Facts on File.

National Center for Health Statistics. (2001, August). Births, marriages, divorces, and deaths for January–December 2000. *National Vital Statistical Reports, 49* (6), 6.

Norwood, R. (1985). *Women who love too much: When you keep wishing and hoping he'll change.* New York: Pocket Books.

Peele, S., with Brodsky, A. (1975). *Love and addiction.* New York: Signet.

Plato. (1960). *The Republic and other works* (B. Jowett, Trans.). Garden City, NY: Dolphin. (Original work published circa 385 B.C.E.)

Russianoff, P. (1981). *Why do I think I am nothing without a man?* New York: Bantam Books.

Shostrom, E., & Kavanaugh, J. (1971). *Between man and woman: The dynamics of intersexual relationships.* New York: Bantam.

Stone, L. (1988, February). A short history of love. *Harper's Magazine,* pp. 26–27.

1

KEY FOUNDATIONAL
TERMS & CONCEPTS

What Do They Mean?

"When I use a word," Humpty Dumpty said, in a rather scornful tone, "it means just what I choose it to mean — neither more nor less." "The question is," said Alice, "whether you can make words mean so many different things." "The question is," said Humpty Dumpty, "which is to be master — that's all."
— Lewis Carroll, *Through the Looking Glass*

his chapter clarifies the meanings of some key terms and concepts that we'll use throughout this book:

- Sex, Love, & Romance
- Mass Media (and Mass Media Influence)
- Unrealistic Portrayals
- Analysis & Criticism.

WHAT ARE "SEX," "LOVE," & "ROMANCE"?

We'll start with **love**, because it's really the larger and more complex concept. **Sex** and **romance** are often discussed as subcategories of love.

"Love"

What is this thing called love? This funny thing called love? ...
That's why I ask the Lawd in Heaven above
What is this thing called love?
— Cole Porter, *What Is This Thing Called Love?*

Limitations of Our Language

The English language has only one word for "this thing called *love*," which we also frequently (mis)use to mean *"like"* (as in "I *love* this movie."). French — the so-called "Language of Love" — has only *"aimer"* ("to love"), which also means *"to*

17

like." Ancient Greek, however, had at least seven words that translate as *"love"* — each with a specific meaning:

- *agape* (pronounced "AH-gah-pay" or "ah-GAH-pay") — selfless, spiritual love; also conceived as love of God
- *eros* — passion; sexual, erotic love; most associated with romance
- *ludus* — playful love
- *mania* — obsessive, clingy love
- *philia* — liking, friendship (even of things, as in *philo*sophy, love of wisdom [*sophia*])
- *pragma* — goal-oriented, functional love
- *storge* (pronounced STORE-GAY) — affection; familial or patriotic love or duty.

In *The Four Loves,* the eminent Oxford University literature professor **C.S. Lewis** (1960) — who wrote quite a bit about "the Lawd above" (and who was portrayed by Anthony Hopkins in *Shadowlands,* the 1993 movie based on the stage play that relates his fascinating love story with an American divorcee he married in his later years) — ranked four of these types of love from "simplest" to "most complex/highest" and presented them in that order:

- Chapter 1: Affection (*storge; pietas* in Latin)
- Chapter 2: Friendship (*philia; amicitia* or *dilectio* in Latin)
- Chapter 3: Eros (*eros; amor* in Latin)
- Chapter 4: Charity (*agape; caritas* in Latin).

One of the most respected and prolific scholars on the subject of love, Yale psychology and education professor **Robert J. Sternberg** (1987, 1998), has acknowledged that no single definition describes *love* throughout the ages or across cultures. Although philosophers, theologians, and poets have investigated the nature of love for centuries, love research as a scientific field is relatively new in the wider array of disciplines that now investigate love — social and behavioral psychology, sociology, cultural anthropology, human communication, women's studies, men's studies, family studies, evolutionary biology, and mass communication. For these experts as well as for the general public, *love* means different things to different people at different historical periods and in different cultures.

The Language of Love

Love is a noun and a verb. Is it a feeling or a thought or a behavior — or all three? This brief list of synonyms generated by my word processing program's *Thesaurus* gives you an idea of how complex the concept really is and why it's so difficult to define, even by people who study it seriously:

affection, affinity, amour, amorousness, attachment, attraction, commitment, compassion, concern, devotion, fondness, heart, kinship, passion, religion, warmth

— and those are just the **nouns**! Here are the **verbs**:

adore, admire, cherish, dote on, idolize, respect, revere, venerate, worship.

When I searched *barnesandnoble.com* for current books with "Love is" in their titles, I got 910, including *Love Is a Special Way of Feeling, Love Is a Family, Love Is a Choice, Love Is a Decision, Love Is Letting Go of Fear, Love Is a Racket, Love Is Stronger than Death, Love Is Forever, Love Is Hell,* and *Love Is a Dog from Hell,* as well as *If Love Is a Game, These Are the Rules* and *Barbie: Love Is Everywhere.*

The title of one of Sternberg's many books, which range from research reports for academics to anthologies and histories for the general public, suggests a definition that neatly fits *our* context of contextualized and mediated messages about love: *Love Is a Story.* (We'll discuss this perspective in Chapter 4.)

The Triangular Theory of Love

Over the last few decades, love researchers have attempted to move from the broad-based assortment of terms and concepts to a more unifying focus. One of the more useful conceptualizations is **Sternberg's Triangular Theory of Love**, which diagrams love as a triangle (not to be confused with a 3-person *love triangle*), each of whose three points represents one of the three components or ingredients that Sternberg (1987, 1988, 1998) claims best represent what love is: **intimacy**, **passion**, and **decision/commitment**.

- *Intimacy* refers to close, connected, and bonded feelings in a loving relationship. It's basically an emotional component.

- *Passion* refers to the drives that lead to romance, physical attraction, and sexual consummation in a loving relationship. It's basically a motivational and psychophysiological component.

- *Decision/commitment* consists of two aspects that are separate: a short-term component, the decision that one loves someone; a long-term component, the commitment to maintain that love. It's basically an intellectual or cognitive component.

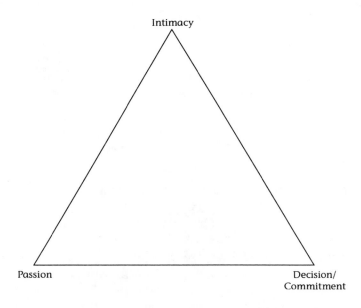

Depending on their relative mixture or combination, these three components generate **eight different kinds of love:**

- **nonlove** (the absence of any of the three components)
- **liking** (only intimacy)
- **infatuated love** (only passion)
- **empty love** (only decision/commitment)
- **romantic love** (intimacy + passion)
- **companionate love** (intimacy + decision/commitment)
- **fatuous (foolish) love** (passion + decision/commitment)
- **consummate (complete) love** (all three components).

Sternberg's model incorporates feelings, beliefs, and actions — all of which are necessary to understand love.

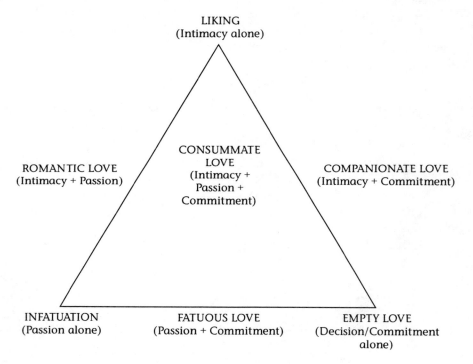

LIKING
(Intimacy alone)

ROMANTIC LOVE
(Intimacy + Passion)

CONSUMMATE
LOVE
(Intimacy +
Passion +
Commitment)

COMPANIONATE LOVE
(Intimacy + Commitment)

INFATUATION
(Passion alone)

FATUOUS LOVE
(Passion + Commitment)

EMPTY LOVE
(Decision/Commitment
alone)

"Colors" of Love

Another attempt to explain the variety of styles of loving is sociologist **John Alan Lee's Typology of Love.** Rather than trying to define love, Lee (1976, 1988) used a color analogy to demonstrate and describe the diversity and richness of different **love-styles.**

Lee's primary colors of love are **eros** (erotic physical attraction), **storge** (friendship or affection), and **ludus** (playful, flirtacious relationship). Lee's secondary colors of love are **mania** (jealous, possessive obsession), **pragma** (practical, sensible, compatible partnership), and **agape** (selfless, giving, altruistic love). In Lee's model (as in Sternberg's) various combinations of these types are likely in reality. Unlike Sternberg, Lee makes no judgment about which love-styles are preferable (As with colors, it's a matter of personal taste, he explains.), but he does suggest that some colors match each other better than others.

As you can see, both *sex* and *romance* — the two terms we'll consider next — figure as part of both Sternberg's and Lee's descriptions of love as well as many other models. (In fact, my computer's *American Heritage Electronic Dictionary* gives as the second definition of love: "A feeling of intense desire and attraction toward a person with whom one is disposed to make a pair; the emotion of **sex** and **romance**.")

"Sex"

Sex was the most frequently searched term on the internet until it was surpassed in July 1999 by "MP3" (Baran, 2002, p. 80).

Let's go back to the *Thesaurus* for some synonyms:

> adultery, classification, coitus, congress, conjugation, copulation, fooling around, foreplay, fornication, gender, intercourse, intimacy, mating, procreation, reproduction, union.

Classification as a synonym for *sex* at first it seems like a mistake, but, as you can see, the term *sex* has different levels of meaning. In fact, the *American Heritage Electronic Dictionary*'s definition #1a (below) clarifies this seeming mistake. (Box 1-1 on the next page shows you how important a clear understanding of this meaning is to our own study.) The other definitions of *sex* provide an overview of the variety of meanings of this complex term:

> — **sex (noun)**
> 1.a. The property or quality by which organisms are classified as female or male on the basis of their reproductive organs and functions. b. Either of the two divisions, designated female and male, of this classification.
> 2. Females or males considered as a group.
> 3. The condition or character of being female or male; the physiological, functional, and psychological differences that distinguish the female and the male.
> 4. The sexual urge or instinct as it manifests itself in behavior.
> 5. Sexual intercourse.
> 6. The genitalia.
>
> — **attributive.**
> 1. Often used to modify another noun.
>
> — **sex (transitive verb)**
> 1. To determine the sex of (an organism, especially a hatching chicken).
> 2. Slang. a. To arouse sexually. Often used with *up*. b. To increase the appeal or attractiveness of. Often used with *up*.

So in addition to being a classification basis (1–3), the term "sex" also refers to a psychophysiological drive (4), an action (5), and body parts (6).

Beyond understanding sex as a classification category, in our study we are also concerned with sex as in definition #4, above: "The sexual urge or instinct as it manifests itself in behavior." In this sense, sex is a key component in romance. This parallels Sternberg's Triangular Theory of Love, in which "passion" is one of the two components of "romantic love."

Box 1-1. Note About the Correct Usage of the Terms "Sex" & "Gender"

Although the classification terms — sex and gender — are often used interchangeably by the media and the public, these two terms are not synonyms. Each has a distinct and different denotation:

- *Sex* refers to biological categorization — that is, male or female (based on reproductive organs).

- *Gender* refers to behavioral categorization — that is, feminine or masculine (based on sociocultural norms and expectations).

As you'll see, it's sometimes awkward to use these terms correctly, but it's important to do so.

Additionally, we will avoid using the inappropriate if not incorrect idiomatic phrase **The Opposite Sex** when we mean **The Other Sex**. Males and females are much more alike than different — both biologically (sex) and behaviorally (gender), so it's ludicrous to focus on these smaller differences and dangerous to polarize the sexes.

Finally, although "male" and "female" are more properly used as adjectives than nouns (which sound clinical or purely biological), these noun forms are used in this book to signify *both* children *and* adults of one sex or the other (rather than the cumbersome alternative — "men and boys and women and girls").

"Romance"

Here are some synonyms:

(**nouns**) affair, adultery, cheating, dalliance, entanglement, fling, flirtation, fooling around, infatuation, intimacy, intrigue, liaison, love affair, playing around, rendezvous, tryst;

(**verbs**) court, woo, attract, encourage, flirt, invite, lure, pursue, solicit, tempt

I'm sure you noticed that the majority of these words connote less than socially sanctioned behavior. What images came to your mind as you read them?

Now let's go to the dictionary:

— **romance (noun)**[1]
1.a. A love affair. b. Ardent emotional attachment or involvement between people, especially that characterized by a high level of purity and devotion; love. c. A strong, sometimes short-lived attachment, fascination, or enthusiasm for something.
2. A mysterious or fascinating quality or appeal, as of something adventurous, heroic, or strangely beautiful.
3.a. A long medieval narrative in prose or verse that tells of the adventures and heroic exploits of chivalric heroes. b. A long, fictitious tale of heroes and extraordinary or mysterious events. c. The class of literature constituted by such tales.

---

[1]If you're a student of languages, you'll note that I deleted the references to the *"Romance"* languages (Italian, French, Portuguese, Romanian, and Spanish as well as Catalan, Provençal, Rhaeto-Romanic, Sardinian, and Ladino), which are so called because they developed from Latin (*Roman*) not because they developed from *romans,* the French stories that give our love literature its name.

4.a. An artistic work, such as a novel, story, or film, that deals with sexual love, especially in an idealized form. b. The class or style of such works.

5. A fictitiously embellished account or explanation.

6. Music. A lyrical, tender, usually sentimental song or short instrumental piece.

— **romance (verb).** romanced, romancing, romances (intransitive).

1. To invent, write, or tell romances.

2. To think or behave in a romantic manner.

— **(transitive) informal.**

1. To make love to; court or woo.

2. To have a love affair with.

The above definitions both denote and connote a refined purity, which might have surprised you — especially in contrast with the rather bawdy synonyms. A puzzling contradiction seems to be operating. In fact, you'll see that's precisely the case: "Romantic love is usually conceived as involving both possessive and altruistic motives, the latter magnified by what its critics regards as an exaggerated idealization of the beloved," as explained by the editors of *The Great Ideas,* which summarizes the *Great Books of the Western World from Homer to Freud* (Hutchins, 1952, p. 1,058).

Hendrix (1992) has argued that "there is no love in romance" (p. 220) because romance is based on unhealthy expectation and illusion. Lindholm (1988) added that romantic love thrives on fantasy, uncertainly, alienation, and loneliness — all "built on the image of absolute mutuality and reciprocity in a dyad" (p. 7). Sternberg (1987) offered *Romeo and Juliet* as the model of his Triangular Theory's romantic love — defined as having intimacy and passion but lacking decision/commitment, whereas "consummate love" (complete love) is a combination of all three components that most people mistakenly seek in *romantic* love (p. 340).

You'll learn more about this conceptually ironic and paradoxical term when we talk about the origins of **romance** in Chapter 2. You'll also notice that the above definitions emphasize a wide variety of mass media as transmitters of romance. Let's define those next.

WHAT ARE "MASS MEDIA" & "THEIR INFLUENCE"?

The medium is the message.
     — Marshall McLuhan, *Understanding Media*

Models of Mass Mediated Communication

A simple verbal model of the mass communication process — provided in the form of a question more than half a century ago by political scientist **Harold Lasswell** (1948) — remains useful today to describe the basic components: *"Who says what to whom through which channel with what effect?"*

- "**Who**" is called a **sender** (or a **source**) in communication theory. In mass communication, the sender is usually a team of professional communicators working within a media institution — like a publishing company or a television network — rather than an individual, although sometimes one individual is clearly the team leader or primary source, like the author of a novel. Mass communicators have **three basic reasons for sending messages: to inform or educate, to entertain, to persuade.** Usually all three of these purposes are combined, but one purpose is dominant. In fulfilling these functions, the mass media also serve a larger purpose or function: **transmitting the culture and socializing us.**

- "What" is a **message** that the sender wants to send or *share.* Another mass comm term for "message" is *content* or *meaning.* Mass media senders create or construct their messages, using symbols such as words or pictures or sounds to convey their meanings. As mentioned above, these messages are either informative/educational, entertaining, or persuasive — or some combination of all **three functions of mass communication.** The media are also **agents of personal and social change.** Many critics argue that the media are the *primary* influencers of personal and social change — although the actual influence is sometimes unintentional.

- "(To) whom" is the **receiver** or **audience.** In a mass communication, the receiver is not in the same place as the sender. Sometimes they're separated by centuries as well — as when we read a book by an author who is no longer living or see a movie of a now-deceased director or film star. Although the receiver might receive the message (say, a TV show) with several friends who are together in the same place (a sports bar), the receiver is not in the same place as *all* of the other receivers of this same message, and some of these receivers might not even be receiving the message at the same time (e.g., movie audiences and magazine readers). In mass communication, these audiences are indeed mass — typically **diverse and very large.** Of course, sending a message doesn't guarantee it will be received.

- "(Through which) channel" is the **vehicle** or **medium**[2] of mass communication: books, newspapers, magazines, comic books, movies and animated films, radio, recorded music, television, music videos, and certain aspects of the internet. These media are technological devices that enable the sender to reach very large audiences dispersed over time and space. The sender has to construct (create) and put the message into a mass medium in the same way that we construct a letter (message) with a pen on paper and put it into an envelope (medium) to send to a recipient.

- "(With what) effect" is the fifth element in the basic model. Communication theory synonyms for *effect* are **impact, influence,** and **consequence.** One effect is **feedback,** which turns the receiver into the sender and the sender into the receiver. Feedback works like radar to help the sender know if and how the message was received and to enable the sender to refine the message, if necessary, to keep it on target for the audience of receivers. Unfortunately, in mass communication the feedback is usually delayed rather than instantaneous. Often it's nonexistent.

Years ago a textbook that I had selected for use by my Mass Media & Society class inadvertently left out this crucial fifth part of Lasswell's description. (The publisher corrected it in the next edition after I provided *feedback.*) It was a small omission, but it was drastic in terms of how it altered the sense of the model.

---

[2]**Medium** is the singular form; the plural form is **media.**

Here's why that omission was so serious. Senders transmit messages to **share meaning** with receivers. Below is a graphic model of this part of the process, which is the same as for interpersonal face-to-face communication between individuals or groups. Animate the circles so that they overlap either a little or a lot. The overlap represents the concept of shared meaning, which is what communication is all about. (Have you ever said or been asked, "Are we together on this?")

The **effect** of that sharing of meaning can be **cognitive** (a thought or perception), **affective** (an emotion or value), or **behavioral** (an action). The effect could

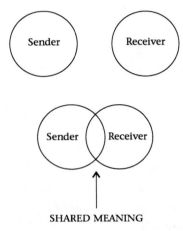

SHARED MEANING

combine all three. But there's always an effect: The receiver is always affected, however slightly.

It's also important to understand that the effects of mass communication are not always the intended ones. Often the effects also depend on our own **psychological filters** — biases — that regulate our exposure, perception, and retention, all of which are selective. As described by Wilson and Wilson (2001) in *Mass Media/ Mass Culture: An Introduction,* we usually prefer to seek out information and ideas that are consistent with our own beliefs, attitudes, and behaviors and we tend to avoid communication that is inconsistent.

We'll cover some specific story-telling devices of the mass media in Chapter 4 and some of the research and theories of mass communication impacts in Chapter 5. But we can't end this discussion of the mass media and their influence without a few words about the man who first applied the term *media* to the means of mass communication: Marshall McLuhan, who greatly influenced what we believe about the influence of the media.

The Mass Media Guru: Marshall McLuhan

In the late 1960s **Marshall McLuhan** — an English professor who directed the Centre for Culture and Technology at the University of Toronto — rocked the world with his groundbreaking best-seller *Understanding Media: The Extensions of Man.* The book transformed him into celebrity who appeared regularly on television programs and magazine covers. According to the book's back cover:

> *Understanding Media* raises two fundamental questions about the modern world: What are communications and how do communications affect mankind? In

answering these questions, Marshall McLuhan interprets the entire process of communication from the invention of movable type throughout the electronic age.

While this would be hype for most books, it's entirely accurate in this case. In fact, it was this Joycean scholar and wordsmith himself who first used and popularized the term *media* to refer to our various vehicles of communication, such as books, magazines, movies, and television. (When the term was new, an "in" joke went like this: *Why is television called a "medium"? — Because it never has anything "rare" or "well done"!*)

McLuhan's choice of the word **medium** (the singular form; the plural form is **media**) was brilliant, reflecting his love of words and their richness. Consider the different shadings of the term, before it came to be used as we use it today:

1. Something, such as an intermediate course of action, that occupies a position or represents a condition midway between extremes.

2. An intervening substance through which something else is transmitted or carried on.

3. An agency by which something is accomplished, conveyed, or transferred.

4. A person thought to have the power to communicate with the spirits of the dead or with agents of another world or dimension. Also called "psychic."

From our discussion of the basic mass communication model above you can see that all four of these different definitions apply perfectly:

1. The media are "mediators" or go-betweens or those in the middle whose position is generally middling or even mediocre to strike some middle ground and reach the broadest possible audience.

2. The media are transmitters and carriers of messages from a sender to a mass of receivers.

3. The media are agents with a goal: informing/educating, entertaining, and persuading through communication — and, whether by intention or accident, the media are agents of social change.

4. The media are frequently accorded mythic status — and, like most mediums or fortunetellers — their methods are sometimes deceptive and suspect.

None of these shadings of meaning would have been lost on McLuhan, whose previous specialty was analysis and criticism of the great novelist and wordplay master James Joyce. McLuhan assuredly chose the word as his new term precisely *because* of these myriad connotations, all of which relate to our current study in this book.

McLuhan's most famous *probe* (as he himself termed his pithy sayings and slogans; others later referred to them as "McLuhanisms") — **"The Medium is the Message"** — summarized his innovative argument nearly 40 years ago that a mass communication medium doesn't merely transmit a message or content: The medium itself also, and more importantly, has a direct impact on how society and individuals think and act. (Later, McLuhan even played with his own most famous statement, reiterating it ironically as *The Medium is the Massage,* to underscore his point.) These media are, McLuhan contended, extensions of our senses; thus, the dominant medium of a society in any given time is the main agent of social change, altering the way people process information and think about the world. The advent of writing was the first such dramatic change in culture — transforming us from a preliterate tribal society to a literate civilization.

WHAT ARE "UNREALISTIC PORTRAYALS"?

Alice laughed: "There's no use trying," she said; "one can't believe impossible things." "I daresay you haven't had much practice," said the Queen. "When I was younger, I always did it for half an hour a day. Why, sometimes I've believed as many as six impossible things before breakfast."
— Lewis Carroll, *Alice's Adventures in Wonderland*

Because the focus of our analysis and criticism is on the mass media's *unrealistic* portrayals of sex, love, and romance, we must come to an understanding of how we'll use terms like *realistic* and *unrealistic*. This discussion necessarily raises the issue of what is **unreal**, as well as what is **ideal** and what is **truth.**

The investigation of the nature of reality goes back centuries. As with the investigation of the nature of love, few conclusions have yet been reached and no universal definition exists, though many philosophers have written many treatises with many different arguments.

Plato suggested that "reality" resided in what he called *Eternal "Forms"* — such as Truth, Justice, Beauty, and Piety. Seeking perfection in these forms was the highest — if totally idealistic — goal.

Today, many critics claim that our reality as individuals and as a society has been shaped and even perverted by the mass media. In fact, some say that *reality* is what the mass media *say* reality is.

For our examination of the mass media's unrealistic portrayals of sex, love, and romance, we'll come to understand **reality** (also: real and realistic) and **non**reality (also: unreal and unrealistic) in terms of their contrasts and in terms of their contexts, such as recommendations of social psychologists and relationship therapists about what constitutes a *realistic relationship as opposed to an unrealistic and, therefore, unhealthy one.*

The term **rational** — "having or exercising the ability to reason; of sound mind; sane; consistent with or based on reason; logical" — is also used frequently by experts to describe healthy thinking and behavior. In fact, a major school of behavioral and clinical psychology (cognitive-behavioral therapy or rational-emotive behavioral therapy)[3] uses the term *rational* in its approach, which is based on scientific research that demonstrates it's our *irrational thinking* that causes counterproductive feelings and behaviors that make us unhappy. The goal of this reality-based psychology is to help people unlearn irrational beliefs and behaviors and relearn more rational ones. We'll examine their models in Chapter 3.

---

[3]The founder of this school and internationally recognized leader in the field is **Albert Ellis.** Originally a Freudian psychoanalyst, he abandoned that practice half a century ago and created **rational-emotive behavioral therapy (REBT),** which advocates "changing people's behavior by confronting them with their irrational beliefs and persuading them to adopt rational ones" (Gregg, 2002, n.p.). He is President of the Institute for Rational-Emotive Therapy in New York and the author of *The Art and Science of Love* (1960) and more than 50 other books as well as more than 600 articles on REBT, sex, and marriage.

Meantime, some simple dictionary definitions are useful in getting a handle on the elusive concepts of the real and the ideal (and their antitheses):

— **reality (noun)**
1. The quality or state of being actual or true.
2. One, such as a person, an entity, or an event, that is actual.
3. The totality of all things possessing actuality, existence, or essence.
4. That which exists objectively and in fact.
5. Philosophy. That which has necessary existence and not contingent existence.

— **real (adjective)**
1.a. Being or occurring in fact or actuality; having verifiable existence. b. True and actual; not imaginary, alleged, or ideal. c. Of or founded on practical matters and concerns.
2. Genuine and authentic; not artificial or spurious.
3. Being no less than what is stated; worthy of the name.
4. Free of pretense, falsehood, or affectation.
5. Not to be taken lightly; serious.
6. Philosophy. Existing objectively in the world regardless of subjectivity or conventions of thought or language.

— **realistic (adjective)**
1. Tending to or expressing an awareness of things as they really are.
2. Of or relating to the representation of objects, actions, or social conditions as they actually are.

— idiom.
for real. (also **realness**). Slang.
Truly so in fact or actuality.

— **unreal (adjective)**.
1. Not real or substantial; illusory.
2. Slang. So remarkable as to elicit disbelief; fantastic.
3. Surreal.

— **ideal (noun)**
1. A conception of something in its absolute perfection.
2. One that is regarded as a standard or model of perfection or excellence.
3. An ultimate object of endeavor; a goal.
4. An honorable or worthy principle or aim.

— **ideal (adjective)**.
1.a. Of, relating to, or embodying an ideal. b. Conforming to an ultimate form or standard of perfection or excellence.
2. Considered the best of its kind.
3. Completely or highly satisfactory.
4.a. Existing only in the mind; imaginary. b. Lacking practicality or the possibility of realization.
5. Of, relating to, or consisting of ideas or mental images.
6. Philosophy. a. Existing as an archetype or pattern, especially as a Platonic idea or perception. b. Of or relating to idealism.

You can see that *reality* is associated with facts and empirical (observable and documentable) evidence. It's like Science. What is *unrealistic* is associated with illusion and fantasy as well as very closely related to the *idealistic* or unattainable perfection that sets a standard or goal toward which we might "strive but not arrive." It's like Art.

Dichotomies of Western Dualism

It's also important to remember that in our Western dualism we tend to dichotomize these conceptual definitions:

- real/unreal,
- realistic/unrealistic,
- real/ideal,
- objective/subjective,
- fact/fiction,
- science/art.

However, these concepts are better understood as ends of a continuum with an almost infinite number of positions between one extreme and the other. Sometimes a blending of the real and the unreal — of Science and Art — can incorporate the benefits of these apparent opposites while diminishing their negative aspects and detrimental effects. In fact, Jungian psychology (which we'll cover in Chapters 2 and 3) focuses on understanding these dualities not as separate and distinct but rather as aspects of the individual *self* of each of us and emphasizes the *integration* of these opposing instincts as the way to achieve personal growth and activate our full human potential.

The Possible vs. the Probable

However, as we begin our study of unrealistic portrayals of sex, love, and romance in the mass media, let's be clear about the distinction between what is *possible* (or "rare-but-true" or "exceptional") and what is *realistic* or *unrealistic* (and "probable" or "normal"). Because we are concerned with guidelines for predicting success in actual behavior that is highly complicated, we're concerned with what is *probable* (based on research and experience) rather than what is clearly *chancy* and *risky* (based on assumptions and exceptions). It's *possible* that you could survive a fall from a 10-story building, but it's also *unrealistic* (and *highly improbable*). And it's *possible* that you could *fall in love at first sight* but — like the fall from the tall building — it's not a very good basis or model for making important decisions about your life.

"Portrayals" & "Models"

Appropriately or inappropriately, many males and females throughout the ages have used mass media portrayals of sex, love, and romance as their primary model. A **portrayal** is a representation or description in words or pictures. *Portrayal* has a dramatic connotation, even when applied to nonfiction.

A **model** is a schematic description of a system, theory, or phenomenon that accounts for its known or inferred properties and can be used for further study of its characteristics. It also means "one serving as an example to be imitated or compared." When we *model* something, we make it "conform to a chosen standard." In zoology, a model is an animal whose appearance is copied by a mimic. Some human behaviors are worthy of our imitation. Others are not.

Ideals and fantasy can serve noble purposes, if we use them constructively. I'm not advocating the abandonment of standards or metaphorical ideals that motivate us to excellence. However, other than in a magic show, illusion — "an erroneous perception of reality" and "an erroneous concept or belief" — is counterproductive because illusion also means "the condition of being deceived by a false perception or belief." Our goal is to *dis*-illusion the portrayals and — in the process — *dis*-illusion *ourselves.* Here's how we'll approach it.

WHAT ARE "ANALYSIS" & "CRITICISM"?

In our analysis and criticism, we'll scrutinize portrayals and models of sex, love, and romance in the mass media that are considered unrealistic and compare them with those that are more realistic. **Analysis** means "separating an intellectual or substantial whole into its constituent parts for individual study." It's often called "deconstruction." **Criticism** builds on analysis. It's "the art, skill, or profession of making discriminating judgments and evaluations, especially of literary or other artistic works." It's also "a review or article expressing such judgment and evaluation."

Those are basic dictionary definitions. However, when it comes to actually conducting mass media analysis and criticism, a great variety of methods and approaches are advocated by different schools of thought with different underlying philosophies and assumptions. Nevertheless, some basic components are consistent across most of them. I've synthesized these common core components of media analysis and criticism and added some specific strategies and skills of **media literacy** to create a seven-step system I believe is most beneficial for us to use to analyze and criticize unrealistic portrayals of sex, love, and romance in the mass media.

Here's an overview of what I call **Dr. Galician's Seven-Step *Dis*-illusioning Directions:**

1. **Detection** (finding/identifying)

2. **Description** (illustrating/exemplifying)

3. **Deconstruction** (analyzing)

4. **Diagnosis** (evaluating/criticizing)

5. **Design** (reconstructing/reframing)

6. **Debriefing** (reconsidering/remedying)

7. **Dissemination** (publishing/broadcasting).

The details of each of these steps are provided in Chapter 6.

The analysis (Step 3) usually flows into the criticism (Step 4) in a single "essay," but each step has its own components:

- In an **analysis of a media portrayal** (usually an entire work, like a movie or book, but sometimes a segment of it, like a specific scene) that you have identified and described, you examine its elements — such as plot and character and media devices — to elaborate on the messages (meanings) you find and the values they support. You specify the underlying myths and stereotypes. You provide *specific examples* of both the content and the form (medium and message) that support your interpretation, which should be clearly stated early in the analysis. You also consider what is omitted. You cited the commentary and research of others to further document your interpretation.

- In a **criticism of a media portrayal**, you make judgments or evaluations *based on your analysis*. Criticism can be positive as well as negative, but it must be *well supported* by clear explanations of how you reached your diagnosis. (Note: Criticism is *not* just an off-hand opinion.) You carefully explain the meaning and possible interpretations of the media text. You compare the portrayal to rational models. You focus on how audience members might experience the portrayal, based on the theories and research of mass media effects. You cite the commentary and research of others, and you might even conduct your own research.

Taking Three Extra Steps

Traditional critical analysis often ends with Step 4: Diagnosis. However, in my seven-step process, *you take three more important steps*.

You suggest *alternate* designs for reframing the portrayals more *realistically* within the context of a professional mass media communication (Step 5: Design). Finally, you reflect on how you yourself have been enlightened by your own criticism (Step 6: Debriefing), and you decide if and how your own raised consciousness will motivate you to *act* constructively as a media consumer or creator to share your insights with others (Step 7: Dissemination).

SUMMARY

No single definition describes "love" throughout the ages or across cultures. One of the more useful conceptualizations is Sternberg's Triangular Theory of Love, which diagrams love as a triangle, each of whose three points represents one of the three components or ingredients of love: intimacy, passion, and decision/commitment. Sternberg's model incorporates feelings, beliefs, and actions — all of which are necessary to understand love. Another model is sociologist John Alan Lee's Typology of Love, which uses a color analogy to demonstrate and describe the diversity and richness of different love-styles.

Love incorporates the concepts of sex and romance. One meaning of sex is as a classification by reproductive organs: male or female. ("Gender" is a sociological term that should not be confused with "sex," which is a biological term.) In addition to being a classification basis, the term sex also refers to a psychophysiological drive, an action, and reproductive organs. Romance is a more contradictory concept that runs the gamut from chaste to erotic.

Harold Lasswell's verbal model of the mass communication process — "Who says what to whom through which channel with what effect?" — describes its five most basic components: sender, message, receiver, medium, effect. Mass communicators have three reasons for sending messages (which are the three mass media functions): to inform or educate, to entertain, to persuade. By transmitting culture, the media are also agents of personal and social change.

In all three functions, senders transmit messages to share meaning, which is what communication is all about. The effect of that sharing of meaning can be cognitive (a thought or perception), affective (an emotion or value), or behavioral (an action).

The term "media" (the plural form of "medium") was first used to signify all the means or conveyors of mass communication by Marshall McLuhan, who conceptualized them as extensions of our senses in his groundbreaking best-seller *Understanding Media: The Extensions of Man.* McLuhan's most famous statement — "The Medium is the Message" —summarized his argument that mass communication media don't merely transmit messages or content but also directly impact how society and individuals think and act. The dominant medium of a society in any given time is the main agent of social change.

Reality has no universal definition. Plato argued that reality resides in *Eternal "Forms."* Today, critics claim that our reality has been shaped and even perverted by the mass media. Reality and nonreality can be understood in terms of their contrasts (e.g., fact vs. fiction; Science vs. Art) and in terms of their contexts. These dichotomous concepts can also be envisioned as ends of a continuum with an almost infinite number of positions between one extreme and the other.

From the wide variety of methods for media analysis and criticism, one that incorporates many of their common features is Dr. Galician's Seven-Step *Disillusioning* Directions (Detection-Description-Deconstruction-Diagnosis-Design-Debriefing-Dissemination), a system of media literacy strategies and skills for conducting analysis and criticism of unrealistic portrayals of sex, love, and romance in the mass media.

SOURCES CITED

American Heritage electronic dictionary. (1991). n.p.: Houghton Mifflin.

Baran, S. J. (2002). *Introduction to mass communication: Media literacy and culture.* New York: McGraw-Hill

Gregg, G. (2002). A sketch of Albert Ellis. Retrieved July 19, 2002 from The Albert Ellis Institute: http://www.rebt.org/titlepages/dr.asp

Hendrix, H. (1992). *Keeping the love you find: A guide for singles.* New York: Pocket Books.

Hutchins, R. M. (Ed.). (1952). *The great ideas: A syntopicon of great books of the Western world* (Vol. 1). Chicago: Encyclopaedia Britannica.

Lasswell, H. D. (1948). The structure and function of communication in society. In L. Bryson (Ed.), *The communication of ideas.* New York: Harper.

Lee, J. A. (1976). *The colors of love.* Englewood Cliffs, NJ: Prentice-Hall.

Lee, J. A. (1988). Love styles. In R. J. Sternberg & M. L. Barnes (Eds.), *The psychology of love* (pp. 38–67). New Haven, CT: Yale University Press.

Lewis, C. S. (1960). *The four loves.* New York: Harcourt Brace Jovanovich.

McLuhan, M. (1964). *Understanding media: The extensions of man.* New York: McGraw-Hill.

Plato. (1960). The Symposium. In *The Republic and other works* (B. Jowett, Trans.). Garden City, NY: Dolphin. (Original work published circa 385 B.C.E.)

Sternberg, R. J. (1987). Liking versus loving: A comparative evaluation of theories. *Psychological Bulletin, 102,* 331–345.

Sternberg, R. J. (1988). Triangulating love. In R. J. Sternberg & M. L. Barnes (Eds.), *The psychology of love* (pp. 119–138). New Haven, CT: Yale University Press.

Sternberg, R. J. (1998). *Cupid's arrow: The course of love through time.* New York: Cambridge University Press.

Wilson, J. R., & Wilson, S. R. (2001). *Mass media/mass culture: An introduction.* New York: McGraw-Hill.

2

IDEALS & ILLUSIONS
(UNREALISTIC MODELS)

Myths & Stereotypes of Love & Coupleship

...[T]he myths of love generally determine our individual behavior, the apparent accidents of our encounters, and the choices we imagine we are making freely.
— Denis de Rougemont, "The Rising Tide of Eros," *Sex in America*

For the most part, we do not first see, and then define, we define first and then see. In the great blooming, buzzing confusion of the outer world we pick out what our culture has already defined for us, and we tend to perceive that which we have picked out in the form stereotyped for us by our culture.
— Walter Lippmann, *Public Opinion*

We can understand, make sense of, and give meaning to the phenomena of our world — including love, sex, and romance — through art and literature, philosophy and religion, natural science, and/or social science. In this chapter, we'll explore some of the universal themes that have attempted to explain human behavior as well as to control it. These themes go back centuries, to the earliest human times for which we have a narrative record (and even before).

In this chapter we'll look at some relevant archetypes, myths, and idealizations in an historical review covering myths of ancient times going back to centuries B.C.E., the establishment of the ideal of "romance" in the 12th century courtly tradition, the revolutionary practice of using love as a basis for choice of a marriage partner in our modern era, and Freud's explanation of sexuality as a driving force. We'll see how myths recurring across time, place, and culture have been summarized as universal themes or archetypes of the "collective unconscious" by psychologist Carl Jung, who viewed them as a way to symbolize and actualize the fragmentation or integration of the individual. Then we'll consider the more recent theory of evolutionary psychology (sociobiology) as a way to interpret natural phenomena and social beliefs and practices about sex, love, and romance in terms of human adaptation rather than preordination. And we'll see how these myths, idealizations, and theories can be molded into stereotypes that can be deceptive and damaging to individuals and society.

WHAT ARE "MYTHS"?

Our word "**myth**" comes from the Greek *mythos* — Aristotle's term for plot or story. Myths are stories that bring the ancient past to the postmodern present through the universal appeal of their *morals,* which have socialized us across the centuries (Vande Berg, Wenner, & Gronbeck, 1998). The focus of a myth, a sacred story that expresses moral values in human terms, is the powers in control of the human world and the relationship between those powers and human beings.

In fact, myths are the stories that determine a society's perspectives about the world, about themselves, about what behaviors and approaches have meaning or value *beyond* the real. As a form of traditional literature, attempting to explain natural phenomena or justify certain practices or beliefs, myths (like all literary fiction) require a willing *suspension of disbelief* — an audience's involvement in a story without questioning the story world or its characters, even though the audience knows rationally that the story couldn't actually occur in "real life."

These narratives are considered both true and sacred in the originating culture, but they are *not* verifiable because their source is usually impossible to document. **Mythology** — a collection of myths from the same group of people — often forms a major part and basis of the group's religion.

Here are some dictionary definitions:

— myth (noun)
1.a. A traditional, typically ancient story dealing with supernatural beings, ancestors, or heroes that serves as a fundamental type in the world view of a people, as by explaining aspects of the natural world or delineating the psychology, customs, or ideals of society. b. Such stories considered as a group.
2. A story, a theme, an object, or a character regarded as embodying an aspect of a culture.
3. A fiction or half-truth, especially one that forms part of an ideology.
4. A fictitious story, person, or thing.

These definitions reinforce an important point: *Myths are not necessarily true, but they're also not necessarily untrue.* Usually, they contain just enough that at least seems credible in their time and place to get them accepted. According to Himmelstein (1994), "Myth transforms the temporal common sense of the dominant ideology into the sacred realm of cultural prehistory and thus of eternal truth" (p. 5). For Eliade (1993), myth is "both a *true story* — because it tells how real things have come to be — and the exemplary model of and justification for the activities of man" (p. 4). Moreover, myth is considered "*true* (because it refers to realities) and *sacred* (because it is the work of Supernatural Beings)" (p. 5).

At any rate, myths can communicate truth; thus, myths have great value as teaching tools — either for the benefit of the believers or for their detriment, as myths can control or even enslave us. As a central force in socialization they always have a moral force. Myths are always about power and control, frequently through sacred stories and religious ritual.

Although myths are stories, they're not always told as complete stories. They're often conveyed piecemeal in epics, legends, rituals, and even the visual arts (like paintings and sculptures). And, like legends and fairy tales, myths were passed on orally for generations before they were first written down. All of these literary forms are closely related. Here are some brief descriptions of these terms (listed alphabetically):

- **Epic**: A long tale in many episodes that relates the exploits of exceptional but human characters such as Beowulf and Gilgamesh.

- **Fable**: A short, simple "preachy" story that illustrates an ethical or moral teaching and ends with a moral (an instruction about what is right), thereby teaching a lesson. Fables usually include animals that talk and act like people.

- **Fairy tale** (also known as a "**wonder tale**"): A folk story about real-life problems, usually with imaginary characters (flat, stock characters who are not meant to be realistic because they are meant to be symbolic, such as the evil stepmother or the handsome prince) and some element of magic (a fairy godmother; transformation of animal to human or human to animal). Fairy tales frequently tell stories about a young person's transition from childhood to adulthood, usually represented by marriage.

- **Folk tale**: Traditional literature of oral origin with a number of subgenres, such as fairy tales.

- **Legend**: A fictional or partly fictional narrative or historical tale of a people that is told as if it were true. Legends were believed by at least some of the original tellers and listeners. These narratives were handed down first in oral and later in written form. A legend is usually an exaggerated story based on an actual person who is made to appear unrealistically great. Although the stories might appear at first to be factual and unique, they actually follow a traditional plot.

Myths, legends, and fairy tales — many of which are as violent and sexually explicit as any contemporary popular entertainment — should be understood as not just delightful stories but also as revelations about human nature and human values with human impact.

Related Classical Mythic Love Stories

If there is one thing anyone can learn from classical love stories, it is that we flatter ourselves when we think that we fall in love totally on our own. The love stories we have heard, and that have been carried on through the ages, set up expectations for ourselves and our partners at all stages of a relationship.
— Robert J. Sternberg, *Cupid's Arrow*

It's ironic that many of the myths about sex, love, and romance that influence us to adopt idealistic and unattainable models for our actual behavior originated with the *rational* Greeks. In *A Natural History of Love,* poet and naturalist Diane Ackerman (1995) explained: "In a world ruled by myth, **Plato** tried to be rational, often using myths as allegories to make a point. His investigations of love in *The Symposium,* around 385 B.C.E., are the oldest surviving attempts to systematically understand love" (p. 95). Unfortunately, we ignore or forget what Plato's purpose actually was.

Classical Greeks considered love an important value, but because women were considered by the great thinkers of the time to be inferior to men in body and spirit, when romantic love was embraced it was more often in the context of a homosexual relationship, typically that of a younger man and an older man. Like the

Greeks, the Romans considered romantic passion to be a type of madness that severely undermined the dominant philosophy of stoicism (Branden, 1980). Of course, love and marriage were two different spheres (with separate gods and goddesses).

Here are some of the classical myths that underlie the 12 major mass media myths that are the focus of our analysis and criticism. I've indicated which myths are related to the items of *Dr. FUN's Mass Media Love Quiz.*

The One & Only Perfect Partner (Myth #1, #3, and #10)

One of Plato's most enduring fictions attempts to account for the *division of the human species into two sexes and their longing for (re)union.* According to this tale (which, in *The Republic,* he puts into the mouth of Aristophanes at a banquet in honor of Eros, God of Love), there were originally three sexes: males, females, and **hermaphrodites.**[1] They were round, with four legs, four arms, one head with two faces (looking in opposite directions) and two sets of genitals. Because they were so strong, they presented a threat to the gods, who decided to divide their bodies in two, thereby both reducing their power and increasing their service to the gods. Zeus split them such that descendants of the male beings would seek sexual union with males; descendants of the female beings would seek sexual union with females; and descendants of the hermaphrodite beings would seek heterosexual union.

Each newly two-legged two-armed, one-faced, single-genitaled creature now longed for its missing half, which it sought relentlessly to become whole again. As the speech concludes: "And the reason is that human nature was originally one and we were a whole, and the desire and pursuit of the whole is called love."

Ackerman relates Plato's description — *of this idealized desire not merely for a mate but rather for a perfect partner who is the one-and-only part of ourselves with whom we long to merge* — to similar mythic accounts of the creation of humanity; for example, to the classical myths of India, where some gods were bisexual, and to the *Bible,* where Eve is created from the very body of the lonely Adam. Further, she recounts the related evolutionary biological theory that "our ultimate ancestor almost certainly was hermaphroditic, and something about that news feels right, not just in our reason but in the part of us that yearns for the other" (p. 97). (We'll discuss evolutionary psychology as it relates to our study later in this chapter.)

While this "urge to merge" encompasses *erotic love,* it's nevertheless more fundamental than pure eroticism and certainly much more than merely physical. It's a spiritual longing as well, for that perfection of the soul in its essential form — a rather complicated Platonic idea. And it relates to the longing for a *soul mate.*

Further, this longing can be understood as *cosmic,* as controlled by the gods and beyond our mental or physical control — all aspects of our own current idealizations of coupleship.

---

[1]The term *hermaphrodite* itself derives from another Greek myth, wherein Hermaphroditus, the son of Hermes (Mercury in Roman myth) and Aphrodite (the Roman's Venus, Goddess of Love), was loved by the Nymph Salmakis, who clung to him and prayed that she could be with him forever. On hearing her prayer, the gods merged their two forms into one, creating a single being that was both male and female. In what is considered medically to be a rare birth defect termed *hermaphroditism,* some humans *do* have sex organs and characteristics of both males and females. These individuals are called *hermaphrodites.*

Cupid's Arrow (Myth #2)

Another classical and universal mythic theme reverberating the idea of the divine causation of *love beyond our own control* involves the ancient **Greek god of love, Eros**, and the **Roman's Cupid**, as well as **Kama**, the **Indian god of desire** — all ironically (and dangerously) frequently blind or blindfolded while shooting the archer's arrow that targets the unsuspecting mortal or even another god, causing heartfelt *love at first sight* of sometimes highly inappropriate objects of instant affection.

Sternberg (1998) noted several concepts illustrated by that imagery: "the swiftness of falling in love, the sometimes arbitrary choice of the beloved, the pain that love can cause, and some kind of external force that is calling the shots. ... Throughout the ages, the idea of inevitability has been at the core of diverse notions of love and especially of love at first sight" (p. 77). He added that this concept "is one of the most unrealistic commonalities in classical love stories and, when applied to modern relationships, one of the most damaging" (p. 77).

Clearly, so many of these early myths describe sex, love, and romance cosmically beyond human control because that is how these phenomena seemed in their world: beyond their control and understanding.

Sex in Myths (Myth #4)

Myths tell how death and sexuality made their appearance in the world (Eliade, 1993). In his comprehensive reference guide to myths from every part of the world, Kenneth McLeish (1996) explained that the impulse to mate — what he calls the *sex-urge* — appeared in two ways in most myth-traditions: In the earlier myths it's a physical equivalent of an irresistible mental urge that started the process of creation; later myths assign responsibility for the sex-urge to specific gods and goddesses, "who combined seductiveness with unpredictability and danger, and who oversaw the fertility of the gods, the universe, and all creation except demons, monsters, and creatures of the Underworld" (p. 549).

In the Mesopotamian region (from Nineveh to Babylon), **Ishtar** (a.k.a. **Astarte** and **Isis**) was **goddess of sex**. Like Eros and Cupid and Kama, Ishtar ("Star") was an archer with arrows of desire, and her songs of lust as goddess of war (an additional duty) became battle cries that "froze the enemies' blood" (McLeish, 1996, p. 296). (Note that **love and war** are frequently coupled in mythology; see Myth #8.) McLeish offered a fascinating descriptive note about another aspect of Ishtar's contradictory nature that remains central in modern-day idealizations and illusions of sex, love, and romance: "Eternally promiscuous, she bathed in a sacred lake each evening to restore her virginity"(p. 296).

Ishtar figures prominently in the Mesopotamian *Epic of Gilgamesh*, which is one of the world's oldest narratives, compiled in the third or second millennium B.C.E. (i.e., as long ago as 5,000 years). Archeologists have found evidence of a real Gilgamesh who lived around 2700 B.C.E. McLeish notes that Gilgamesh might also be *The Bible*'s "Nimrod, son of Cush." In the *Epic,* Ishtar — insulted by Gilgamesh's rejection — destroys him and his bosom buddy Enkidu, a beast who earlier in the legend is seduced by a beautiful prostitute who tames and "civilizes" him by teaching him the art of sex as well as washing, wearing clothes, and drinking alcohol (see Myth #7).

The Love of the Beautiful (Myth #5 and #7)

In *The Symposium,* Plato presented his theory that love is the desire to possess **the good** (or **the beautiful**) forever. For Plato, who tried to explain concepts rationally and idealistically, the most admirable lovers are those who move from the love of the physical and individual to the love of the intellectual and general.

Ironically, in a skewed interpretation of Plato, the physical has been emphasized and elevated. Throughout the ages, beauty and goodness are frequently linked together in mythology and legend, so that being beautiful or handsome *equates to* being good. In reality, of course, physical beauty is a poor basis for lasting committed relationships.

McLeish (1996) asserted:

> All myth-traditions treated physical beauty as one of the absolutes of existence, a possession as character-defining as skill in crafts or prophecy, a force as irresistible as lust or rage. It had the power to enhance other qualities in the possessor, so that (for example) a gentle beauty was overwhelmingly desirable .... Also, since beauty required an admirer as well as a possessor it involved relationships and was often the catalyst for enormous events of creation or destruction in the existence of mortals and gods alike. (p. 87)

When the angry gods removed beauty from someone, the good creature became a demon. On the other hand, love is **transformational**. Perhaps that is why the Roman poet Ovid (whom Ackerman [1995, p. 39] called "love's scribe and laborer") selected *Metamorphoses* as the title for his poetic epic. Beauty can tame a beast — as in the *Epic of Gilgamesh*. Myths often show a *male* **testing** a *female* (rarely the reverse), who must prove she is virtuous by liking a man who looks horrible but becomes handsome through her virtuous love. Fairy tales frequently present such plots. *Beauty and the Beast* is the classic.

Rescue Fantasies (Myth #6, #7, and #10)

Tales of damsels-in-distress rescued by knights-in-shining-armor and stories like *Beauty and the Beast* can be read as narratives of **codependency** — an unhealthy dependence of two people on each other who reinforce each other's need to be needed and/or rescued. Codependents are people who let another person's behavior affect them and who are obsessed with controlling that person's behavior (Beattie, 1987). Many couples exhibit this dysfunction, which, at the extreme, can lead to abuse and even death.

According to Transactional Analysis therapist **Stephen Karpman** (1968), "Fairy tales help inculcate the norms of society into young minds consciously, but subconsciously may provide an attractive stereotyped number of roles, locations, and timetables for an errant life script" (p. 39). Using fairy tales and Script Drama Analysis, he developed the **Karpman Drama Triangle** to help clients visualize and analyze dysfunctional roles they play in codependent relationships. The triangle diagrams three primary roles, which parallel the three changing roles in Greek drama: hero/heroine (called the **rescuer** in this triangular model), **victim**, and villain (**persecutor**). These roles are manipulative, inauthentic, and destructive of self and others. Rescuers have martyr tendencies and power issues, seeking power and love by helping and controlling their victim and feeling resentful if they are unsuccessful. Victims frequently begin to resent their loss of autonomy and the strings attached to the rescue. Then they become persecutors of their rescuers, who become victims. If rescuers aren't appreciated sufficiently, they might become persecutors. Persecutors are often critical and abusive — verbally, emotionally, or physically. They are frequently the victims of counterattacks. It's a chaotic cycle.

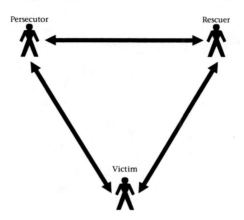

Although we all play these roles from time to time, codependents get stuck in them. The therapeutic goal is to exit from the triangle. One way to do this is to nurture yourself and stop usurping responsibility for romantic partners. Another is to stop expecting that a partner can complete you and make your dreams come true.

Feminist poet and cultural critic Adrienne Rich (1980/1993) argued that women have been conditioned to believe that they are incomplete and abnormal without a man and that this conditioning — which she termed "**compulsory heterosexuality**" and viewed as criminal — can lead to the acceptance of counterproductive and even abusive relationships to which women will cling in desperation to meet that cultural norm:

> In Western tradition, one layer — the romantic — asserts that women are inevitably, even if rashly and tragically, drawn to men; that even when that attraction is suicidal (e.g., *Tristan and Isolde,* Kate Chopin's *The Awakening),* it is still an organic imperative. In the tradition of the social sciences it asserts that primary love between the sexes is "normal"; that women *need* men as social and economic protectors, for adult sexuality, and for psychological completion ... (p. 221)

Barriers & Battles *(Myth #8 and #9)*

Tests are frequent in myths and fairy tales. For lovers, **tests of societal disapproval** and **tests of separation** commonly test their commitment. The idea of the contest is so often central to infatuation that modern psychology has named the concept of intensification of passion due to obstruction "**the Romeo and Juliet effect**" (Fisher, 1992, p. 48). In its purest and most spiritual sense, love is always envisioned as conquering every barrier, even death. In this ideology, lovers with conflicting values can easily overcome these differences, which fade in the face of love's power.

And, as noted earlier, love in myth often combines with war and its images. In *The Art of Love,* the Roman poet Ovid wrote: "Love is a kind of war [or war story], and no assignment for cowards." The plays of Shakespeare, who adapted many of these classical myths, are filled with verbal sparring — a parallel to the more **physical contests and competitions** in ancient myths (Sternberg, 1998, p. 85). The *Kama Sutra,* Sternberg also pointed out, includes entire chapters on techniques for striking and biting a lover as well as advice on how to have love quarrels.

In some ways, these contests represent *ludic* love with its gameplayers who range from innocent jokesters to sinister manipulators. In their darker aspect, these contests represent the frightening side of *manic, passionate* love, with out-of-control victims of slings and arrows. Of course, if partners have vastly values, conflicts are inevitable.

Heroes & Love (Myth #6 and #11)

Swaggering around the world, fighting battles and undertaking quests — "primarily in a macho dimension" (McLeish, 1996, p. 258) — were the mythic **heroes**. In Greek mythology this term signified the offspring of one mortal and one immortal parent, so Greek heroes spend a lot of time trying to balance their dual divine-yet-human nature. In all traditions, whether semi-god or not, they were leaders of human communities.

Until the 12th century, the dominant form of coupleship remained under the **heroic love model**, whose main theme is the "pursuit and capture of woman by the man" (Hendrix, 1988, p.244). But in the 12th century, troubadours popularized a major revolution in the idealized conception of love: "romance" and chivalry, or courtly love.

Related Myths of "Courtly Love"

French poets, in the 11th century,[2] discovered or invented, or were the first to express, that romantic species of passion which English poets were still writing about in the 19th. They effected a change which has left no corner of our ethics, our imagination, or our daily life untouched …. Compared with this revolution, the Renaissance is a mere ripple.

— C. S. Lewis, *The Allegory of Love*

Courtly love, developed by aristocratic ladies and disseminated by **troubadours** in the courts of the nobility in 12th century France, was "truly revolutionary," according to medieval literature scholar Andrea Hopkins (1994), who wrote *The Book of Courtly Love: The Passionate Code of the Troubadours*, "because it placed women, who technically had no power in medieval society, in a position of complete dominance over their lovers" (p. 11). The troubadours — precursors of today's popular recording artists — were musicians who composed and sang poetry about love in almost religious terms, with the woman (often unnamed but usually the wife of the troubadour's lord) "venerated as an object of worship" in a sort of religious cult of love "with its own deities — Venus and Cupid — and its own temples, rites, prayers, priests, and commandments" (p. 11). Thus, they combined the myths and rituals of earlier pagan religions and Platonic ideals with their own contemporary Christianity. In fact, once Christianity gained popularity, love came to include a quality indicative of a spiritual kind of selflessness (*agape*).

Courtly love was idealized and spiritualized, non-marital and non-intimate, but it was also intense and emotional, passionate (in the religious sense) and painful (because unconsummated). Marriage was still regarded primarily as an economic and political union (Branden, 1980; Hendrick & Hendrick, 1992; Stone, 1988), but the beginning of the modern concept of romantic love — emphasizing heterosexual love as well as the principles of free choice and mutual admiration —

---

[2]Some scholars place the beginning of courtly love in the 11th century; most, however, place it in the 12th.

originated with this courtly love code in which sexuality was scorned as were many types of worldly pleasures. In this model, women were indeed placed on pedestals for adoration from afar.

Through the code of chivalry (so-called from the French for a man on horseback or a knight), the warrior-hero was modified and civilized into the courtier and gentleman (Hopkins, 1994) who balanced warfare and love, as well as an occasional tournament. Mass Media Myth #7 is firmly rooted in this concept, as is Myth #6. The impact of this idealized woman was, as Hendrick and Hendrick (1992) put it, "the ennoblement of the male from a rather loutish brute at best to heights of self-sacrifice, pure thoughts, and loving consideration of his chosen lady" (p. 84).

Thus, during the Middle Ages this new concept of romantic love was viewed as a humanizing experience and a refining influence. According to Hopkins: "For the first time in post-classical Europe, a man's status as a civilized being, a member of courtly society, was judged partly by his behavior towards women" (p. 13). Indeed, our word *courtesy* derives from these rules of courtly behavior. Likewise, some of the highly stylized and ritualized forms and symbolic acts of courtly love persist today in an evolved form, which we call *courting* (Hendrick & Hendrick, 1992).

This form of love and its very name (both of which derive from the French love stories, *romans*) were anglicized into "romance" and found expression in stories, songs, poems, and plays. From this setting came "all the great themes that form the basis of our romantic literature," including and especially knights-in-shining-armor and fair ladies who share a "holy passion" and "unattainable ideal" (Johnson, 1983, pp. 46–47) — Tristan and Isolde, Arthur and His Roundtable Knights, Lancelot and Guinevere.

Romantic love, added Johnson, is "story-book" love (p. 46) — a very poor basis for coupleship. For example, in the world of the courtly lover, Hopkins observed, love is always at first sight (p. 17). Likewise, barriers such as parental prohibitions and physical separations were believed to make love intensify as well as to make the tales of love more interesting (pp. 55–59). Even more common in these tales of romance is the interference of jealous husbands (p. 59). "It should be remembered," Hopkins advised, "that courtly love was partly conceived as an imaginative escape from the horrors of a loveless marriage" (p. 69).

A Revolutionary Concept: Marriage Based on "Love"

Although the dominance of the troubadours died out after a century, the evolution toward a joyful notion of romantic love continued into the Renaissance of the 16th century and was further nurtured by the rise of Protestantism during the Reformation, which gave way to a culture that secularized much of Europe and shunned much of the antiwoman, antisexuality doctrine of the Medieval Catholic Church (Branden, 1980). Love was advocated as a natural precondition of marriage, as evidenced in the literature of the period (e.g., Shakespeare's plays) (Branden, 1980; Stone, 1988) — even though this new practice remained scandalous to the majority of traditionalists (Hendrick & Hendrick, 1992).

As Ackerman (1995) explained: "*Romeo and Juliet* is but one Renaissance example of a radical idea spreading through the bourgeoisie — that romance might be combined with marriage. ...The bourgeoisie wanted to indulge in the delights of courtly love, but without feeling sinful" (p. 74).

Of course, it took about 400 years for love to establish itself (at least in the Western world) as the primary basis for marriage. At first love was only one of several other more important factors, including status, family alliances, and economic security (Hendrick & Hendrick, 1992). Nevertheless, the emerging middle class was becoming a force for expanded possibilities, "though rationality was supposed to be the basis of marriage," which was still arranged by families (Branden, 1980, p. 25).

Then, came the Age of Reason — the so-called era of the Enlightenment, lasting from the mid-17th century to the early part of the 19th century, and with it came many expansive new theories, including the presumption that humans had the right to happiness and pleasure. "For the first time in human history," Branden noted, "it was explicitly recognized that human beings *should be free to choose their own commitments*" (p. 29). Most marriages remained economically or politically motivated, but a revolutionary notion was gathering momentum: "Couples might grow to love each other after they were married."

According to Fisher (1992), the Industrial Revolution that began in the late 1700s and early 1800s changed Europe and the United States from agrarian cultures in which "farming couples needed each other to survive" (p. 106) to mechanized urban cultures in which men — and women — earned money and had individual discretion about their lives in a way never before possible. Even divorce was becoming a more widespread possibility, particularly in non-Catholic countries.

The rise of the importance of the individual and the economic changes in society encouraged a new view of relationships. This new view considered as a *right* the ability of men and women to choose to marry one another on the basis of emotion rather than economic need or family pressure (Stone, 1988). In addition to the impact of the Industrial Revolution, the Romantic movement in literature affected male/female relationships in the 19th century. Indeed, as Branden[3] (1980) put it, "...finding one's 'soul mate', choosing the appropriate person, was of the highest importance" (p. 33)

Ackerman (1995) noted: "[Romantics] urged people to follow the heart rather than the head" — and love was again a high value" (p. 82). After the rationalism of the 18th century's Enlightenment, Romanticism became fashionable. Perhaps encouraged by its more secular culture, immigrant population, and frontier mentality, America set the standard for the rest of the Western world in this area (Branden, 1980).

Then, as the 20th century was dawning, Freud ironically paved the way for the liberating sexual revolution — despite his paradoxically antiromantic misogynistic views (see next section of this chapter).

Hendrick and Hendrick (1992) noted that, over the past 200 years, finally free-to-choose individuals have gradually came to realize that similiarity of backgrounds and values are important to successful coupleship because these qualities reduce conflict potential. In our own time, we have also come to see the value of

---

[3]Branden complained, however, that the writers of this Romantic era could not escape their time. Their novels were unrealistic and sentimental escapist fare, typically set in the past without relevance to the problems of their own day. He argued:

> But what romantic love requires, and what the Romantic vision of the nineteenth century utterly failed to provide, is an *integration* of reason and passion — a balance between the subject and the objective that human beings can live with. To express the same thought differently: What romantic love requires, and what Romantic writers fail to provide, is *psychological realism*. (p.36)

His point is relevant to our study of Romantic media forms.

ongoing communication. Love remains glorified in the United States; in fact, marriages for economic convenience or reasons other than love are regarded as simply un-American (Blumstein & Schwartz, 1983).

Related Interpretation of Mythic Themes in Psychoanalysis

Freud's View of Love

Myths about sex and love were both shattered and reestablished by the father of psychoanalysis, **Sigmund Freud**, more than 100 years ago. Although many have discredited his theories, his influence is still felt, and his methods are still widely utilized by many practicing therapists as well as by media critics. He viewed love as **sublimated sexuality** — a means of rechanneling unacceptable sexual desire in a socially acceptable fashion. Freud believed that when we fall in love, we regress to a childish state and *idealize our partner* in much the same way we once idealized our parents. His theory was based on his belief that our emotional lives as adults are greatly influenced by our early childhood relationships with those who raised us.

Freud utilized Platonic ideals and ancient myths to develop his theories. One of the most famous examples is his use of the **Oedipus and Electra myths** to describe our childhood frustration and disappointment at discovering our passion for our other-sex parent cannot be consummated. Hurt by perceived parental rejection, we repress our sexual desires for some time and even feel and express antagonism for the other sex. Later we begin looking for someone to love who reminds us of the other-sex parent. Of course, much of this process occurs on the subconscious level.

Many others have built on Freud's ideas. For example, psychoanalytic theory is the basis of famous child psychologist Bruno Bettelheim's *The Uses of Enchantment: The Meaning and Importance of Fairy Tales* (1976).

Carl Jung's Universal Archetypes

Some universal themes about sex, love, and romance transcend both time and space. For example, Shakespeare transformed the ancient Greek myth of *Pyramus and Thisbe* into his Elizabethan *Romeo and Juliet,* which Leonard Bernstein, Stephen Sondheim, and Arthur Laurents transformed into the stage and movie musical *West Side Story. Cinderella* has counterparts in both Chinese literature (*The Golden Carp*) and Russian literature (*Vassilissa, the Fair*) (Sternberg, 1998, pp. 75–76).

These are classics for a reason. They convey some central concepts that touch human beings in every generation across the centuries. Is it because they reveal truths about human nature — or is it because they reveal larger-than-life drama we'd *like* to be true but isn't? (Sternberg suggested that we might cherish these stories precisely *because* they're unrealistic!)

Over the last century, analysts have examined the purpose and effect of myth on our modern culture. **Freud** saw myths as expressing repressed impulses commonly found in the personal unconscious; for example, the myth of Oedipus expresses a boy's socially unacceptable desire to kill his father and have sex with his mother.

However, whereas Freud saw the unconscious as being entirely personal, the product of a lifetime's repressed sexual urges, **Carl Jung** (one of Freud's students) imagined another layer of consciousness below this: **the collective unconscious** — a vast psychic pool of energized symbols shared by humanity as a whole and filled with **archetypes** or symbolic figures, such as the Mother and the Father. An archetype is an unlearned tendency to experience things in a certain way. These archetypes form the *dramatis personae* of myth. Thus myths offer a way for cultures to explore their collective impulses.

Everyone has a more superficial Personal Unconscious, but Jung's Collective Unconscious is universal, predating the individual and comprising all religious, spiritual, and mythological symbols and experiences. For Jung, these archetypes were the conceptual matrixes or patterns behind all our religious and mythological concepts and even our general thinking processes — a kind of genetic memory or "psychic inheritance," the repository of our experiences as a species. Some experiences show the effects of the collective unconscious more clearly than others: for example, love at first sight or *deja vu* (the feeling that you've been in a specific setting before even though you haven't).

Although not everyone agrees with Jung's ideas, the influence of his theories has been vast. Jung's basic concept, as Holtsmark (2001) put it, is "what is at heart mythic is at heart universal" (p. 49), and his analysis frees myth from culture specificity and puts it on a deeply human basis. Like Freudian analysis, Jungian psychology is a major branch of the field, with worldwide Jungian "Societies" dedicated to its study and application. Therapists as well as arts and media scholars employ Jung's archetypes and his other theories of intuition and integration. (The goal of Jungian analysis is the *integration* of the seemingly opposite urges *within* each of us.) Mythicist Joseph Campbell's popular 1988 PBS television series *The Power of Myth with Bill Moyers* (one year after Campbell's death) introduced Jungian analysis of the hero archetype to a general audience of millions of people. And George Lucas has acknowledged using the hero archetype in the creation of his *Star Wars* trilogy.

Jung's major archetypal patterns related to our study are:

- **Mother**
- **Shadow**
- **Anima/Animus**
- **Syzygy (Divine Couple)**
- **Self.**

The infinite variety of all myths and dreams derive from these archetypal patterns and images, which Jung believed operated at the unconscious level in every culture and in every time period of human history. In Jungian psychology, even the theories of the natural sciences — such as biological evolution, for example — can be seen as mythic constructs relating to one or more of the archetypes.

The Mother is our built-in ability to recognize the relationship of "mothering." Everyone had a mother, so this archetype is universally experienced. Even when an archetype doesn't have a particular real person available, we tend to personify the archetype, that is, turn it into a mythological "story-book" character who symbolizes the archetype. **Father** is also an important archetype we can all understand, even if we don't personally know our own. In Christianity, God is "Our Father." **The Child and the Family** are also archetypes.

The Shadow — or "dark side" — is the personification of that part of us that we deny in ourselves and project onto "others," interpreting them as "enemies" or as "exotic" presences that fascinate us. The shadow is potential but amoral evil that derives from our prehuman past, when our concerns were limited to survival and reproduction and when we weren't self-conscious. We see the shadow everywhere in popular culture (the "wicked stepmother" or the "beast"). The devil is the great shadow image of religion. The great themes of literature revolve around conflict between good and evil that sometimes manifests itself between individuals and sometimes is within an individual. The goal of personality integration is to integrate the "bad," rejected, inferior side of our life into our total experience and to take responsibility for it.

The Anima & Animus ("soul" in its feminine and masculine forms) archetype represents our inner opposite: males their anima, and females their animus. It is also the archetype that is responsible for much of our love life. As in ancient Greek myth, we're always looking for our other half, which the Gods took from us, when we encounter members of the other sex. Consider Superman and Lois Lane. Clark Kent is the inferior, shadow side of Superman, but he is also closer to ordinary people. Lois Lane has no interest in Clark. She is infatuated with Superman, her animus or the masculine completion of her own personality. Jung argued that most people experience only half of themselves — either the anima or the animus. As small children we are conscious that we are either male or female. Both our biological construction and our subsequent cultural conditioning play a significant part in how we perceive ourselves and how we perceive others of the same and the other sex. Though we have progressed through many millennia, the fundamental male-female issues portrayed in the mass media are not much different from those in ancient times.

The Syzygy (**The Divine Couple**) represents a pattern of wholeness and integration. If one comes to terms with the dualities in the shadow and in the soul, one will encounter the enchanted castle with its king and queen, where the opposites of the outer and the inner life are now joined in marriage. Great power arises from this integration.

The Self is the ultimate and most important archetype or pattern, the unity of the personality wherein human self and divine self are incapable of distinction. For Jung this is the God-image of perfection, which we don't achieve on earth but nevertheless seek all our lives.

Related Biological Bases of Myth in Evolutionary Psychology (Sociobiology)

While the mythic archetypes advanced by Jung spring at least in part from our biology — anima/animus, mother/father, family, the goal of Jungian analysis is to *integrate* the seemingly opposite or conflicting aspects of these archetypes in one's self. A different (and controversial) perspective that focuses on the prehistoric influence of *segregated* sex-roles is **evolutionary psychology** or **sociobiology**, a relatively new discipline whose own theoretical breakthroughs came from the work of psychologists teamed with anthropologists led by **social psychologist David M. Buss** in 1970s and 1980s. Their purpose was to study and explain human mating behavior based on **Darwin's theory of sexual selection.** Darwin had posited two key processes by which evolutionary change can occur: preferences for a mate and competition for a mate (Buss, 1994, p.3). Buss and his team tried to identify psychological mechanisms that were the product of evolution.

The central conclusion of the evolutionary psychologists or sociobiologists is that only prehistoric humans with certain genetic advantages were able to survive and reproduce. These genes have been passed to modern humans, who are influenced by vestiges of these reproductive strategies.

According to sociobiologists, *the major function of romantic love is to aid the continuation of the human species through sexual intercourse.* In other words, behaviors that we think of as love have evolved because they supported increased reproductive success. They are now "instinctive." For the male, this means propagating the species by sowing his seeds and thereby his genes with as many healthy females as possible. (In this theory, health is signaled by *youth and attractiveness).* Females, on the other hand, must screen these male candidates and carefully select and secure the male or males who offer the *best resources* to take care of them and their offspring and who are *ready to commit* to doing so.

From this overall framework, Buss has suggested evolutionary rather than purely cultural explanations for some of the myths and stereotypes that are the focus of our study — particularly Mass Media Myths #4, #5, #6, and #8. In *The Evolution of Desire: Strategies of Human Mating*, he describes some of them; for example:

- The reason men prefer women who are young and attractive might be that these attributes signal good health and, therefore, reproductive advantage.

- The reason women prefer men who are older might be that older men tend to have higher social status and greater resources.

- Taller men also have higher social status in most cultures.

- Women also want stronger males for protection. (To illustrate this evolutionary preference, Buss describes an animal behavior — female frogs who bump the males to test their strength — that seems almost a spoof of the bickering and battling that some couples then justify as demonstrations of love.)

- Similarly, playing hard-to-get and indifferent to the pursuer has been an effective mate-attracting strategy for women. In *The Anatomy of Love,* anthropologist Helen Fisher (1992) also reported that barriers actually help provoke the "mystery and madness essential to romantic love" (p. 48) and that hard-to-get is an important motivational tool, as described earlier in the *Romeo & Juliet effect.*

- The so-called battle of the sexes might be over resources and sexual access, two areas in which men and women have different and sometimes conflicting sexual strategies.

Although its arguments are indeed interesting, this theory is only that: *a theory.* In that sense, it's like mythic or even Freudian interpretations and explanations of the human experience. And sociobiology has been attacked by critics from a variety of disciplines, many of whom find it too biological and not sufficiently sociological.

The proponents of the evolutionary psychology theory claim it *blends both the biological and the cultural approaches.* Buss (1994) countered: "Evolutionary psychology represents a true interactionist view [between biological determinism and environmental determinism], which identifies the historical, developmental, cultural, and situational features that formed human psychology and guide that psychology today" (p. 17).

Nevertheless, not everyone is enthusiastic about the theory, as Buss himself acknowledged:

> Resistance to evolutionary psychology comes from [among others] the feminist movement. Many feminists worry that evolutionary explanations imply an inequality between the sexes, support restrictions on the roles that men and women can adopt, encourage stereotypes about the sexes, perpetuate the exclusion of women from power and resources and foster pessimism about the possibilities for changing the status quo ...yet evolutionary psychology does not carry these feared implications for human mating. In evolutionary terms, men and women are identical in many or most domains, differing only in the limited areas in which they have faced recurrently different adaptive problems over human evolutionary history. For example, they diverge primarily in their preferences for a particular sexual strategy, not in their innate ability to exercise the full range of human sexual strategies. (pp. 17–18)

Buss added: "A final source of resistance to evolutionary psychology comes from the idealistic views of romance, sexual harmony, and lifelong love to which we all cling" (p. 18).

Let's take a closer look at how these myths, idealizations, and theories can be molded into stereotypes that can be deceptive and damaging to individuals and society.

WHAT ARE "STEREOTYPES"?

What matters is the character of the stereotypes, and the gullibility with which we employ them.

— Walter Lippmann, *Public Opinion*

Although myths and other interpretations of human experience of sex, love, and romance can be useful as background to understanding why we function as we do, they can also be harmful **stereotypes** — positive or negative characterizations of a group of people based only on expectations or assumptions about the group, thus erasing the features of individuals and turning us all into rag-dolls and robots. Stereotypes are "mental cookie-cutters" (*Meaning and Significance,* n.d.) that force a simplistic narrow pattern on a whole group and preclude individuality, spontaneity, and independence (such as "Men only want one thing." or "Women are all gold-diggers."). Moreover, they might be completely false.

Consider these definitions:

— **stereotype (noun)**
1. A conventional, formulaic, and oversimplified conception, opinion, or image.
2. One that is regarded as embodying or conforming to a set image or type.
3. Printing. A metal printing plate cast from a matrix molded from a raised printing surface, such as type.

— **stereotype (transitive verb)**
1. To make a stereotype of.
2. To characterize by a stereotype.
3. To give a fixed, unvarying form to.
4. To print from a stereotype.

As you can see, the term *stereotype* has journalistic origins. First of all, a *stereotype* was a kind of printing stamp to make multiple copies from a single model or mold. Then in 1922, journalist and commentator **Walter Lippmann** used the term metaphorically in his pioneering book *Public Opinion* to describe the way we (as a society and as individuals) categorize *people* — "stamping" human beings with a set of characteristics and creating what he called "pictures inside our head" (p. 4). But these pictures don't necessarily correspond to the world outside our heads.

Lippmann explained there's a gap — often huge — between the world as it really is and the world as we envision it through those pictures in our own head — a "fiction" or representation we've created. "To traverse the world," Lippman wrote, "men must have maps of the world. Their persistent difficulty is to secure maps on which their own need, or someone else's need, has not sketched in the coast of Bohemia" (p.16).

Characteristics of Stereotypes

Consider these **four characteristics of stereotypes** (*Meaning and Significance,* n.d.):

1. **Simple:** They're far more simple than reality and often expressed in two to three sentences.

2. **Acquired secondhand:** We acquire (and absorb) stereotypes from cultural mediators (like the mass media) rather than from our own direct experience with the stereotyped groups. The culture "distills" reality and then expresses its beliefs and values in stereotypical images that convince audiences of the "truth" of the stereotype by placing it in a carefully controlled context in which *there is a measure of truth to the image.*

3. **Erroneous:** All stereotypes are false — although some are less false than others, and (more importantly) some are less harmful than others. Because they claim that each and every individual human being in a certain group shares a set of common qualities, stereotypes are a logical impossibility. Even countertypes presented as the "new" truth about a group are false unless presented as *possibilities* rather than *actualities.*

4. **Resistant to change:** Even though race and sex inequalities have alerted most of us to the tragic consequences of stereotypes, old stereotypes nevertheless still color our perceptions. Fortunately, stereotypes *can* change when we decide to break the mold and recast those pictures in our heads.

If we cling too tightly to stereotypes, we can hurt others as well as ourselves. However, stereotypes can help us make sense of the world if we follow Lippmann's advice "to hold them lightly, to modify them gladly" (p. 91) thereby constructing clearer and more productive pictures of reality inside our heads.

Countertypes

In and of itself, stereotyping is morally neutral. In fact, stereotyping can be useful in a constructive way — such as simplifying complex realities to better determine actions in given circumstances. Classifications of individuals can be useful if employed to benefit rather than disadvantage others in a positive manner, arousing "good" emotions and associating a group with socially approved characteristics.

One such positive stereotype is the **countertype**, which evolves as an attempt to replace or "counter" a previously applied negative stereotype (*Meaning and Significance,* n.d.). While countertypes are important reflections (and shapers) of popular beliefs and values, we should remember two things:

1. **Countertypes are still stereotypes.** They, too, are oversimplified views of the group being stereotyped, so we can't accept them at face value any more than the negative stereotype they're seeking to replace or ameliorate.

2. **Countertypes are often merely surface correctives.** Under many countertypes are the slightly disguised old stereotypes — like the "successful career woman ...who really needs a man."

Conventional Characters & Stereotypic Idealizations in the Mass Media

Stereotyping of characters — for example in novels and movies — is a traditional tool of mass communicators to easily make a point and move the action forward quickly. There's the prostitute with the heart of gold, the tough boss who's going to relent, the bad guy with the black cowboy hat and ugly scar. But these stereotypes also represent cultural beliefs, feelings, and actions that are real and deeply held by the audience as well as the creator. As such, they're powerful reinforcers, usually of the status quo and of false images. We'll include stereotyping in our list of mass media storytelling techniques in Chapter 4.

Counterproductive Stereotypes in So-Called Self-Help Books

Before we conclude this chapter about how myths and stereotypes can foster the establishment of ideals and illusions and, thereby, unrealistic expectations about sex, love, and romance, let's reflect on the impact of even seemingly positive stereotypes in the mass media. Through these stereotypes, the media socialize us into specific roles and rituals, thus tragically limiting our human capacity. Remember: Stereotypes were originally metal molds that insured absolute uniformity. Anything that deviated from the mold was destroyed as useless.

Today, many of us uncritically accept the blinders that stereotypes impose on us, particularly in one of the most important areas of our lives: *love.* From the unhealthy stereotypes of what we should look like (*Bigger breasts! Thinner waists! Thicker hair! Tighter abs!*) to how we should behave (*A diamond is forever: This anniversary, show her how much she means to you!* and *Nothing says lovin' like something from the oven!*), the mass media creators of fiction, advertising, and even the news dictate what we as men and women and boys and girls should be to fit into those molds and patterns — regardless of our uniqueness.

And that goes for **harmful stereotypes presented to us as self-help strategies** we "should" use to improve our love live — for example, *The Rules* and John Gray's *Men Are From Mars/Women Are From Venus,* two extraordinarily popular books bought by millions of people in the United States and around the world.

Sadly, *The Rules* (a primer on manipulative "ludic" relationships) insulted the intelligence and assaulted the integrity of both the men it sought to control and the women it pretended to empower. (Apparently it didn't even work for one of the co-authors, who was divorced between editions.)

John Gray's *Men Are From Mars/Women Are From Venus,* which one Amazon.com reader/reviewer described as "Dark Ages stuff," presents accurate descriptions of some *communication style differences* that are *typically* found in males and females — although in actual practice, many females employ communication styles that Gray stereotypically terms "Martian," and many males are "Venusian." However, what he then offers as advice about dealing with those differences is, indeed, simplistic, male-chauvinistic, and ultimately counter-productive to good communication and good relationships. For example, for males to simply "go off to their caves" (It *does* sound prehistoric, doesn't it?) for indefinite periods is actually abusive, as is that behavior in females. And for men to just "listen" to women (or vice versa) without any input has been appropriately attacked in the academic literature. Moreover, the National Association of Cognitive-Behavioral Therapists, which has created a seminar called "Men and Women Are Earthlings: A Cognitive-Behavioral Approach to Marital Problems," cautions that "men and women are more alike than different" and "irrational metaphors, such as 'Mars & Venus', only make matters worse for couples who are having problems" (n.d.).

Now that you've read this chapter about ideals and illusions, you know precisely *why* simplistic, stereotyped advice strikes such a deep chord in so many people who are longing for the easy answers. Like quick-weight-loss schemes, these silly solutions might *seem* to work in the short run, but in the end you wind up worse than when you started.

The strategies for realistic and healthy coupleship presented in Chapter 3 have been researched and validated. They derive from scientific study and the scholarly literature. They're not as easy to implement as some of the fluffier stuff because they require genuine self-reflection and analysis, self-determination to change unhealthy patterns, and the refusal to indulge in self-destructive irrational thinking and behavior. But they work over the long term, and their benefits are astounding.

These realistic models actually can help us achieve the more magnificent, rewarding lives and loves that mythic and stereotyped models merely ape on a far lower and less satisfying level that's empty and sickening. (Can you imagine the effect of eating nothing but candy all your life?)

Unfortunately, we don't see the realistic models very often in the mass media.

SUMMARY

Myths are stories that influence a society's perspectives about the world, about themselves, about what behaviors and approaches have meaning or value. The focus of a myth, a sacred story that expresses moral values in human terms, is the powers in control of the human world and the relationship between those powers and human beings. These narratives are considered both true and sacred in the originating culture, but they are not verifiable because their source is usually impossible to document. Related narratives include epics, fables, fairy tales, folks tales, and legends.

Many of the myths about sex, love, and romance that influence us to adopt idealistic and unattainable models for our actual behavior originated with the ancient Greeks. Some of the themes in classical mythology that relate to the 12 major mass media myths in *Dr. FUN's Mass Media Love Quiz* include The One and Only Perfect Partner (based on Plato three sexes/hermaphrodite fable), Cupid's Arrow (cross-cultural metaphor), Sex in Myths (related to the creation process as well as to the sex-urge), The Love of the Beautiful (equated with the transformational power of the Good), Rescue Fantasies (codependency dramas described by Karpman), Barriers and Battles (tests of love), and Heroes and Love.

Courtly love, developed by aristocratic ladies and disseminated by troubadours in the courts of the nobility in 12th century France, revolutionized European views of love and of women, placing them on a pedestal and idealizing the coupled relationship, which was rarely physical. Other terms for courtly love are chivalric love and romance, which derives from the French word for love stories. Although this love was rarely between husband and wife, the movement nevertheless signaled the beginning of love as a precondition for marriage.

The Protestant Reformation, the Age of Reason, the Industrial Revolution, and the Romantic Era created an even more secularized society in which human beings had rights and were considered capable of choosing to marry one another on the basis of emotion rather than economic need or family pressure.

Myths about sex and love were both shattered and reestablished by the father of psychoanalysis, Sigmund Freud, who viewed love as sublimated sexuality and utilized Platonic ideals and ancient myths to develop his theories. Whereas Freud saw the unconscious as being entirely personal, the product of a lifetime's repressed sexual urges, Carl Jung imagined another layer of consciousness below this: a collective unconscious of universal archetypes, such as Mother, Shadow, Anima/Animus, Syzygy (Divine Couple), and Self. All myths and dreams derive from these archetypal patterns and images, which Jung found at the unconscious level in every culture and in every time period of human history.

Evolutionary psychology (sociobiology), developed by social psychologist David M. Buss, attempts to explain human mating behavior based on Darwin's theory. According to evolutionary theory, the major function of romantic love is to aid the continuation of the human species through sexual intercourse. In other words, behaviors that we think of as love have evolved because they supported increased reproductive success. This theory relates to some of the 12 major mass media myths in *Dr. FUN's Mass Media Love Quiz:* the so-called battle of the sexes, males' preference for attractive younger females, and females' preference for males who are older, taller, and stronger. Like myths, however, these explanations are theories based on interpretations.

Stereotypes, a term first used by Walter Lippmann in 1922, are positive or negative characterizations and categorizations of a group of people based only on expectations or assumptions about the group rather than on individuals who compose the group. Four basics of stereotypes are that they are (1) simple, (2) acquired secondhand, (3) erroneous, and (4) resistant to change. Stereotypes can be positive, such as countertypes. Stock characters in the mass media are stereotypes that can help media consumers more quickly and easily understand the narratives, but these characterizations can also be harmful in perpetuating false images. Stereotypes diminish the personhood of others and ourselves, often socializing us without our full knowledge and consent. We should be more critical of stereotyped messages, including self-help books that purport to offer easy simplistic solutions to the problems of coupleship and its enhancement.

SOURCES CITED

Ackerman, D. (1995). *A natural history of love.* New York: Vintage Books.

Beatty, M. (1987). *Codependent no more: How to stop controlling others and start caring for yourself.* New York: HarperCollins.

Blumstein, P., & Schwartz, P. (1983). *American couples.* New York: William Morrow.

Branden, N. (1980). *The psychology of romantic love.* New York: Bantam.

Buss, D. M. (1994). *The evolution of desire: Strategies of human mating.* New York: Basic Books.

de Rougemont, D. (1964). "The rising tide of Eros." In H.A. Grunwald (Ed.), *Sex in America* (pp. 291–311). New York: Bantam Books.

Eliade, M. (1993). "Toward a definition of myth." In Y. Bonnefoy (Comp.), *American, African, and old European mythologies.* Chicago: The University of Chicago Press.

Fisher, H. (1992). *Anatomy of love: A natural history of mating, marriage, and why we stray.* New York: Fawcett Columbine.

Hendrick, S., & Hendrick, C. (1992). *Liking, loving, and relating* (2nd ed.). Pacific Grove, CA: Brooks/Cole.

Hendrix. H. (1988). *Getting the love you want: A guide for couples.* New York: Henry Holt.

Himmelstein, H. (1994). *Television myth and the American mind* (2nd ed.). Westport, CT: Praeger.

Holtsmark, E. B. (2001). "The katabasis theme in modern cinema." In M.M. Winkler (Ed.), *Classical myth and culture in the cinema.* New York: Oxford University Press.

Hopkins, A. (1994). *The book of courtly love: The passionate code of the troubadours.* New York: HarperSanFrancisco.

Johnson, R. A. (1983). *WE: Understanding the psychology of romantic love.* San Francisco: Harper & Row.

Karpman, S. (1968). Fairy tales and script drama analysis. *Transactional Analysis Bulletin, 7* (26), 39-43.

Lippmann, W. (1922). *Public opinion.* New York: Harcourt-Brace.

McLeish, K. (1996). *Myth: Myths and legends of the world explored.* New York: Facts on File.

Meaning and significance of stereotypes in popular culture, The. (n.d.). Retrieved November 12, 2001, from http://www.serve.com/shea/stereodf.htm

National Association of Cognitive-Behavioral Therapists. (n.d.). Retrieved November 10, 2001, from http://www.nacbt.org/menandwomenareearthlings.htm

Plato. (1960). The Symposium. In *The Republic and other works* (B. Jowett, Trans.). Garden City, NY: Dolphin. (Original work published circa 385 B.C.E.)

Rich, A. C. (1993). "Compulsory heterosexuality and the lesbian existence." In B. C. Gelpi & A. Gelpi (Eds.), *Adrienne Rich's poetry and prose: Poems, prose, reviews, and criticism* (pp. 203–224). New York: W.W. Norton. (Original work published in 1980)

Sternberg, R. J. (1998). *Cupid's arrow: The course of love through time.* New York: Cambridge University Press.

Stone, L. (1988, February). A short history of love. *Harper's Magazine,* pp. 26–27.

Vande Berg, L. R., Wenner, L. A., & Gronbeck, B. E. (1998). *Critical approaches to television.* Boston: Houghton Mifflin.

3
DIAGNOSES & *DIS*-ILLUSIONS (REALISTIC MODELS)

Designs for Rational Love & Coupleship

To agree in the widest sense with reality can only mean to be guided either straight up to it or into its surroundings, or to be put into such working touch with it as to handle either it or something connected with it better than if we disagreed.

— William James, *The Meaning of Truth*

The key difference between true love and false love is that false love often ends with the honeymoon.

— Stan Katz & Aimee Liu, *False Love and Other Romantic Illusions*

As we saw in Chapter 2, myths and stereotypes can foster the establishment of ideals and illusions and, thereby, unrealistic expectations for males and females about sex, love, and romance. Through these stereotypes, the mass media socialize us into specific roles and rituals, thus unnecessarily and tragically limiting our human capacity.

Are there more realistic models of more appropriate coupleship?

Social psychology and cognitive-behavioral therapy offer many scientifically researched and validated models, strategies, and skills for realistic and healthy coupleship. In this chapter we'll review some of them that address the 12 major mass media myths that form the focus of our study. I've synthesized these recommendations as the 12 *Dr. Galician's Prescriptions*™ (see page 55) that serve as "antidotes" to the myths and stereotypes and as the basis of our analysis and criticism in Part II. Unfortunately, we don't see these healthy, rational models of sex, love, and romance very often in the mass media.

*"DIS-*ILLUSION"

In "I Know Things Now," one of my favorite songs from the brilliant Broadway play *Into the Woods: A New Musical* (in which Stephen Sondheim and James Lapine weave a variety of fairy tales into a satiric yet uplifting story), Little Red Riding Hood explains her escape from the wolf:

So we wait in the dark
Until someone sets us free,
And we're brought into the light,
And we're back at the start.

Noting that she now knows "many valuable things," she adds wistfully:

Isn't it nice to know a lot!
And a little bit not.

The definition of **dis**-illusion (both a noun and a transitive verb) is "to *free* or *deprive* of illusion." In other words, *dis*-illusioning ourselves and others can be either a good thing (freedom) or a bad thing (deprivation)! Many people choose to participate in what cultural critics call "their own oppression" by refusing to see the truth. It's easier to believe the myths and stereotypes than to construct our own worldview. Staying stuck in myths and stereotypes allows you to avoid responsibility for your own actions — irrationally blaming Cupid's arrows or even our own biological heritage as the cause of our romantic problems and wishing for magic forces or fairy godmothers to fix things. As Katz and Liu (1988) advise: "Living happily-ever-after requires a lot more hard work than magic" (p. 2).

To **dis**-illusion also means "to *dis*enchant" — as in to break a spell or bewitching or trance (the good part); the downside is we might feel we're going to be less "delighted" (another meaning of *enchant*).

In fact, nothing could be farther from the truth than the seeming downside of *dis*-illusion.

In *Dr. Galician's Prescriptions™ for Getting Real About Romance: How Mass Media Myths About Love Can Hurt You*, I advise readers to "Get real!" Substituting facts for fictions and taking responsibility for ourselves isn't a dreary undertaking. It's exhilarating. It's liberating. It's where the FUN *really* is.

Let's examine some *non*-mythic practices that can help people *get real* and improve their **coupled relationships** (often called "**close relationships**" in the scholarly literature).

Remember: Our ultimate goal is analysis and criticism of unrealistic portrayals in the mass media. The realistic models provide a benchmark for us.

THE RELATIONSHIP BETWEEN EXPECTATION & SATISFACTION

Certainly for the most part, the way we see things is a combination of what is there and what we expected to find. The heavens are not the same to the astronomer as to a pair of lovers.

Walter Lippmann, *Public Opinion*

A great many social psychologists, psychotherapists, marital counselors, and relationship researchers have listed **unrealistic expectations** of sex, love, and romance as a primary cause of dissatisfaction in real coupleships (Crosby, 1991; Ellis, 1969; Eidelson and Epstein, 1982; Epstein and Eidelson, 1981; Fromme, 1956; Galician, 1995, 1997, 1998, 2001; Hendrix, 1988; Katz & Liu, 1988; Laner & Russell, 1994, 1995; Lauer & Lauer, 1994; Lazarus, 1991; Peele & Brodsky, 1976; Tennov, 1979).

Major Mass Media Myths
& Corresponding Prescriptions™ for Healthy Coupleship

> Numbered items = *Dr. FUN's Mass Media Love Quiz©*
> Rx = *Dr. Galician's Prescriptions™ for Getting Real About Romance*

PARTNER IS PREDESTINED ...
1. Your perfect partner is cosmically predestined, so nothing/nobody can ultimately separate you.
   Rx: CONSIDER COUNTLESS CANDIDATES.

RIGHT AWAY, YOU KNOW ...
2. There's such a thing as "love at first sight."
   Rx: CONSULT your CALENDAR and COUNT CAREFULLY.

EXPRESSION NOT NECESSARY ...
3. Your true soul mate should KNOW what you're thinking or feeling (without your having to tell).
   Rx: COMMUNICATE COURAGEOUSLY.

SEXUAL PERFECTION ...
4. If your partner is truly meant for you, sex is easy and wonderful.
   Rx: CONCENTRATE on COMMITMENT and CONSTANCY.

CENTERFOLDS PREFERRED ...
5. To attract and keep a man, a woman should look like a model or a centerfold.
   Rx: CHERISH COMPLETENESS in COMPANIONS (not just the COVER).

ROLE OF GENDER (OR "REAL MEN") ...
6. The man should NOT be shorter, weaker, younger, poorer, or less successful than the woman.
   Rx: CREATE COEQUALITY; COOPERATE.

INTO A PRINCE (FROM BEAST) ...
7. The love of a good and faithful true woman can change a man from a "beast" into a "prince."
   Rx: CEASE CORRECTING and CONTROLLING; you CAN'T CHANGE others (only yourself!).

PUGILISM = PASSION ...
8. Bickering and fighting a lot mean that a man and a woman really love each other passionately.
   Rx: COURTESY COUNTS; CONSTANT CONFLICTS CREATE CHAOS.

TOTALLY OPPOSITE VALUES ...
9. All you really need is love, so it doesn't matter if you and your lover have very different values.
   Rx: CRAVE COMMON CORE-VALUES.

INCOMPLETE WITHOUT MATE ...
10. The right mate "completes you" — filling your needs and making your dreams come true.
   Rx: CULTIVATE your own COMPLETENESS.

OFTEN, ACTORS = ROLES ...
11. In real life, actors and actresses are often very much like the romantic characters they portray.
   Rx: (DE)CONSTRUCT CELEBRITIES.

NOT REAL/NO EFFECT ...
12. Since mass media portrayals of romance aren't "real," they don't really affect you.
   Rx: CALCULATE the very real CONSEQUENCES of unreal media.

Northwestern University Medical School psychiatry professor Richard Carroll (as cited in Bertagnoli, 2001) recently highlighted the need for becoming *dis*-illusioned: "During the courtship stage, people live in a fantasy stage. The challenge is moving beyond fantasy" (p. E1).

In a Rutgers University National Marriage Project study of 1,003 young adults ages 20 to 29 — "The State of Our Unions: The Social Health of Marriage in America 2001" — an overwhelming majority (94%) of the never-married singles had a romantic, unrealistic view of marriage that includes staying single until they find a "perfect" mate, evidenced by their agreement with the statement: "When you marry you want your spouse to be your soul mate, first and foremost" (Whitehead & Popenoe, 2001).

Katz & Liu's "False Love Syndrome"

Katz and Liu (1988) formulated what they call the **"false love syndrome,"** whose criteria "describe not lasting love, but illusion — illusion so powerful that it becomes difficult even to imagine any more realistic kind of love" (pp. 3–4). The false love criteria, which relate to several of the mass media myths and stereotypes, include:

- Finding the one person who is right for you
- Being intensely attracted to your partner
- Feeling excited whenever you're with your partner
- Rarely fighting
- Rarely wanting to be apart from your partner
- Having great sex
- Never being sexually attracted to anyone else
- Enjoying constant romance
- Never needing anyone but your partner in your life
- Complete fulfillment.

Conversely, they explained that the key ingredients of true love are **shared goals and commitment** — "as unromantic as it may seem" (Katz & Liu, 1988, p. 4). In addition, genuine love includes a balance of mutual supportiveness and independence and welcomes change and personal growth rather than fearing it. Understanding, trust, intimacy, and enjoyment with your partner are paramount to a successful relationship. But such relationships require an investment of time, energy, and dedication. Additionally, advocating realistic and rewarding models of love, Katz and Liu warned about expecting "perfection": "While it is not wise to enter into love with someone who lacks the characteristics you consider critical, neither is it sensible to create a fixed image of your 'ideal beloved'" (p. 6). Katz and Liu advised: Since we're not perfect, we shouldn't expect others to be.

Eidelson & Epstein's Relationship Beliefs Inventory (RBI)

To systematically assess unrealistic or **dysfunctional** expectations that lead to distress in intimate relationships, cognitive-behavioral psychologists **Roy J. Eidelson** and **Norman Epstein** (1982) developed the **Relationship Beliefs Inventory** (RBI), a 40-item questionnaire that yields five scales (with 8 items each). The scales, which also relate to our mass media myths and stereotypes, are:

- *Disagreement Is Destructive* (which can lead to attempts at conflict resolution by coercion or avoidance)

- *Mind Reading Is Expected* (which generally results in disappointment, misperception, and escalation of conflict)

- *Partners Cannot Change* (a "terminal hypothesis" [p. 715] that suggests no hope for problem amelioration)

- *Sexual Perfectionism* (which, ironically, can inhibit sexual responsiveness)

- *The Sexes Are Different* (a stereotyped perceptual field).

With an earlier version of their RBI, Epstein and Eidelson (1981) found that married couples with unrealistic beliefs about romantic love rated both their *marital satisfaction levels and their chances for an improved relationship lower than average.* (They noted that *"unrealistic"* and *"irrational"* have been used interchangeably in the literature.) In particular, the marital satisfaction of couples in their study was negatively correlated with three of the scales on the RBI: Mind Reading Is Expected, Disagreement Is Destructive, and Partners Cannot Change.

Expectation Differences Between the Sexes

Further complicating the problem is that males and females in general are socialized toward different expectations. Using scales adapted in part from a 12th century treatise about courtly love, Rechtien and Fiedler (1988) found that both men and women agree that 20th century women have expectations of male partners that are similar to those central to the 12th century notion of courtly love. When **expectations of relationships differ by sex**, successful relationships may be difficult to achieve without a conscious effort by the partners to understand each other.

In another study of sex differences regarding seven dimensions of romantic love, Cimbalo and Novell (1993) found that men scored significantly higher on sexual behavior and aberrant sexual behavior. The researchers concluded that romantic love is a multidimensional concept whose dimensions hold different amounts of importance for men and women: Women appear to respond to security-based stimuli, men to sexuality-based stimuli. (The findings of this research offer an interesting parallel to the arguments of Buss and his evolutionary psychology colleagues, described in Chapter 2.)

The Difficulty of Changing Unrealistic Beliefs

The problem is that it's not easy to change these unrealistic beliefs.

In fact, some experts (Peele & Brodsky, 1976; Tennov, 1979) believe that at the obsessive extreme, "romantic" relationships are a form of addiction. (This type of love corresponds to the Greek "mania.") **Peele** viewed it as a form of **sickness** ("pathology"). **Tennov** has termed it **"limerence,"** an emotionally disabling attachment filled with anxiety, fantasy, over-dependence and enmeshment, and frightening obsession. Like Katz and Liu, these psychologists have delineated the differences between real love — which is productive, enlarging, and joyful — and false love, which is often mythic and stereotypic.

Another physical phenomenon that contributes to the confusion between real love and false love is called the **misattribution of arousal**, described by social psychologists (Berscheid & Walster, 1974; Gold, Rickman, & Mosley, 1984; Schachter & Singer, 1962; White, Fishbein, & Rutstein, 1981; all as cited in Lauer & Lauer, 1994). These researchers have conducted classic experiments demonstrating that, in some cases, the arousal someone attributes to the feeling of love might actually be physical arousal — such as a pounding heart from exercise or caffeine or media stimulation. For example, misattribution of arousal can be responsible for the feeling of love "at first sight" (see Mass Media Myth #2).

Our education in rational love should start early. Sociologists **Laner and Russell** (1994) found that a semester-long university courtship and marriage class was able to lower marital expectations of never-married students *only slightly and only among women.* These unmarried young adults also had significantly higher marital expectations than did a group of subjects married 10 or more years. When the researchers repeated this study with a larger sample and an improved design, they found *no change* in expectations (Laner & Russell, 1995). Laner and Russell concluded that one class might not be enough to offset the influence of the students' nearly 20 years of other socialization agents (e.g., peers, religion, the mass media). This distressing finding led the researchers to recommend that high schools and even grade schools institute reality-focused courses with a specific component on unrealistic expectations.

MODELS OF REALISTIC LOVE

The most illuminating writing about close relationships has come from storytellers and playwrights, not from psychologists and sociologists.
— Zick Rubin, "Preface" to *The Psychology of Love*

Since 1984 when Rubin lamented the failure of his colleagues to research this most vital and serious area, the field has changed. Many scholarly studies have been published in a variety of academic journals, and countless books spanning the spectrum from scholarly to "pop" psychology have appeared.

Lazarus's *Marital Myths*

One of these books most closely related to our topic is *Marital Myths: Two Dozen Mistaken Beliefs that Can Ruin a Marriage (or Make a Bad One Worse)* by psychotherapist **Arnold Lazarus**, author of 10 books and 130 articles. Lazarus exposed 24 widely held but mistaken beliefs about marriage.[1] He selected the myths from those he found most prevalent among his own clients over a 25-year period, considering them to be "the most common mistaken beliefs that result in marital dissatisfaction" (p. 6). After stating each myth, he offers more realistic alternatives to the unhealthy models.

His book is both tied to valid theory and practice (cognitive-behavioral) and extremely down-to-earth (practical). Several of Lazarus' myths relate directly to the 12 in my *Dr. FUN's Mass Media Love Quiz*[2] and to our study of mediated

---

[1]Many studies of sex, love, and romance use the term *marriage,* but their relevance extends to coupleships that do not include marriage.

portrayals. Here they are, with a summary of Lazarus' recommendations to *dis*-illusion each of the myths:

- **"Romantic love makes a good marriage."** Opposing this myth, Lazarus explained: "The affection that enables a marriage to endure is something finer, deeper, and more rewarding than the romantic love of the story books." He argued that these key qualities are vital: kindness, consideration, communication, harmonious adjustment to each other's habits, joint participation in several activities, consensus on important values and issues, reciprocity rather than coercion, and clear evidence of respect for one another — to build profound acceptance of each other. Building these qualities requires the passage of time. He added that the idea of one "Mr. or Mrs. Right" is "hogwash," as there are "literally hundreds — perhaps thousands" — of compatible people who could make a good partner for you (see Mass Media Myth #1).

- **"Good spouses should make their partners happy."** Lazarus noted: "One of the most unfortunate errors that many people make is to accept and assume responsibility for other people's feelings. ...Preoccupation with happiness often leads to unhappiness. ... Happiness is a byproduct of other activities." Lazarus reiterated the ancient wisdom of philosophers that we're not influenced or upset by events but rather by our interpretation of them and he urged us to "take charge of your own gratification and fulfillment" (see Mass Media Myth #10).

- **"Marrying can fulfill all your dreams."** Lazarus attributed this belief to social conditioning — noting, "Mature love never transforms the other person into 'emotional oxygen'" (see Mass Media Myth #10).

- **"True lovers automatically know each other's thoughts and feelings."** Lazarus acknowledged that "one might learn to read one another's reactions quite accurately ..., [but] there are no mind readers!" He noted that this is an especially unfortunate — but prevalent — myth in the area of sexual intimacy. In all cases, the healthier model is to ask for what you want as well as never to tell others that you "know" what they're thinking or feeling (see Mass Media Myth #3).

- **"Competition between spouses adds sparkle to a marriage."** Lazarus explained: "Competition is corrosive. Good marriages rely on cooperative, collaborative, and unified levels of functioning." He added that couples who engage in constant ego contests and power battles are insecure and deficient in self-worth. Instead, noncompetitive, healthy — and safe — relationships foster the trust and confidence that make lovers a team that doesn't merely cooperate but moreover collaborates (see Mass Media Myth #8).

- **"You should make your spouse over into a 'better person'."** The toxic aspect of these "rescue fantasies," Lazarus explained, is that "to satisfy the rescuer's desire for power, approval, or control, the recipient must continue to be (or appear to be) needy ...and forever-more beholden." But it's usually

---

[2]In fact, Norman Epstein, whose RBI I used to assess the beliefs of the participants in my own large surveys, recommended Lazarus' book to me early in my research when I told him about the myths in my *Quiz.*

the rescuer who is the real emotional weakling, requiring eternal gratitude. We can't change others, he advised, so we should carefully select those who don't need much changing (see Mass Media Myth #7).

- **"Opposites attract and complement each other."** Although short-term flings with people who are very different can be quite exciting, and *some* difference can be enriching and stimulating, Lazarus explained that "long-term relationships usually flourish when similarity rather than dissimilarity prevails" (see Mass Media Myth #9).

We'll return to Lazarus' authoritative guidelines in Part II when we conduct our analyses and criticisms of unrealistic mass media portrayals of sex, love, and romance.

Sills' Psychologically Driven Criteria for Mate Selection

Another clinical psychologist with a scientific basis for down-to-earth strategies for realistic romance is **Judith Sills**. I bought her book years ago because I loved the title — *How to Stop Looking for Someone Perfect and Find Someone to Love* — and because the book offered advice to both men and women. (Too many books speak only to one sex.) In addition to her lively articulation of some serious therapeutic principles — "Life is a Blue Plate Special: You want the chicken, it comes with the peas. You want the roast beef, you get brussels sprouts — NO SUBSTITUTIONS!" (1984, p. 41) — she provides an analysis and comparison of **biological needs** and **psychological needs**. Specifically, she called attention to an important aspect of a healthy model of contemporary love by drawing a key distinction between these needs: "At the same time that these biologically-based motivations for mating have declined, the psychological motivations for mating have increased" (p. 64). Nevertheless, many of us still use coupleship models that were more fitting for our cave-dwelling ancestors.

Sills also offers a useful side-by-side comparison of **biologically driven criteria** and **psychologically driven criteria** for mate selection. Her recommendations serve as a good bridge from the sociobiological approach developed by Buss (1994) (Chapter 2) and appropriate application of that theory. (Remember that even Buss himself suggested that we shouldn't use the information his theory presents as the basis of a model for our own modern-day behaviors.)

Prehistory in the Postmodern World

Sills makes sense. When I was asked the question — "But doesn't female preference for taller men go back to prehistoric times?" — by a newspaper reporter (who was interviewing me to get the realistic romance angle for her article "Size: Does it Matter?"), I pointed out:

> But we're not in prehistoric times anymore. And while some things that are imprinted into our being need to be understood and honored today, many other ones, like our appendix, have lost their usefulness and can only serve to hurt us. ... And they block many potentially wonderful relationships from ever getting started. We mustn't equate height with strength. What we should look for is stature in terms of character in each other. (Galician as cited in Whetstone, 2000, p. D1)

By the way, that same article named Nicole Kidman (taller-woman) and Tom Cruise (shorter-man) as a then-"happy" *countertype* couple. Ironically, soon after, the newly Cruise-less Kidman appeared on *The Late Show with David Letterman* — reverting to (stereo)type by telling the world: "*Well, I can wear heels now*" (see Mass Media Myth #6).

Sternberg's Triangular Theory

In Chapter 1, you read about the **Triangular Theory of Love** devised by **Sternberg** (1987, 1988, 1998), who maintains that what best represents genuine love are the qualities he calls **intimacy**, **passion**, and **decision/commitment**. Of the eight different kinds love these components can yield alone or in combination, the one that combines all three components — *consummate* (complete) *love* — is the one Sternberg ranks as most desirable as well as realistic. In addition, he notes that his model incorporates feelings, beliefs, and actions — all of which are necessary for love. It's important to note that sex (*passion*) and *romance* are clearly a *part* of consummate love but in equilibrium with the other two components. Sex (passion) alone is *infatuated love;* romantic love — passion + intimacy — lacks the stabilizing ingredient of decision/commitment (the "after-the-honeymoon" of Katz & Liu).

Gottman's Positive Interactions

Another realistic model focuses on the role of **friendship** and the **communication** component (which Sternberg calls **intimacy**). Psychologist **John Gottman**, a researcher and therapist for more than 25 years, has emphasized communication, negotiation, and conflict resolution as the keys to successful partnerships. Over the years, Gottman and his colleagues have found that satisfied married couples had five positive interactions to every one negative interaction (Gottman, 1994). Couples who are very dissatisfied with their relationships typically engage in more negative interactions than positive (see Mass Media Myth #8). Thus, he recommends that partners verbally compliment and encourage one another.

In *The Seven Principles for Making Marriage Work,* Gottman (1999) argued that he has come to believe the most important strategy is to increase **positive interactions**. If the two partners feel positively toward each other, they'll have less trouble resolving their resolvable conflicts and be accepting of their unresolvable conflicts. Three of Gottman's seven principles are guidelines for implementing this approach:

1. Know each other. Learn all about each other's likes, dislikes, wishes, hopes, dreams, etc.

2. Focus on each other's positive qualities, positive feelings for each other, and the good times you have shared with each other.

3. Interact frequently; tell each other about your day, your thoughts, your experiences. Romance is fueled not by candlelight dinners, but by interacting with your partner in numerous little ways.

The remaining four principles are basic communication, negotiation, and conflict resolution principles, the core of his earlier work:

4. "Let your partner influence you." Share power.

5. "Solve your solvable problems." Criticize behavior without criticizing your partner. Compromise.

6. "Overcome gridlock." Understand your partner's underlying feelings that are preventing resolution of the conflict.

7. "Create shared meaning." Share values, attitudes, interests, traditions (see Mass Media Myth #9).

Like Gottman, many experts advise that conflict resolution is vital for successful coupleship. While airing of differences is healthy, constant conflict is not. According to Northwestern University Medical School psychiatry professor and marriage counselor Richard Carroll (as cited in Bertagnoli, 2001), "Being able to resolve conflict is the most important survival tool a couple has" (p. E1).

Hendrix' Imago Relationship Therapy

A model that focuses on establishing deep constructive communication and conflict resolution as well as deepening the friendship of the couple is **Imago** (ih-MAH-go) **Relationship Therapy**, developed by former pastoral counselor and now Jungian analyst **Harville Hendrix**, founder and president of New York's Institute for Relationship Therapy. He brings together a variety of therapeutic traditions that emphasize self-understanding and growth to literally *dis*-illusion the partners and bring about a healthy, realistic, and loving relationship. His complex but easily understandable theories and strategies are delineated in his two popular books, *Getting the Love You Want: A Guide for Couples* (1988) and *Keeping the Love You Find: A Guide for Singles* (1992), both of which urge us to integrate the "lost," "false," and "disowned" parts of ourselves, such as our *anima/animus* (see Mass Media Myths #6 and #7). "Even when love fails," he advised, "it provides us with a glimpse of our better self and a reminder of our potential for wholeness" (1992, p. 219).

In *Keeping the Love You Find*, Hendrix (1992) explained the metaphorical meanings of love and the quest for wholeness that only individuals can give to themselves:

> The notion that we love other people for themselves, just as they are, with their peculiar needs and quirks, is an illusion. Romantic love is not at all what it appears to be. We are in love with the projection of our Missing Self, and the expectation of what our beloved can give us through our association with them. The Imago bond creates a spurious wholeness. Our attempt to get through another what is missing in ourselves never works, for personal emptiness cannot be filled by a partner. (p. 220)

He adds that it's a good thing that someone else cannot do this for us, as it would compromise "our own chances to deal with our issues of self-completion." Noting that romantic love is supposed to end, he gently offered: "I hate to say it, but *there is no love in romance*. Real love is something entirely different — and better" (p. 220).

For Hendrix, the bottom line is that we must do the work of becoming more complete in ourselves, and then "you will become a picture of someone who ... is more healthy and whole. You will fall in love with a healthier partner. A healthier partner will fall in love with you" (p. 221). But it takes work. It doesn't happen by magic.

Bem's Psychological Androgyny

Several realistic models refute Mass Media Myth #6. Based in extensive research, they offer healthier alternatives for more balanced, equitable relationships that benefit both sexes.

One freer and freeing alternative to traditional sex role-typing is **psychological androgyny** — a less limiting self-concept that incorporates both masculine and feminine attributes and behaviors — posited most notably by **Sandra Bem** (1974). She argued that androgynous individuals are healthier and more adaptable (thanks to their greater repertoire of traits and behaviors), and she developed her widely used **Bem Sex-Role Inventory (BSRI)** for measuring traditional "feminine" and "masculine" self-concepts as well as androgynous self-concept. Her intention was that the BSRI might encourage researchers

> to question the traditional assumption that it is the sex-typed individual who typifies mental health and to begin focusing on the behavioral and societal consequences of more flexible sex-role self-concepts. In a society where rigid sex-role differentiation has already outlived its utility, perhaps the **androgynous person** will come to define a more human standard of psychological health. (pp. 161–162)

Using the BSRI, Pedersen and Bond (1985) found that following several decades of cultural change (including the women's movement) sex-role attitudes were moving away from traditional male/female stereotypes. Also using the BSRI in their study of 100 dual-worker couples, Cooper, Chassin, and Zeiss (1985) found that androgynous dual-worker couples reported the greatest marital satisfaction and personal adjustment. This was true for both men and women and across occupational levels. In addition, congruence between spouses' sex-role attitudes was associated with greater marital satisfaction.

Schwartz' Peer Marriage

Peer marriage is another model of nontraditional egalitarian relationship described by **Pepper Schwartz** (1994), a sociologist who studied 100 couples (approximately half of whom had traditional hegemonic/patriarchal marriages) over a three-year period. In contrast to traditional marriage, wherein separate roles frequently lead to separate lives, peer marriage is characterized by intense companionship, deep knowledge of the other's personality, an inclination to negotiate and converse more than other couples, and no visible yearning for attention and affection. Schwartz has argued that peer marriages are superior to traditional marriages: The peer couples' defining principle is deep friendship whereas the defining principles of traditional couples are idealization and hierarchy, which can destroy intimacy. However, she also reported that the close friendship of the peer couples could be inhibiting to passionate sexuality.

SUMMARY

Social psychology and marital therapy offer many models, strategies, and skills for realistic and healthy coupleship that derive from the scholarly literature and have been researched and validated. Some of these models *dis*-illusion and provide alternatives to the 12 major mass media myths that form the focus of our study — encapsulated in *Dr. FUN's Mass Media Love Quiz*. These recommendations for healthy coupleship, which serve as antidotes to each of the 12 myths in the *Quiz*, have been synthesized to form *Dr. Galician's Prescriptions™ for Getting Real About Romance*.

Many social psychologists, psychotherapists, marital counselors, and relationship researchers have listed unrealistic expectations of sex, love, and romance as a primary cause of dissatisfaction in real coupleships. Katz and Liu formulated what they call the "false love syndrome." To systematically assess unrealistic or dysfunctional expectations that lead to distress in intimate relationships, cognitive-behavioral psychologists Roy J. Eidelson and Norman Epstein developed the Relationship Beliefs Inventory (RBI), a 40-item questionnaire that yields five scales. Some researchers have found differences in the expectations of males and females. Peele viewed obsessive romanticized love as a form of sickness ("pathology"), and Tennov has termed it "limerence." But these unrealistic expectations and models are difficult to change; for example, Laner and Russell found little *dis*-illusioning after students had taken a college-level marriage and courtship class.

Lazarus exposed 24 widely-held but mistaken beliefs about marriage and offered realistic strategies in their place. Sills highlighted the differences between biologically driven criteria and psychologically driven criteria for mate selection; she suggested we abandon counterproductive outdated strategies. Researchers have also described another illusion to avoid, called the misattribution of arousal (our confusing of love with other physical phenomena).

Sternberg posited the best and most balanced type of love is what he called consummate love, combining all three basic components of his Triangular Theory of Love and including passion and romance. Gottman also focused on the role of friendship and positive interactions in successful coupleships as well as on intimacy (communication), negotiation, and conflict resolution. Hendrix developed Imago Relationship Therapy, a Jungian-based approach that incorporates other therapeutic traditions to foster self-understanding and growth to literally *dis*-illusion the partners and integrate the "lost," "false," and "disowned" parts of ourselves.

Bem advocated psychological androgyny as an alternative to traditional sex role-typing, and researchers who have used her Bem Sex-Role Inventory (BSRI) have found that nontraditional (androgynous dual-worker) couples reported the greatest marital satisfaction and personal adjustment. Schwartz has argued that peer marriages are superior to traditional marriages: The peer couples' defining principle is deep friendship whereas the defining principles of traditional couples are idealization and hierarchy, which can destroy intimacy.

SOURCES CITED

Bem, S. L. (1974). The measurement of psychological androgyny. *Journal of Consulting and Clinical Psychology, 42*, 155–162.

Bertagnoli, L. (2001, July 11). Expert tells engaged pairs to talk tough. *Arizona Republic*, p. E1.

Buss, D. M. (1994). *The evolution of desire: Strategies of human mating*. New York: Basic Books.

Cimbalo, R. S., & Novell, D. A. (1993). Sex differences in romantic love attitudes among college students. *Psychological Reports, 73*(1), 15–18.

Crosby, J. F. (1991). *Illusion and disillusion: The self in love and marriage* (4th ed.). Belmont, CA: Wadsworth.

Cooper, K., Chassin, L., & Zeiss, A. (1985). The relation of sex-role attitudes to the marital satisfaction and personal adjustment of dual-worker couples with preschool children. *Sex Roles, 12*(1/2), 227–241.

Eidelson, R. J., & Epstein, N. (1982). Cognition and relationship maladjustment: Development of a measure of dysfunctional relationship beliefs. *Journal of Consulting and Clinical Psychology, 50,* 715–720.

Ellis, A. (1969). *The art and science of love.* New York: Bantam.

Epstein, N., & Eidelson, R. J. (1981). Unrealistic beliefs of clinical couples: Their relationship to expectations, goals and satisfaction. *The American Journal of Family Therapy, 9*(4), 13–22.

Fromm, E. (1956). *The art of loving.* New York: Bantam Books

Galician, M.-L. (1995, October). *The romanticization of love in the mass media: A comparison of the relationship among unrealistic romantic expectations, ideal role models, heterosexual coupleship satisfaction, and mass media usage of Baby Boomers and Generation Xers.* Paper presented at the annual meeting of The Organization for the Study of Communication, Language, and Gender, Minneapolis/St. Paul, MN.

Galician, M.-L. (1997, February). *The romanticization of love in the mass media: The relationship of mass communication media usage, unrealistic romantic expectations, coupleship dissatisfactions of Baby Boomer and Generation X males and females.* Paper presented at the annual meeting of the Western States Communication Association, Monterey Bay, CA.

Galician, M.-L. (1998). Popular culture and mass media myths about romantic love. In J. Wilson & S. L. R. Wilson, *Mass media/mass culture: An introduction* (4th ed., pp. 34–35). New York: McGraw-Hill.

Galician, M.-L. (2001). Media literacy: Popular culture and mass media myths about romantic love. In J. Wilson & S. L. R. Wilson, *Mass media /mass culture: An introduction* (5th ed., pp. 33–34). New York: McGraw-Hill.

Gottman, J. (1994). *Why marriages succeed or fail … and how you can make yours last.* New York: Simon and Schuster.

Gottman, J. (1999). *The seven principles for making marriage work.* New York: Crown.

Hendrix. H. (1988). *Getting the love you want: A guide for couples.* New York: Henry Holt.

Hendrix, H. (1992). *Keeping the love you find: A guide for singles.* New York: Pocket Books.

Katz, S. J., & Liu, A. E. (1988). *False love and other romantic illusions.* New York: Pocket Books.

Laner, M. R., & Russell, J. N. (1994). Course content and change in students: Are marital expectations altered by marriage education? *Teaching Sociology, 22,* 10–18.

Laner, M. R., & Russell, J. N. (1995). Marital expectations and level of premarital involvement: Does marriage education make a difference? *Teaching Sociology, 23,* 1–7.

Lauer, R. H., & Lauer, J. C. (1994). *Marriage and family: The quest for intimacy* (2nd ed.). Madison, WI: William C. Brown.

Lazarus, A. A. (1985). *Marital myths: Two dozen mistaken beliefs that can ruin a marriage or make a bad one worse.* San Luis Obispo, CA: Impact.

Lippmann, W. (1922). *Public opinion.* New York: Harcourt-Brace.

Pederson, D. M., & Bond, B. L. (1985). Shifts in sex role after a decade of cultural change. *Psychological Reports, 57,* 43–48.

Peele, S., with Brodsky, A. (1975). *Love and addiction.* New York: Signet.

Rechtien, J. G., & Fiedler, E. (1988). Courtly love today: Romance and socialization in interpersonal scripts. *Psychological Reports, 63,* 683–695.

Rubin, Z. (1984). Toward a science of relationships. *Contemporary Psychology, 29,* 856–858.

Schwartz, P. (1994). *Peer marriage: How love between equals really works.* New York: The Free Press.

Shapiro, J., & Kroeger, L. (1991). Is life just a romantic novel? The relationship between attitudes about intimate relationships and the popular media. *American Journal of Family Therapy, 19*(3), 226–236.

Sills, J. (1984). *How to stop looking for someone perfect and find someone to love.* New York: St. Martin's.

Sternberg, R. J. (1987). Liking versus loving: A comparative evaluation of theories. *Psychological Bulletin, 102,* 331–345.

Sternberg, R. J. (1988). Triangulating love. In R. J. Sternberg & M. L. Barnes (Eds.), *The psychology of love* (pp. 119–138). New Haven, CT: Yale University Press.

Tennov, D. (1979). *Love and limerence: The experience of being in love.* New York: Stein & Day.

Whetstone, L. (2000, January 10). Size: Does it matter?/Some Valley women know. *Tribune* [Scottsdale/Mesa/Tempe & Chandler, AZ], pp. D1–D2.

Whitehead, B. D., & Popenoe, D. (2001). Who wants to marry a soul mate?: New survey findings on young adults' attitudes about love and marriage. *The state of our unions: The social health of marriage in America 2001.* Retrieved July 14, 2001 from http://www.marriage.rutgers.edu

4

MASS MEDIA NARRATIVE CONSTRUCTIONS

Mass Media Storytelling Approaches, Techniques, & Devices

You furnish the pictures, and I'll furnish the war.
— William Randolph Hearst to Frederic Remington,
reported by James Creelman, *On the Great Highway*

The medium is the message.
— Marshall McLuhan, *Understanding Media*

The medium is the massage.
— Marshall McLuhan, *The Medium Is the Massage*

Preliterate societies were oral, and their storytellers were highly valued as "meaning makers" (Baran, 2002, p. 39) who passed on what was important to the culture. In such societies, people rely on each other for survival, so roles are clearly defined. Their stories — which intertwine history and myth — teach important lessons and preserve important cultural traditions and values. In general, preliterate societies have been shown to have been more egalitarian than more developed societies, with considerable harmony between the sexes. Many of these preliterate societies were **matriarchal**: Both men and women worshiped goddesses, women served as chief priests, and property even passed through the female line (Shlain, 1998).

About 5,000 years ago, the introduction of **literacy** — writing and reading through an *alphabet* — changed society drastically, as McLuhan (1964) argued and as few deny. In his provocative book *The Alphabet versus the Goddess: The Conflict Between Word and Image*, Leonard Shlain — a vascular surgeon and medical school professor who has studied the brain, anthropology, and McLuhan — proposed an intriguing "neuroanatomical hypothesis":

> [W]hen a critical mass of people within a society acquire literacy, especially alphabet literacy, left hemispheric modes of thought are reinforced at the expense of right hemispheric ones, which manifests as a decline in the status of images, women's rights, and goddess worship. (p viii)

While Shlain's focus is on the single issue of how the invention of the alphabet and "left-brain" literacy upset the balance of power between men and women and fostered centuries of patriarchy and misogyny that began to change only with the 19th century development of image-centered "right-brain" photography and film and, more important, the 20th century inventions of television and computers, his proposition is nevertheless useful for our own study because of our focus on mass media portrayals of sex, love, and romance.

We see *images* concretely and simultaneously, in an "all-at-once" manner that we receive as a holistic pattern, as McLuhan put it earlier. This is cross-culturally perceived as *feminine.* We see *words* abstractly and analytically, in a linear sequence using reduction. It's *masculine.* Computer use requires males and females to utilize and reintegrate both right and left brains. Of course, as Schlain emphasized: *Every* human is a *blend* of the so-called feminine and masculine.

The point is that different media engage us differently, and their influence on us as individuals and as a society comes not just from their *content* but also from their *form.*

This chapter focuses on mass media storytelling approaches, techniques, and devices that frame narrative constructions of sex, love, and romance in both print (books, newspapers, magazines, comics) and electronic forms (movies and animated features, radio, recorded music, television, music videos, and the internet). Box 4-1 provides a brief history of these mass media. We'll examine nonfiction and fiction in entertainment, information/news, and persuasion messages. In examining these mediated narrative conventions, you'll discover reasons why the mass media rarely depict the more healthy rational relationships discussed in Chapter 3.

Each medium has its own unique aesthetic, codes, and conventions, and each medium's content is closely related to its form — so newspapers present the world to us in a very different way from television. Each medium has its own specific creative language: scary music heightens fear, camera close-ups convey intimacy, big headlines signal significance.

Mass media both shape and reflect us. As we'll discuss in Chapter 5, some experts consider mass media our *primary* socializing agents. Understanding their narrative approaches, techniques, and devices increases our appreciation and enjoyment of media experiences and helps us to be less susceptible to manipulation by their messages.

> ### Box 4-1. A Brief History of the Mass Media
>
> **Books** are considered the first mass medium. **Johannes Gutenberg**'s invention of **movable type** in 1456 changed the world forever. Printing presses made of clay or wood existed long before this, but Gutenberg's revolutionary contribution to the printing press was the use of *metal molds* ("stereotypes") to make individual letters and set the "types" line by line to *mass produce* books, the first of which was *The Bible* (from the Greek *byblos,* "the book"). Within just a few decades, books were being mass produced all over Europe. Exact mechanized duplication through movable type permitted standardization and created a model for the Industrial Revolution of the 18th century. Eventually, people with more money and more leisure began to rely on books for information and entertainment. Thus, a **mass market** evolved.
>
> In America the media became "mass" in 1833, when the cost of a daily **newspaper** came down to a penny and, thus, reached a truly mass audience. **Books and magazines** — with their more elaborate production process and therefore higher cost — took a few decades longer to enter the popular culture here. Literacy rates increased as print media became affordable.
>
> **Movies** (silent at first) — the first electronic medium — signaled another minirevolution, becoming a mass medium almost immediately upon their introduction at the end of the 19th century. **Radio** and **recorded music** entered the popular culture in the early 1920s. For these media, reading was no longer an essential skill. They brought exciting new messages to an entire nation.
>
> And then came **television** in the early 1950s, right after World War II. A decade later, nearly every home (90%) had one. Our world was shrinking. We were in an **Age of Information**. The **personal computer and the internet** combined the old media into new interactive forms, making the concept of a global village less of a metaphor and more of a reality.

MEDIATED STORIES OR NARRATIVES

We risk being the first people in history to have been able to make their illusions so vivid, so persuasive, so "realistic" that they can live in them.
— Daniel Boorstein, *The Image: A Guide to Pseudo-Events in America*

As noted in Chapter 1, the mass media disseminate messages that inform us, entertain us, and persuade us. They also transmit the culture and socialize us. And they do it all through **stories**. Another media term for "stories" is "**narratives**." The term "**text**" is also used to mean any work that can be "read" — a book, a comic strip, a movie, a popular song, a television commercial; in other words, a "text" is not just a print form. (Recall from our earlier discussion in Chapter 2 that *myths* are generally considered "sacred stories.")

A culture's values and beliefs reside in the stories it tells, according to Baran (2002). Our stories "help us define our realities" (p. 20), shaping and reflecting the ways we think, feel, and act. Mediated stories — whether fiction or nonfiction — thus have great power. Baran urged media consumers to be mindful of this power:

> [Y]ou, the audience for these stories, also have opportunities and responsibilities. You use these stories not only to be entertained but to learn about the world around you, to understand the values, the way things work, and how the pieces fit together. You have a responsibility to question the storytellers and their stories, to interpret the stories in ways consistent with larger or more important cultural values and truths, to be thoughtful, to reflect on the stories' meanings and what they say about you and your culture. To do less is to miss an opportunity to construct your own meaning and, thereby, culture. (p. 20)

Chapter 6 provides details about specific analysis and criticism tools and strategies that will enable you, as Baran exhorted, to "question the storytellers and their stories" — and to *dis*-illusion them. However, to be able to deconstruct the mass media's stories, you first need an understanding of what those stories are and how they are constructed.

In *Love Is a Story: A New Theory of Relationships,* Sternberg (1998) goes beyond his Triangular Theory of Love and addresses the question: **"What does it mean for love to be a story?"** The key to better relationships, his book asserts, is understanding what love stories are and why they are important (p. 1). Explaining their use in therapy, Sternberg observed:

> Stories about love have existed throughout the ages, and the basic themes and plots of these stories have changed little. What has changed, however, is how these stories play out in day-to-day living, as well as the popularity of some stories compared with others. (p. 5)

> We imagine ... that we replace a "fiction" with the "reality" of nonfiction. But if we think about first impressions, about the rituals surrounding mating and marriage, this replacement is often not what really happens. We come to relationships with many preconceived ideas. ... What are viewed as "realities" are rather perceptions of realities — stories. (p. 7)

Most of the mass media's stories — especially its stories of sex, love, and romance — are mythic and, therefore, stereotypic and archetypal. Silverblatt, Ferry, and Finan (1999) asserted that "the media has assumed a vital role in the transmission of cultural myths" (p. 176), and Olson (1999) argued that "cinematic and televisual language is almost always mythic" (p. 24). Olson explained why these myths seem real to us:

> They appear to the reader to convey some deeper, self-evident, and universal truth about life. ... This is no less so for myths conveyed via television or films, which seem to successfully convey to their audiences that what they portray "is so." ... Visual media seem to function as though they are a window to the world they depict, whereas they are as conventionalized and formulaic in their presentation of the world as any pulp romance. (p. 108)

The Appeal of Mediated Myths & Stereotypes

Mediated myths and stereotypes are powerful. Let's consider their characteristics. Perhaps first and foremost, they're *sometimes* true, setting the stage for us to imagine that they are *frequently* if not *usually* true. (In fact, such "intermittent reinforcement" is the basis of much addiction, wherein those who are only sometimes reinforced constantly seek the reward and work harder and harder to achieve it.) Another characteristic of myths and stereotypes is that they are simple and simplistic, which fits well with the needs of the mass media for simple stories (see the Checklist in the next section). Myths and stereotypes are mostly acquired second-hand; in that sense, just as we have no direct experience that provides evidence to validate them, we likewise have none to invalidate them. Ironically, myths are "sacred" stories with larger-than-life appeal, yet we want them to be true. (This irony helps to explain our disappointment when our media celebrities in sports, politics, and show business demonstrate their too-human qualities.) These sacred stories are usually accompanied by dramatic symbols that further manipulate us into believing them or being swayed by them.

Further, as Olson explained, myths are "inclusive"; thus, "the reader senses from myth that it is speaking directly to him or her, that it has something relevant and useful to convey" (p. 25). Nearly a century ago, Lippmann (1922) offered an intriguing analysis of why mediated stories of sex, love, romance are so appealing:

> The audience must have something to do, and the contemplation of the true, the good, and the beautiful is not something to do. In order not to sit inertly in the presence of the picture, and this applies as much to newspaper stories as to fiction and the cinema, the audience must be exercised by the image. Now there are two forms of exercise which far transcend all others, both as to ease with which they are aroused, and eagerness with which stimuli for them are sought. They are sexual passion and fighting, and the two have so many associations with each other, blend into each other so intimately, that a fight about sex outranks every other theme in the breadth of its appeal. There is none so engrossing or so careless of distinctions of cultures and frontiers. (p. 163)

Ackerman provided an interesting perspective about the importance of conflict and "the contest" in these stories: "Love games appeal to us because they test our wits, and remind us of childhood. In fact, they're the principal ways adults play" (p. 86). She added that people love this sports-like aspect of love because it offers the "hope of winning and being rewarded."

It's important to note that our wishes and hopes of "winning and being rewarded" in terms of these mythic stories are often just that — wishes and hopes. A large measure of the appeal of these magical stories is that we don't have to do any work to make them come true for us. We're absolved of personal responsibility and effort for achieving our goals.

In fact, in his classic *Anatomy of Criticism,* **Northrop Frye**[1] asserted: "The romance is nearest of all literary forms to the wish-fulfilment dream .... The perennially childlike quality of romance is marked by its extraordinarily persistent nostalgia, its search for some kind of imaginative golden age in time or space" (p. 186). He characterized the Romance as primarily dealing with idealized human forms in idealized worlds (p. 367). Frye also explained that in such stories, conflict is the basis or archetypal theme and "subtlety and complexity are not much favored" (p. 193).

Box 4-2 lists mass-mediated love stories whose couples are so appealing that they have become icons. Some are fictional and some are real, although even the "reality" of the nonfictional couples is mass-mediated and thereby mythical. In addition to "great lovers" who appear in the research literature, this list includes recommendations from my students and research respondents.

---

[1] Frye was the first literary critic to apply the scientific approach to study mythic themes and archetypes. Anyone interested in media criticism should read his book.

Box 4-2. Iconic Couples: Mass-Mediated Love Stories

Here are some couples — real and fictional — known to us through the mass media. These "great lovers," who are considered icons of sex, love, and romance, were suggested by my students and research respondents as well as the research literature. (You'll note that some of these couples are no longer together, but their influence continues.)

· Which couples represent mass media manifestations of unrealistic or unhealthy relationships? Which myths/stereotypes in *Dr. FUN's Mass Media Love Quiz* do they exemplify?

· Which couples represent realistic romance or healthy relationships? Which *Dr. Galician's Prescriptions™* do they demonstrate?

· Why do you think the listed couples are considered to be icons? Why are their love stories so appealing? Which others would you add — and why?

Classic Couples — Fictional & Nonfictional

    Caesar & Cleopatra
    Cinderella & Prince Charming
    Helen of Troy & Prince Paris
    Heloise & Abelard
    Lancelot & Guinevere
    Mickey & Minnie
    Pyramus & Thisbe
    Queen Victoria & Prince Albert
    Romeo & Juliet
    Tristan & Isolde

Movie Couples

Note: # refers to American Film Institute's 2002 list of the 100 most romantic movies of all time

    "Baby" (Jennifer Grey) & Johnny Castle (Patrick Swayze) in *Dirty Dancing* (#93)
    Belle & The Beast in *Beauty and the Beast* (#34)
    Burt Lancaster & Deborah Kerr in *From Here to Eternity* (#20)
    Deborah Kerr & Cary Grant in *An Affair to Remember* (#5)
    Doris Day & Rock Hudson in *Pillow Talk* (#99)
    Elle (Reese Witherspoon) & Emmett (Luke Wilson) in *Legally Blonde*
    Gwen (Sandra Bullock) & Jasper (Dominic West) in *28 Days*
    Harry (Billy Crystal) & Sally (Meg Ryan) in *When Harry Met Sally* (#25)
    Ilsa (Ingrid Bergman) & Rick (Humphrey Bogart) in *Casablanca* (#1)
    Jerry (Tom Cruise) & Dorothy (Renee Zellweger) in *Jerry Maguire* (#100)
    Lady & Tramp in *Lady and the Tramp* (#95)
    Meg Ryan & Tom Hanks in *Sleepless in Seattle* (#45)
    Rose (Kate Winslet) & Jack (Leonardo DiCaprio) in *Titanic* (#37)
    Ryan O'Neal & Ali McGraw in *Love Story* (#9)
    Scarlet O'Hara (Vivien Leigh) & Rhett Butler (Clark Gable) in *Gone with the Wind* (#2)
    Vivian (Julia Roberts) & Edward (Richard Gere) in *Pretty Woman* (#21)

TV Couples

    Carol & Mike Brady in the *Brady Bunch*
    Carrie & Mr. Big in *Sex and the City*
    Chandler & Monica in *Friends*
    Dawson & Joey in *Dawson's Creek*
    Dharma & Greg in *Dharma and Greg*
    Heathcliff & Clair Huxtable in the *Cosby Show*
    Homer & Marge in *The Simpsons*
    June & Ward Cleaver in *Leave It to Beaver*
    Kermit & Miss Piggy in *Sesame Street*
    Ozzie & Harriet in *The Ozzie and Harriet Show*
    Paul & Jamie in *Mad About You*
    Ricky & Lucy in *I Love Lucy*
    Roseanne & Dan in *Roseanne*

Comic Book & Cartoon Strip Couples

    Blondie & Dagwood
    Popeye & Olive Oyl
    Superman & Lois Lane

Real-life Couples

    Annette Bening & Warren Beatty
    Bill & Hillary Clinton
    Brad Pitt & Jennifer Aniston
    Demi Moore & Bruce Willis
    Elizabeth Taylor & Richard Burton
    Goldie Hawn & Kurt Russell
    Jada Pinkett & Will Smith
    Joanne Woodward & Paul Newman
    Madonna & Guy Ritchie
    Nicole Kidman & Tom Cruise
    Oprah & Stedman
    Ronald & Nancy Reagan
    Roy Rogers & Dale Evans
    Sonny & Cher
    Spencer Tracy & Katherine Hepburn

Here are some reasons my students and research respondents have given for the great and universal appeal of love stories, the romantic genre, and portrayals of sex in the mass media:

- Since sex and romance are not easily found on a regular basis, these stories give you hope for your own romantic relationships.

- Portrayals of sex stimulate people's minds sensually. They're fantasies, so they're exciting.

- We watch these stories because they offer us something that is unattainable — a perfect relationship with a blissful ending. We look for clues to help us out in our own relationships, and we often try to apply what we learned to our own life.

- In the movies, sex is perfect. Two beautiful people go at it for as long as they want and we are left in awe. We think sex will be that way for us, too, if we find the right partner.

- What we see is what we think is reality. It is so appealing because it cuts away any negative aspect of real life and makes everything look picture-perfect.

- I think it's the idea that love is easy, and when you find your supposed "soul mate," the rest is history with a fairytale ending. As humans, we all want to experience the "happily-ever-after."

- It's so appealing because the portrayals all make it seem so easy. Everything always works out for the best, sex is easy, and complications in relationships are always resolved with very little effort.

It's also important to consider how these universal archetypes reinforce the ideology of the prevailing culture. Olson (1999) warned that "because myths are stories with credibility, authority, and a claim to truth, they can be used forcefully for any number of reactionary or revolutionary purposes" and that myth in movies and television "tends to be a conservative force, one that reinforces the status quo" (p. 112).

CHECKLIST OF MASS MEDIA STORYTELLING TACTICS & TECHNIQUES

Unrealistic portrayals of sex, love, and romance appear in a variety of mass media: books (including fairy tales, romance novels, action stories, and even nonfiction works, such as the "love stories" of real people and "tell-all" biographies of celebrities); newspapers (from the *New York Times* to the *Enquirer*); magazines (from *Playboy* to *Cosmo,* from teenzines to porn); comic books; movies & animated features (including romantic and action stories); radio & recorded music; television & music videos; and the internet.[2]

---

[2]Shlain (1998) asserted that the computer's unique features have "shifted the collective cultural consciousness of the men and women who use them" toward a right-hemispheric mode, leading to a diminution of male dominance and patriarchy. The formats are holistic and iconic. The processes integrate left and right brain; for example, typing, which uses both hands and is used now not just by females but also by males who in a past generation would have considered typing a *female* activity. And the communication is often interactive. Cyberspace is a "computer-generated extension of the human mind into another dimension" (pp. 417–418).

To better *dis*-illusion these portrayals, we need to consider how the media create their narratives. Below is a checklist of just some of the storytelling approaches, techniques, and devices used by the mass media. (In Chapter 6, we'll examine specific strategies and skills of mass media literacy and review the seven-step process we'll use for our formal analysis and criticism.)

As you study the checklist, be aware that nearly all our mass media today are *commercial entities* whose major (sometimes *only*) **goal is to make money.** Mass media are businesses — really *big* businesses — so "**saleability**" is of the utmost importance. Even the content of the news media is heavily commercialized.

Moreover, in these commercial media, something in addition to the communication itself is *always* being **sold.** It's not always just the apparent product or service of a sponsor in an ad. As often as not, mass media narratives are also selling an idea. In other words, even though it's not often explicitly stated, they're persuading us to adopt a viewpoint and take an action. They're socializing us.

Here's a checklist[3] of some tactics and techniques they use:

❏ Simplification (& Shortening)

"K.I.S.S." is *not* a romance strategy. It's a sales formula: "Keep it simple, stupid." Because the mass audience is so diverse and unspecific, media senders have to aim for the lowest common denominator (or they risk losing much of their audience). So simplification is the rule, and **shortening** is part of this technique. As another rule, books are less simple and short than magazines, which are less simple and short than newspapers. The print media are less simple and short than the electronic media. That's why some of the characters you loved the most in a novel are often cut out of the movie version. **Strictures** that necessitate editing concern **space** (in print media) and **time** (in electronic media). Because the media reduce the complex to the simple, richly complicated themes and issues with a variety of positions are often depicted in dichotomous terms such as black/white and good/evil. Media narratives are focused on **specifics**, eliminating a great deal of the detail of real life.

❏ Stereotypes & Symbols of Drama

As mentioned in Chapter 2, the stereotyping of characters and the utilizing of stock characters are traditional tools of mass communicators to easily make a point and move the action forward quickly. Stereotypes frequently work with symbols. There's the prostitute with the heart of gold, the tough boss who's going to relent, the bad guy with the black cowboy hat and ugly scar. They're also powerful reinforcers, usually of the status quo and of false images. **Objectification** of persons is also a part of stereotyping — such as music videos' objectifying of women.

❏ Slant & Skew

Whether intentional or unintentional, all media narratives have a certain slant or *angle* (or **point of view**) that represents a skew or *bias*. It's not always possible to determine if the slant and skew are intentional or unintentional. Nonfiction and the news have a slant as well, of course. In fact, a require-

---

[3]I used words beginning with "S" for each item in the checklist to remind you of the underlying concepts of saleability and socialization. Parts of the descriptions under my headers are based on Berger (1997), Silverblatt (1995), and Silverblatt, Ferry, & Finan (1999), which I recommend you consult for details.

ment of news is that it have an angle (which seems strange when we consider that news is supposed to be objective; but humans cannot be objective, though journalists should strive to be *fair,* a better term). The **tone** of the text is often a key to the slant and skew. **Selection** is a vital aspect of media narrative construction, and what is left out is often as important for us to consider as what is included. Media presentations generally assume the point of view of the dominant culture.

❏ Seriousness (Tragedy/Comedy)

Closely related to slant and skew is the *seriousness* of the narrative, by which I mean whether the narrative is presented as a **tragedy or a comedy** (if fiction) or as a matter of grave concern or as a lighthearted note (if nonfiction). The seriousness of the text is a clue to how we are to interpret and internalize the message. Traditionally, tragedy is a serious story about a character facing a moral issue of universal importance. Tragedy arouses pity and fear because the sympathetic main character is defeated in the struggle by superior forces. Comedy is less profound, and we usually view it with more detachment than we read tragic texts. In reading love stories of romantic comedy, we tend to be emotionally involved but not so profoundly as with genuine tragedy. The eminent film critic **Roger Ebert** (2000) said love stories are comedies and not tragedies because "it is funny when we lose control of ourselves despite our best efforts to remain dignified. A man in love has stepped on an emotional banana peel. When a woman falls in love with an unavailable man, he *is* a banana peel" (p. 297). **Sentimentality** — appealing to the sentiments, especially to romantic feelings — is another related clue that indicates the creator of the text is trying to reach us emotionally rather than by reason or realism. We see this emotional appeal in ads and the news, not just in romance novels or movies.

❏ Script & Storyline (Plot)

The storyline or plot is a summary of the action, particularly the patterns involving the conflict (see next item on checklist). While the storyline is not the theme or the meaning of a story, it's an important element in how the underlying meaning is conveyed. It should always be summarized in an analysis and criticism.

❏ Suspense (& Conflict)

Without suspense and conflict, we have no story. (This point is illustrated by Andy Warhol's film of nothing but a man sleeping.) Conflict is opposition between characters or forces, especially opposition that motivates or shapes the action of the plot. In an ad, the conflict is represented as a problem for which the commodity being sold is the solution. In the news, conflict is an important factor, though some journalists don't like to acknowledge it. Sporting events are all about conflict within a ritualized setting. Suspense is pleasurable excitement and anticipation regarding an outcome, such as the ending of a romance novel or the resolution of a news story. Conflict and suspense fuel our adrenalin and keep our attention riveted.

❏ Sensationalism & Sex

Increasingly, the media attempt to arouse and maintain the interest of the audience through the inclusion of exaggerated or lurid details. Frequently, it's sex that is sensationalized in the news, entertainment, and advertising narratives of both print and electronic forms. Sex is usually *dichotomized,* especially in terms of the depictions of females: In ads, movies, and other narratives, women are usually portrayed either as good or bad, virgins or whores. Sex is used to sell a variety of products that have nothing to do with sex, such as cars. *Sex sells.* And unrealistic sensationalistic sex sells best.

❏ Subtexts (Support or Subversion)

In addition to the primary plotline and ostensible theme (or "manifest message"), media texts have subtexts — the implicit meaning or theme (or "latent message"). Manifest messages are clear and straightforward. Latent messages or subtext are indirect and beneath the surface. As such, they might **support** (reinforce) or **subvert** (contradict) the manifest message. One form of subtext is **satire** (comedy that evaluates human conduct in terms of behavioral norms, using irony, sarcasm, or caustic wit to attack or expose folly, vice, or stupidity).

❏ Speaker

As with subtexts, it's important to understand who is *really* speaking in a novel, movie, music video, news report, advertisement, etc. The speaker could be a teenage heartthrob or a housewife baking brownies with love, but **whose point of view** are these characters really articulating?

❏ Sender or Sponsor

The immediately apparent sender or sponsor of a mass mediated message is the **specific producer or creator** of it. But in all mass mediated communication, the sender is rarely a solo act but rather a part of an institution team. In addition to learning more about who the direct sender is, readers of media texts should investigate the indirect source: the **media conglomerate** with corporate interests that actually underwrites and disseminates the message.

❏ Setting

In many stories, the action is so closely related to the setting that it's determined by it. In other narratives, setting provides atmosphere, influencing our reception of the message. Setting can also be **symbolic**, suggesting attitudes and feelings. Sometimes the setting is an **actual** place, though a great deal of selection might be reshaping it. Sets, of course, are not at all real. Related to setting is the other "orientation device," **time** — past, present, or future.

❏ Style & Structure

Style and structure (or **production elements**) can set the mood that reinforces messages and themes. These elements, which vary by medium, include **color, lighting, texture, phrasing, arrangement and positioning, typeface, costumes, makeup, and sound.** Sound includes **sound effects and music.** (Music is especially powerful.) **Sequencing** — the order in which the elements are arranged — can also affect the story and our reception of it. Unlike real life, media narratives have a clear beginning, middle, and end. Also unlike real life, they're focused on **specifics**, as noted previously.

❏ Special Effects

In addition to the other factors above that make media stories different from real life stories and increase their influential power, special effects further alter and enhance the presentations. Today, computers can work literal magic. Beauty and perfection can be digitally supplied in both print and electronic media. Sometimes these effects are so realistic that it's hard to accept that they're **fake**.

❏ Superhumans & Scale

In addition to special effects, media narratives frequently rely on superhumans who are stronger than normal people — physically, intellectually, or emotionally. These mythic and stereotypic characters are usually contrasted with their opposites, resulting in dichotomous portrayals of good/evil, smart/dumb, beautiful/ugly, young/old. In general, scale — of individuals as well as of objects in media texts — influences our perceptions and determines our responses.

❏ Superstars

Celebrities abound in today's global village, serving as the heroes and heroines or gods and goddesses of myth. Superstars populate the news and information media as well as the more fictional forms. As powerful cultural **icons**, their presence (or absence) provides a subtext that demands analysis. Of course, their presence in persuasive messages requires even more scrutiny.

❏ Suspension of Disbelief

Media narratives require audiences to suspend their disbelief: in other words, to discard our *dis*-illusioning skills and strategies. Their stories usually offer not reality or truth but the suggestion of it, known as **verisimilitude**. We also accord fictional accounts **dramatic license**. All of this is fine, but after "reading" a media text, we must *re*activate our disbelief as well as our beliefs about reality — via a healthy dose of analysis and criticism.

❏ Socialization & Shaping

All of the techniques listed here contribute to socialization and shaping of the audiences. It's important to remember that. Even if we're overly analytical, it doesn't hurt. We can adjust our criticism to consider actual impacts once we've completed our analysis.

❏ Status Quo (& Social Stability)

The direction of our socialization and shaping is generally toward the status quo or **dominant cultural norms**. This is true in persuasive messages, entertainment messages, and even information/news messages. By selling not just the product or service but also a way of life that can only be gained by adherence to some predominant system and the use of the sponsored item, advertising reinforces the status quo. Entertainment programs reinforce the status quo by romanticizing the established order and those who run it. Informational media rarely seriously challenge the social order even when they question aspects of it. It's important to carefully analyze the **solutions** offered or suggested by the text, including the *happily-ever-after* **ending** that is usually an unrealistic projection. Ebert (2000) commented: "There's an emotional conservatism that runs much deeper in movie audiences than any other form of belief, and which teaches: If a movie shows us a boy and a girl who are really in love, there *must* be a happy ending" (p. 297).

SUMMARY

Preliterate societies were oral, and their storytellers were highly valued as " meaning makers" who intertwined history and myth to teach important lessons and preserve important cultural traditions and values. Many of these preliterate societies were matriarchal or egalitarian. About 5,000 years ago, the introduction of literacy — writing and reading through an alphabet — changed society drastically.

Shlain proposed that the invention of the alphabet and "left-brain" literacy upset the balance of power between men and women and fostered centuries of patriarchy and misogyny that began to change only with the 19th century development of image-centered "right-brain" photography and film and, more important, the 20th century inventions of television and computers. Different media engage us differently, and their influence on us as individuals and as a society comes not just from their content but also from their form.

Mediated myths and stereotypes are powerful because of their simplicity, dramatic symbols, and conflict. The Romance is the nearest literary form to the wish-fulfilment dream.

Each medium has its own unique aesthetic, codes, and conventions, and each medium's content is closely related to its form. Understanding their narrative approaches, techniques, and devices increases our appreciation and enjoyment of media experiences and helps us to be less susceptible to manipulation by their messages.

Books are considered the first mass medium. Johannes Gutenberg's invention of movable type in 1456 changed the world forever. In America the media became "mass" in 1833, when the cost of a daily newspaper came down to a penny and, thus, reached a truly mass audience. Books and magazines — with their more elaborate production process and therefore higher cost — took a few decades longer to enter the popular culture here. Literacy rates increased as print media became affordable. Movies (silent at first) — the first electronic medium — signaled another minirevolution, becoming a mass medium almost immediately upon their introduction at the end of the 19th century. Radio and recorded music entered the popular culture in the early 1920s. For these media, reading was no longer an essential skill. They brought exciting new messages to an entire nation. By the 1960s television was in nearly every home in America. The personal computer and the internet combined the old media into new interactive forms.

These mass media disseminate messages that inform us, entertain us, and persuade us. They also transmit the culture and socialize us. And they do it all through stories ("narratives" or "texts"). A society's values and beliefs reside in these stories, which help us define our realities.

Nearly all our mass media today are commercial entities — big businesses whose major goal is to make money, so "saleability" is of the utmost importance. In these commercial media, something in addition to the communication itself is always being sold, and we're always being socialized by them.

SOURCES CITED

Ackerman, D. (1995). *A natural history of love.* New York: Vintage Books.
Baran, S. J. (2002). *Introduction to mass communication: Media literacy and culture.* New York: McGraw-Hill.

Berger, A. A. (1997). *Narratives in popular culture, media, and everyday life.* Thousand Oaks, CA: Sage.

Creelman, J. (1901). *On the great highway.* Boston: Lothrop.

Ebert, R. (2000). *Roger Ebert's movie yearbook 2001.* Kansas City, MO: Andrews McMeel.

Frye, N. (1957). *Anatomy of criticism: Four essays.* Princeton: Princeton University Press.

Lippmann, W. (1922). *Public opinion.* New York: Harcourt-Brace.

McLuhan, M. (1964). *Understanding media: The extensions of man.* New York: McGraw-Hill.

McLuhan, M., & Fiore, Q. (1967). *The medium is the massage.* New York: Simon & Schuster.

Olson, S. R. (1999). *Hollywood planet: Global media and the competitive advantage of narrative transparency.* Mahwah, NJ: Lawrence Erlbaum Associates.

Shlain, L. (1998). *The alphabet versus the goddess: The conflict between word and image.* New York: Penguin.

Silverblatt, A. (1995). *Media literacy: Keys to interpreting media messages.* Westport, CT: Praeger.

Silverblatt, A., Ferry, J., & Finan, B. (1999). *Approaches to media literacy: A handbook.* Armonk, NY: M.E. Sharpe.

Sternberg, R. J. (1998). *Love is a story: A new theory of relationships.* New York: Oxford University Press.

5

THE INFLUENCE
OF THE MASS MEDIA

Research & Theories of Mass Media Effects on Individuals & Society

Young people love mass-media entertainment radio, television, music, videos, film, comic books, and more. The entertainment media love young people, too; much of mass media entertainment is aimed at young adults, who, even in many developing countries, often spend substantial amounts of money on entertainment. Love, romance, and sex are favorite topics of this entertainment, and many young people say that this is where they learn about sex.

— Media/Materials Clearinghouse,
Johns Hopkins Population Information Program

It's a difficult task to find anything in the media that has much to teach us about the realities of love.

— Robert J. Sternberg, *Cupid's Arrow*

While most of us would agree with critics and scholars and the person on the street that the mass media influence individuals and society in a variety of ways, we'd probably think that these influences are, of course, on *other* people. And even if we admit that we are personally influenced, we prefer to think that it's only on rare occasions and that *other* people are influenced much more. This impression fits with a tendency that Stanford psychologist Philip Zimbardo observed years ago and called **the illusion of personal invulnerability** (Zimbardo, Ebbesen, & Maslach, 1977). It's part of a larger theory known as **the third-person effect** (Davison, 1983; Shah, Faber, & Youn, 1999).

Another important consideration for our analysis and criticism of mediated portrayals is that we don't just get influenced by persuasive media messages like those in advertising and public relations. In fact, we might be more influenced by messages that are basically entertaining. The explanation for this — called **the elaboration likelihood model of persuasion**, developed by Richard Petty and John Cacioppo (1986) — says that we're persuaded through one of two major pathways: the **central route** to persuasion or the **peripheral route**.

In the *central route*, we've got our antennas up and windows bolted against an argumentative assault that we know is coming. We're alert and in our analytic mode. Somebody's trying hard to sell us something. But it's difficult to reach people this way. In *peripheral-route* persuasion, they're sneaking around from the back to persuade or influence us, usually distracting us with entertainment. We sit back and relax and let our defenses down. And just when we think we're not being subtly influenced, lo and behold: We've been massaged, as McLuhan would say. Sometimes we don't even realize it until much later.

Similarly, a study of soap opera impact found that viewers were more likely to embrace the values and messages of these programs when their motives for viewing were **ritualistic** (i.e., enjoyment or boredom) rather than **instrumental** (i.e., goal-oriented reality explorations or character identification) (Carveth & Alexander, 1985; see also Fink & Galician, 1996; Perse, 1986; Perse & Rubin, 1988; Rubin, 1985). In other words, these soap fans "learned more" when they weren't seeking information.

Before we look at more research of mass media effects, let's take a moment for a reality check to make sure we haven't fallen victim to the illusion of personal invulnerability. After all, this book is all about *dis-illusioning ourselves.* Let's simply agree that to some degree at some times *we're all influenced by the mass media.* (Remember: I'm not asking you to do anything I haven't done. I've already told you that I myself was greatly influenced by media portrayals of sex, love, and romance — even though I didn't realize it and even though I worked in the mass media, researched it, and consumed it significantly.)

There's a huge difference between our *education* and our *enculturation* (see Baran, 2002, p. 374). And our enculturated attitudes and emotions are the hardest to change — even when we "know better" and sincerely *want* to change.

Using the information about mass media presented in Chapter 1, let's also agree that *mass media both shape us and reflect us.* Indeed, the mass media are powerful **socializing agents.**

MASS MEDIA AS SOCIALIZING AGENTS

Socialization is the process whereby individuals are made aware of the behavior that others expect of them regarding the norms, values, and culture of their society. **Agents of socialization** include the family, school, friendship groups, religious institutions, and the *mass media.* A body of theory suggests that the mass media are indeed powerful socialization agents from which we learn and model many behaviors — both healthy and unhealthy.

Specifically, **social learning theory** (later termed **social cognitive theory**) — associated most closely with work of social psychologist **Albert Bandura** — considers the mass media to be primary socialization agents, along with family, peers, and classroom teachers (Bandura, 1969, 1971, 1977, 1986). This well-regarded theory asserts that we learn by "**modeling**" the behavior of in-person or mediated real people or fictional characters through **imitation** (exact replication of behavior) and **identification** (more generalized but directly related behavior). Identification is obviously more subtle and, therefore, more difficult to trace to the source. Both imitation and identification result from three processes: **observational learning** (basically copying what we see or hear), **inhibitory effects** (avoiding behaviors that we see punished), and **disinhibitory effects** (copying behaviors that we see rewarded).

Bandura argued that children can learn social roles and behaviors solely by watching real or fictional models, although not all learned behaviors will necessarily be enacted ("modeled") without reinforcement; in other words, many mass media messages *do* offer considerable inducements and rewards related to specific ideas, feelings, and behaviors. Bandura's theory suggests that exposure to mediated models of sex-roles and coupleship should promote related attitudes and feelings and, under certain conditions of reinforcement, related behaviors. (For example, I used to think that men *liked* women who were sassy and sarcastic because the women in some of my favorite classic movies acted that way and got rewarded — even though I never did.)

Media guru **Marshall McLuhan** viewed the mass media as *extensions of our very senses,* as described in Chapter 1 of this book. The media supplement the natural reach of our eyes, our ears, our brain — even our touch, giving us the "feel" or a sense of the parts of world well beyond our own neighborhood and our own century. Because of the mass media, our world has become what he called a global village, where no one can escape the effects of the mass media — whether intentional or not. And, according to McLuhan, these effects are massive, for the mass media alter our senses and our society permanently and immeasurably.

But McLuhan was not a researcher. He was a "prober" — a stimulator of ideas and perceptions through his metaphors and his visions.

SCIENTIFIC RESEARCH OF MASS MEDIA EFFECTS

Methodologies

Conducting mass media effects research using *the scientific method* is difficult indeed. And slow. Through continued replicated research studies, the scholarly discipline of mass communication gradually begins to build **theories** that can be tested with more research studies that support or reject the theories, which then get altered as they attempt to accurately describe the actual processes they study. Moreover, many different approaches are employed, some of which conflict with each other in their underlying assumptions and in their interpreted conclusions.

Nevertheless, those of us who study mass media effects forge on and make small connections that might be useful in better understanding our mass media and how they affect us. Some of us use more **quantitative/deductive methods** (facts and statistics and, usually, larger numbers of participants, who are studied broadly); others use more **qualitative/inductive methods** (impressions and words and, usually, fewer participants, who are studied in more depth). Some of us combine these approaches. But no matter what method or approach, all scientific research shares certain basic characteristics:

- **systematic** — following prescribed steps and traditions of the particular approach (so others can more easily follow and evaluate it),

- **objective** — attempting to be impartial in seeking answers to research questions and solutions to research problems (so the findings can be less biased),

- **empirical** — relying on observable documentable *evidence* rather than opinions (so we can more easily open our minds to considering their merit),

- **cumulative** — building on existing knowledge, theories, and research (so we can further our knowledge rather than reinventing the wheel each time).

The mass media effects studies we'll consider span many different approaches along the quantitative/inductive–qualitative/deductive continuum: experiments, content analyses, textual analyses (or reception analyses), surveys, historical and legal studies, intensive interviews, ethnographies, case studies, critical and cultural studies, and feminist studies. Many of these approaches borrow techniques from other fields, such as sociology and psychology.

No one method or approach can completely cover all the questions and problems we'd like to investigate and that demand our attention. In fact, no single method can adequately cover even one small issue — much less an entire phenomenon. Each method has its strong suit, and each has its limitations. Together, they begin to offer a picture that's *not* "just in our head" (to recall Walter Lippmann's phrase).

Further, unlike Inspector Morse or Inspector Colombo (two of my favorite TV detectives who also span a wide continuum of investigative methodologies), we rarely *prove* anything in research. Instead, we move *toward* proof, supporting some theories in which we develop more confidence and rejecting others as inadequate. It's also important to understand these theories, because merely studying the *content* of a portrayal doesn't tell us about the potential *effects* on its audiences.

A Brief History of Mass Media Effects Research

The study of mass media effects began in the early part of the last century, when public concern about the impact of movies on children and adolescents prompted the privately funded Payne Studies (a series of 13 studies from 1928–1932). These and other studies of that time period helped establish a "legacy of fear" that mass media messages were indeed powerful agents of social change whose influence could be dangerous and damaging (Baran & Davis, 2000; Lowery & DeFleur, 1983; Sparks, 2002). (One famous example is the impressive major impact of the 1938 radio broadcast of Orson Welles' dramatic adaptation of H. G. Wells' *War of the Worlds* on actual behavior nationwide.) The theories of mass communication effects of this era have been characterized by scholars as the **magic bullet theories** or the **hypodermic needle theories** because of the belief that the effect of media is like a powerful bullet or drug that hits and penetrates everyone powerfully and uniformly — and from which no one could escape. These theories comprise what is generally considered the **powerful effects model**.

In the 1940s, newer and more sophisticated scientific techniques for mass media research were introduced that somewhat discredited the simplistic powerful effects model and diminished its popularity in the research community. One important finding of the new era was that individual differences among audience members result in differences in media influence. Another important finding — at least in terms of political communication — was that mass media users are less likely to be *converted* by messages they receive than to have their already existing views *reinforced* by the media they select. In other words, we seek out the media that reinforce the views we already hold and avoid those messages that conflict with our already-held viewpoints. Studies like these became more prominent, leading to a generalized research view that mass media exert only **limited or minimalist effects**.

However, the advent of television on the national scene in the 1950s transformed the limited effects model as well. Television was the first national mass medium to provide both video and audio in our homes. At the same time, the public was concerned about the impact of comic books on young people. Because both these media seemed to present a great deal of graphic violence, the government began offering large grants to scholars who focused on the relationship between media use and violence. (Nevertheless, after 50 years the findings of hundreds of these studies form no single conclusive theory that explains and predicts behavior in this area.)

By the 1960s, the paradigm shifted once more — to the overall view that there simply *isn't* an overall view. Today, we acknowledge that mass media effects are very complicated and extremely difficult to study. Mass media consumers are both active and passive, individual and communal. The limited effects theory is clearly inadequate to describe the power of the 24/7 global mass media conglomerates and their messages of news/information, entertainment, and persuasion; but the powerful effects theories are too simplistic.

Most scholars today agree that reality is *socially constructed,* and **Bandura's social cognitive theory** (discussed earlier) has gained widespread acceptance by the more quantitative social/behavioral theories as well as by the more qualitative cultural/critical theorists. In fact, our current era has been called the **"era of cultural theory"** by **Stanley Baran** (2002, p. 387ff), who is himself a cultural theory scholar. Cultural critical theorists view the mass media — which have a stake in political, social, and economic structures as they currently exist — as rarely challenging the system that has enriched them; thus the media are **hegemonic**, that is, reinforcing the status quo by deliberately engineering mass consent to the established order, usually by making the empowered dominant group's ideas and assumptions seem commonsensical and normal. This theory also posits that although the effects of the mass media are potentially very powerful, media consumers either enhance or thwart these influences by the way they *interpret*[1] meaning from these mediated cultural messages. Of course, not all researchers have adopted the cultural theory model.

We need many ways to examine the effects of mass media on us as individuals and as a society. By considering a variety of approaches, we can begin to formulate some basic understandings that can help us get a better handle on the specific mass media influence issues that concern us.

Relevant Theories & Studies of Mediated Portrayals of Sex, Love, & Romance

We'll consider specific findings of research of mediated portrayals of sex, love, and romance in Part II's chapters, each of which focuses on one of the 12 major mass media myths in *Dr. FUN's Mass Media Love Quiz.* Here, though, are summaries of a few studies that offer food for thought — a kind of appetizer, if you will.

First, let's sample three studies that examine sex role socialization. Then we'll review some studies that focus on specific media. Finally, we'll review one of the few studies examining the relationship between both sexes' attitudes about coupleship and a wide variety of mass media — research (directed by Joan Shapiro)

---

[1]We'll cover three ways mass media consumers interpret media messages or "texts" — *preferred, negotiated,* or *oppositional* — in Chapter 6.

that formed the basis of my quantitative Baby Boomer/Generation Xer studies, one of which is abstracted at the end of this chapter.

Sex Role Socialization

From his examination of decades of research concerning children's sex-role socialization, Comstock (1991) concluded that a relationship exists between mass media and traditional beliefs about **sex roles**. Further, he argued that mass media portrayals can foster children's expectations of themselves as well as of others; for example, "Portrayals in television and other media of highly attractive persons may encourage dissatisfaction or lowered evaluations of the attractiveness of those of the pertinent sex in real life" (p. 176).

From his review of studies of television portrayals of sex roles, Tan (1985) concluded that television portrays females in traditional roles, that children use television as a guide to appropriate sex-role behaviors in real life, and that television also can effectively change sex-role expectations of children.

Inaccurate portrayals of how Americans behave sexually can produce **sexual dissatisfaction** in college students as well as young children. Baran's 1976 survey of college students supported his suggestion that "the media may indeed serve as a contributing factor to an individual's picture of his or her sexual self" (p. 473). For the most part, cinema and television portrayals tended to increase sexual expectations and thus decrease personal sexual satisfaction levels among survey respondents.

Fairy Tales & Romance Novels

Women in fairy tales are magical figures who are often defined by beauty, danger, innocence, malice, and greed (Dworkin, 1974). These images have profound effects on mass media audiences: "...We have not formed that ancient world — it has formed us" (p. 32). Calling fairy and folk tales the primary source of information about a culture, Dworkin argued that humans cannot help acting out roles taught to them by these tales, which specify gendered romantic roles. Because women are depicted as either evil or saintly, the real terror of fairy tales, she suggested, lies in the romantic message — that is, a woman who is not passive, innocent, and helpless must, then, be evil.

Romance novels are another potential source of illusions and expectations about love relationships. Barreca (1993) warned: "Consider the 'wisdom' imparted to millions of devoted readers by Barbara Cartland [best-selling romance writer] when she says that 'women have always been fascinated by abduction by a brutal, determined villain who, of course, eventually is reformed by love'" (p. 163). Schwartz (1994) also addressed the impact of romance novels:

> The more traditional the woman is, the more her ideal of love and sex is fulfilled best by gothic romance novel stereotypes: The hypermasculine hero overwhelms a finally submissive maiden, covers her with kisses and manly need, falls in love with her, takes her, and then marries her (not necessarily in that order).
>
> Men in ordinary marriage cannot live up to this fantasy imagery. (p. 77)

Romance novels, one of publishing's most lucrative categories, captivate millions of female readers. Radway (1991), who conducted an extended case study of a group of regular readers as well as of the industry itself, argued that at least part of the reason for the popularity of the successful romance novel lies in its ability to help readers resolve fundamental sexual and cultural ambiguities in their own lives. In the new (1991) introduction to the study, originally published in 1984 as *Reading the Romance,* she acknowledged that "romance reading is a profoundly conflicted activity centered upon a profoundly conflicted form" (p. 14). She explained:

> ...in ideal romances the hero is constructed androgynously. Although the women were clearly taken with his spectacularly masculine phallic power, in their voluntary comments and in their revealed preferences they emphasized that his capacity for tenderness and attentive concern was essential as well. (pp. 13-14)

Magazines

In an experimental study (Kenrick, Neuberg, Zierk, & Krones, as cited in Buss, 1994), men who viewed pictures of attractive women thereafter judged their actual partner to be less attractive than did the men who had viewed analogous pictures of women who were average in attractiveness — *and* (more importantly) these men (who viewed the attractive women) then rated themselves less committed, less satisfied, less serious, and less close to their actual partners. A study of nudes had similar results (Kenrick, Gutierres, & Goldberg, as cited in Buss, 1994). Buss explained: "The reason for these distressing changes are [*sic*] found in the unrealistic nature of the images" (p. 65). Magazines with photographs like these select only a few models from thousands of applicants, pick the best shots of them in the best settings and poses (from thousands of photos taken[2]), and then airbrush or digitally enhance them.

Movies

In an analysis of Hollywood's romantic comedies from the "screwball" movies (1934 to 1942) to the "nervous" romances of the 1980s, Krutnik (1990) highlighted some of the romantic fantasies and attendant unrealistic expectations that characterized the output of the Dream Factory. In the screwball romantic comedies, the woman was often presented a clear choice between marriage for money and marriage for love (the latter was presented as a "magical force which would triumph over all manner of real or imagined obstructions" [p. 58]), but in the 1950s and 1960s, the emphasis shifted from love and marriage to sex and the playboy fantasy ("a vision of bachelorhood as an idealized state of phallic omnipotence" [p. 60]). In the latter model, playful courtship is replaced by hostile antagonism and competition between the sexes. By the 1970s and 1980s, nervous romances — in which feminism is characterized as corruptive narcissism — exhibited a nostalgic yearning for the lost possibility of romance along with a more cynical awareness of the difficulty.

Schwartz (1994; see also Barreca, 1993) wrote that even well into the 1980s film fantasy imagery about sexual relations falls into the pattern of a woman meeting Prince Charming, being pursued by him, and then saved by him; for example, in *Pretty Woman* (1989) a prostitute uses her good looks and sexual talents to gain the status of the wife of a respectable and wealthy man, and in *An Officer and a Gentleman* (1982) a rising star in the military toys with a poor female factory

---

[2]Buss noted that *Playboy* "is reputed to shoot 6,000 pictures for its centerfold each month."

worker, falls in love with her, and rescues her from a life of drudgery. Portrayals of romance such as these may influence attitudes about normal courtship behavior.

Television

Gerbner's Cultivation Analysis. Although focused on the socializing agency of only one medium, "**cultivation analysis**" (or "enculturation research") conducted by **George Gerbner and his associates** (who coined the term) has presented an impressive amount of data covering more than three decades to show how television influences or "cultivates" its audiences. Cultivation theory assumes that heavy viewers are more likely to hold a view of reality that is congruent with television depictions. Beginning in 1967 with their first "Cultural Indicators" research project, Gerbner et al. have tracked television's dramatic content and its impact on children and adults over long periods of time (Gerbner, Gross, Morgan, & Signorielli, 1986). The primary focus of the project is television *violence*;[3] however, the project has also examined how television viewing contributes to audience perceptions of social reality in a variety of realms, including coupleship. For example, Signorielli (1991) concluded that "television might be the single most common and pervasive source of conceptions and actions related to marriage and intimate personal relationships for large segments of the population" (p. 12).

The general television viewing study of Potter and Chang (1990) contributed to mass communication researchers' efforts to strengthen the basic methodology of cultivation analysis by attempting to identify the best predictor of cultivation in teens: total viewing, type of program viewed, or a weighted proportion of program viewing. The investigators found that in predicting the amount of social learning occurring from television use, it is less important to know whether television dominates viewers' time than what *genre* (i.e., type) of program dominates their viewing.

In a more recent cultivation study, genre-specific programming was a significant factor. Segrin and Nabi (2002) surveyed 285 never-married university students to examine whether television viewing cultivated idealistic expectations about marriage and intentions to marry. They found that overall television viewing had a negative association with idealistic marriage expectations; however, viewing of romantic genre programming (e.g., romantic comedies, soap operas) was positively associated with idealistic expectations about marriage. They also found a strong and positive association between these expectations and marital intentions.

General TV Programming and Sex, Love, & Romance. Toner (1988) examined four television programs to see if the American notion of romance is directly related to the romance portrayed on television. Among the mass media–created expectations he found were that television separates sex from commitment but also abandons sex for romance, a couple is happy when they look good together, and intimacy and physical attraction are the path toward establishing a relationship (rather than vice versa). Toner postulated that some of the far-reaching consequences of the unattainable concept of love that dominated the programs he

---

[3]Cultivation analysis has found that network television presents far more violence than real life and that heavy television viewers overestimate the incidence of actual violence and believe the world to be "mean."

analyzed included the notion that the search for true love never ends and so viewers are forced to withdraw into their own fantasies to find satisfaction.

Sociologist Mary Laner — an expert on dating, courtship, and marriage — suggested that the depersonalization inherent in our mass media society might lead to overly high expectations and longings for a close relationship in which one person will satisfy every need — as in the "*Ozzie and Harriet*[4] mythology" (as cited in Blanc, 1994, p. 14).

Changes in women's images in family shows from prefeminist to postfeminist fictional television were the focus of an analysis by Press and Strathman (1993). Early programs such as *I Love Lucy* depicted women teaming up with other women against men (often their husbands) in order to escape the domestic realm. Programs at the height of the feminist movement portrayed single women in the workplace focusing on personal achievement rather than the inherent patriarchy of that workplace, such as *Charlie's Angels,* who were led by two men, one of whom never appeared in person. Postfeminist programs such as *The Cosby Show* placed women back in the nurturing role of the home at the same time as they held careers. However, even 1990s television portrayals of women — such as Roseanne and Clair Huxtable — are idealized and typically romanticized, failing to realistically represent the pressure of balancing a family, work, child care, and budgets.

TV Soap Operas. Lowry, Love, and Kirby (1981), whose content analysis of daytime soap operas counted 6.58 sex acts per hour and twice as many characters engaging in intercourse outside of marriage as within it, expressed concern that a "steady viewing diet of role models who engage in fornication and adultery may influence or cultivate viewers' attitudes and values concerning what is 'normal' and 'proper' in society" (p. 96). Similarly, the results of another content analysis of soap operas (Greenberg, Abelman, & Neuendorf, 1981) that showed that these daytime shows contain more sexual content (usually adulterous) than do prime-time programs (although prime-time intimacies are racier) prompted the researchers to express concern about young viewers' sexual socialization.

To explore the actual impact of such constructions of social reality from the distorted world views presented systematically by television, Buerkel-Rothfuss and Mayes (1981) conducted a cultivation study to see if heavy viewers of daytime soaps would exaggerate the prevalence of soap opera "problems" in the real world. They concluded:

> There appears to be an important relationship between what a person watches on daytime serials and what he or she believes to be true about those aspects of the "real world" which tend to be portrayed with exaggerated frequency on soap operas. (p. 114)

As noted earlier, a similar study by Carveth and Alexander (1985) found that the cultivation effect on viewers of soap operas seemed strongest when the motives for viewing were ritualistic (i.e., enjoyment or boredom) rather than instrumental (i.e., reality explorations or character identification).

---

[4]A popular network television sit-com (1952-1966) that featured a fictionalized and idealized version of a real-life family — the Nelsons: father Ozzie, mother Harriet, and sons David and Ricky (who became a popular teen recording artist). This long-running family show was in the tradition of *Father Knows Best* and *The Donna Reed Show.*

Radio & Popular Music

In his best-selling self-help book *Your Erroneous Zones*, psychologist Wayne Dyer (1976) cautioned readers about the negative but subtle impact on romantic reality of such popular song lyrics as "I can't live, if living is without you," "You make me so very happy," "You're nobody till somebody cares," and "You make me feel like a natural woman": "Those sweet harmless lyrics may be more damaging than you realize," he warned (p. 69). Though he advised rewriting[5] the songs to fit a less dependent image, he admitted that songs with healthier but less "romantic" messages (e.g., "I chose to love you. I must have wanted to do it then, but now I've changed my mind.") probably wouldn't sell (pp. 69–70).

Advertising

Dyer (1976) also analyzed the psychological manipulations of commercial advertising messages that rely on social conditioning to focus consumers on the external rewards of cultural norms. Tan (1985) summarized research that showed that exposure to beauty commercials can cause adolescent girls to place more importance on beauty-related characteristic in real life.

Wilson (1995) — illustrating how motivational research (MR) "discovered just how subtle and complex sexual fantasies are in influencing consumer buying patterns" (pp. 276–277) — described one example of MR's application of romantic idealizing: the creation of the "compromise car" to satisfy male automobile buyers who were lured by regular convertibles, which symbolized a mistress, but who usually bought sedans, symbolizing the "girl they would marry because she would make a good wife and mother" (p. 277). (The hardtop convertible was the solution.)

Shapiro's Studies of the Effects of Unrealistic Portrayals of Sex, Love, & Romance Across a Wide Variety of Mass Media

All of the studies discussed above focused on individual media; however, my research and this book focus on all mass media. Surprisingly, an extensive review of the scholarly literature found only *one* other researcher who has investigated the relationship between a wide variety of mass media and the expectations and satisfactions of both sexes.

Joan Shapiro, a marital psychotherapist, directed two ambitious studies (Shapiro & Kroeger, 1991; Shapiro, Kroeger, & Warren, n.d.) that examined the effects of the cultivation of unrealistic romantic expectations across a wide variety of mass communication media. One study focused on adults, and the other focused on adolescents.

Adults

In the first study, Shapiro and Kroeger (1991) investigated the relationship between attitudes about intimate relationships and popular culture media exposure.

---

[5]In Step 5 (Design) of the Seven-Step Dis-illusioning Directions (detailed in Chapter 6), you will learn how to follow this excellent advice.

A convenience sample of 109 adults involved in intimate relationships completed three questionnaires: Eidelson and Epstein's Relationship Beliefs Inventory (RBI), the Satisfaction Subscale of Spanier's Dyadic Adjustment Scale (DAS), and a mass media use questionnaire created by the researchers.

As expected, respondents with *more unrealistic beliefs* about romantic love reported significantly *less satisfaction* with their current relationship, significantly *more exposure* to popular media, and significantly less exposure to TV news and documentaries than those who endorsed more realistic views. There was a trend for married women who reported more exposure to popular media to rate themselves as less satisfied with their current intimate relationship. No significant differences on the RBI were found based on age or sex.

The researchers, who cautioned that this correlational study could not provide a clear indication of causation, raised an important question:

> Do the media create dysfunctional beliefs about relationships or do people with dysfunctional beliefs expose themselves more to the popular media to confirm or reinforce those beliefs? Or is this related to some third variable?

The authors speculated that the direction of influence might be "circular, rather like the chicken-egg phenomenon" (Shapiro & Kroeger, 1991, p. 233).

Shapiro and Kroeger recommended the replication of the study with diverse populations, especially adolescents — who, along with children, might be most in danger of the potentially dysfunctional socializing impacts of unrealistic mass media. To counteract this danger, they suggested that "parents, educators, and mental health professional teach critical thinking and independent decision-making to children and adolescents, as well as practice it themselves" (p. 234).

Adolescents

Following their own recommendation, Shapiro et al. (n.d.) studied the perceived influences on attitudes about romantic relationships of 123 late adolescents between the ages of 18 and 20, who completed the three questionnaires used in the 1991 study. Adolescents who perceived themselves to be *highly influenced* by the mass media during the ages of 13 to 15 held *more unrealistic beliefs*. Although the researchers had found significant correlations between exposure to romantic media and attitudes about romantic relationships in their 1991 study of adults, this later study of adolescents did not; however, some specific types of mass media (e.g., romance/drama movies and tabloids) did seem to correlate with unrealistic attitudes.

Galician's Continuing Research of the Effects of Unrealistic Portrayals of Sex, Love, & Romance Across a Wide Variety of Mass Media

As I've mentioned, I direct an ongoing research project to study what I've termed "The Romanticization of Love in the Mass Media." I've conducted large-scale quantitative surveys of hundreds of male and female Baby Boomers and Generation Xers, and I'm continually summarizing the responses from the thousands of people who take my *Dr. FUN's Mass Media Love Quiz*. To get qualitative data, I conducted in-depth interviews with males and females from the age of 3 to 103, and hundreds of students in my classes have shared anecdotal reports about mass media influences as have members of the audiences I address. More recently, I created the 12 *Dr. Galician's Prescriptions™ for Getting Real About Romance* by synthesizing a wide variety of recommendations for healthy coupleship that serve as *antidotes* to each of the 12 myths in the *Quiz.*

I'll share the findings of my studies with you in the Additional Research & Commentary Related to This Mass Media Myth section of the relevant chapters of Part II. In addition, all 12 chapters begin with several case studies, and every chapter includes a box containing male and female university students' responses to that chapter's *Quiz* item.

In the meantime, here's an extended summary of my survey of the romantic expectations, satisfactions, and mass media usage of male and female Baby Boomers and Generation Xers (Galician, 1995, 1997), for which Shapiro's studies formed the basis.

The survey examined what 381 women and men of two different age cohorts —Generation Xers and Baby Boomers—learn from the mass media in terms of expectations about romantic love in heterosexual coupleship as well as how their own partnerships are affected by unrealistic models and mythic or stereotyped portrayals in the entertainment, news, and advertising messages of a wide variety of mass media: romance novels and movies, television soap operas and sitcoms, radio music and MTV, newscasts and talkshows, newspapers, advice columns, fashion magazines, and others.

Respondents anonymously completed a Romantic Love and the Mass Media Questionnaire, which included the Relationship Belief Inventory (RBI) (Eidelson & Epstein, 1982), the 10-item Dyadic Satisfaction Subscale of the complete 32-item Dyadic Adjustment Scale (DAS) (Spanier, 1976), and several parts that I created to assess respondents' ideals and models, current relationships, media usage, and demographics.

Demographic Comparison

The median age of the 148 *Baby Boomers* was 38 (birth-year 1957), with a range of 31 to 49 (1964–1946); the median age of the 233 *Generation Xers* was 20 (birth-year 1975), with a range of 17 to 29 (1978–1966). Most Boomers (64%) were married, and the median length of their longest committed romantic relationship was 10.5 years; Xers mostly were either not dating (34%) or were "going steady" (34%) (Only 3% were married and 10% were living together.), and their longest relationship averaged 2 years. Many more Boomers (25%) than Xers (only 2%) had been divorced, but there were fewer divorces or separations among Baby Boomers' parents (22%) than Xers' parents (33%). More Boomers (91%) than Xers (79%) had grown up in dual-parent homes, and fewer mothers of Boomers (61%) than Xers (71%) worked outside the home before their children were teenagers.

Though roughly the same majority of both groups (71% of Boomers and 69% of Xers) resorted to mutual give-and-take in a disagreement, more Xers (17%) than Boomers (10%) reported men giving in. And although the majority of both groups said the man and woman are fairly equal in dominance, the proportion of Boomers was larger (60%, compared with 52% for Xers), whereas twice as many Xers (20% compared with 10% for Boomers) said the woman is dominant; 30% of both groups age cohorts said the man is dominant.

Ideal Romantic Role Models

When asked about "real people you know personally who have achieved ideal coupleship," Baby Boomers more frequently named friends, whereas Generation Xers named their parents. Xers also evaluated their parents as having happier marriages than Boomers did, despite higher rates of divorce and single-parenting in Xers' families. Their "celebrity" models were primarily entertainment figures but some were political leaders — though in all named political couples it was the man who is the politician. Xers' frequent naming of "Romeo and Juliet" as a fictional ideal is troubling — considering the obvious dysfunction and realistic failure of that relationship.

The Relationship Between Romantic Expectations & Satisfactions

Further validating the studies of Shapiro and Kroeger (1991) and Shapiro et al. (n.d.), as well as those of Epstein and Eidelson (1981) and Eidelson and Epstein (1982), my study found strong support for a negative or inverse relationship between romanticized hegemonic beliefs about coupleship and satisfaction in actual current coupleship.

The Relationship Between Mass Media Usage
& Romantic Expectations

As in Shapiro's studies, unrealistic romanticized attitudes about intimate relationships were related to some measures of mass media usage. In my study, unrealistic attitudes were linked to both romantic and non-romantic movies as well as men's and women's magazines focused on appearance (i.e., fashion, sports/fitness) and television (including music videos).

Differences Between the Two Age Cohorts

Some key findings of the cross-generational aspect of this study of two different age cohorts are that Generation Xers appeared to use more mass media in general. These Xers also had more unrealistic expectations of coupleship in terms of expecting mindreading in partners and sexual perfection of themselves as well as holding more stereotypic hegemonic gender-role models. These findings support studies of Laner and Russell (1994, 1995). What is not clear from the quantitative self-reported nature of the data is whether these differences are a function of a genuinely different demographic grouping ("Xers") or of a maturing process; that is, many more Boomers were in long-term relationships and marriages, whereas Xers were basically in shorter-term dating relationships.

Differences Between the Two Sexes

Overall, men in my study were (surprisingly) less realistic in their romantic attitudes than women. (Usually, women are thought to be more "romantic" and less realistic.) The one clear unrealistic expectation of men in both age cohorts appears to be sexual perfectionism. Apparently, this aspect of romance remains a traditionally male domain despite decades of "sexual equality." Another interesting finding is that while men of both age cohorts seem to share the same romantic beliefs, women in the younger groups appear more unrealistic than their older "sisters" of the Baby Boom generation, particularly in the mind-reading expectation. Again, it would be interesting to know whether age cohort or maturation determine these differences.

Implications of This Study

The findings of this study suggest that there is a relationship between mass media usage and the romantic ideals and expectations of both men and women. Mass media may indeed influence or at least reinforce dysfunctional unrealistic belief about heterosexual coupleship that could lead to unhappiness and harm. Few models of healthy coupleship can be found in the popular culture. Researchers have much work to do to attempt to discover the process of media myth construction and cultivation.

SUMMARY

The illusion of personal invulnerability and the third-person effect describe our tendency to believe the effects of mass media are greater on other people than on ourselves. The elaboration likelihood model of persuasion says that we're persuaded through one of two major pathways: the central route (where we're more aware and less likely to be persuaded) and the peripheral route (where we're less suspecting and more likely to be persuaded, frequently by entertainment). These pathways are similar to the influences under instrumental and ritualistic motivations for media usage.

Mass media are powerful socialization agents from which we learn and model many behaviors — both healthy and unhealthy. Social learning theory (associated most closely with work of social psychologist Albert Bandura) considers the mass media to be primary socialization agents, along with family, peers, and classroom teachers. This widely regarded theory asserts that we learn by modeling the behavior of in-person or mediated real people or fictional characters through imitation and identification resulting from three processes: observational learning, inhibitory effects, and disinhibitory effects. Media guru Marshall McLuhan argued that because of the mass media the world has become what he called a global village, where no one can escape the effects of the mass media.

Through replicated research studies, the discipline of mass communication gradually begins to build theories that can be tested. Quantitative/deductive methods utilize facts and statistics and, usually, larger numbers of participants, who are studied broadly; qualitative/inductive methods utilize impressions and words and, usually, fewer participants, who are studied in more depth. All scientific research is systematic, objective, empirical, and cumulative.

Generalized conceptions about mass media effects have evolved from the early belief that mass media have powerful effects like magic bullets or hypodermic needles to a later reversal in the limited effects theory that emphasized the reinforcing rather than revolutionizing nature of media effects. By the 1960s, the paradigm shifted once more — to the overall view that there simply isn't an overall view. Most scholars today agree that reality is socially constructed, and Bandura's social cognitive theory has gained widespread acceptance both by the quantitative social/behavioral theorists and by the more qualitative cultural/critical theorists.

Cultural critical theorists view the mass media as hegemonic. By studying the research of various approaches, we gain a broader understanding.

A variety of studies of mass media portrayals and their effects are related to our focus. For example, cultivation analysis (or "enculturation research") conducted by George Gerbner and his associates shows how television influences or "cultivates" its audiences.

Joan Shapiro directed two studies that examined the effects of the cultivation of unrealistic romantic expectations across a wide variety of mass communication media. Respondents with more unrealistic beliefs about romantic love reported significantly less satisfaction with their current relationship and significantly more exposure to popular media. These studies formed the basis of one of my own studies, a large-scale quantitative survey of hundreds of male and female Baby Boomers and Generation Xers that also found a relationship between their mass media usage and their attitudes toward coupleship. The findings suggest that mass media may indeed influence or at least reinforce dysfunctional unrealistic beliefs about coupleship that could lead to unhappiness and harm.

SOURCES CITED

Bandura, A. (1969). *Principles of behavior modification.* New York: Holt, Rinehart & Winston.

Bandura, A. (1977). *Social learning theory.* Englewood Cliffs, NJ: Prentice-Hall.

Bandura, A. (Ed.). (1971). *Psychological modeling: Conflicting theories.* New York: Aldine-Atherton.

Bandura, A. (1986). *Social foundations of thought and action: A social cognitive theory.* Englewood Cliffs, NJ: Prentice-Hall.

Baran, S. J. (1976). How tv and film portrayals affect sexual satisfaction in college students. *Journalism Quarterly, 53,* 468–473.

Baran, S. J. (2002). *Introduction to mass communication: Foundations, ferment, and future.* Belmont, CA: Wadsworth.

Baran, S. J., & Davis, D. K. (2000). *Mass communication theory: Foundations, ferment, and future.* Belmont, CA: Wadsworth.

Barreca, R. (1993). *Perfect husbands & other fairy tales: Demystifying marriage, men, and romance.* New York: Harmony Books.

Blanc, T. (1994, Spring/Summer). Marriage mythology. *ASU Research,* pp. 13–15.

Buerkel-Rothfuss, N. L., & Mayes, S. (1981). Soap opera viewing: The cultivation effect. *Journal of Communication, 31*(3), 108–115.

Buss, D. M. (1994). *The evolution of desire: Strategies of human mating.* New York: Basic Books.

Carveth, R., & Alexander, A. (1985). Soap opera viewing motivations and the cultivation process. *Journal of Broadcasting & Electronic Media, 29,* 259–273.

Comstock, G. (1991). *Television and the American child.* San Diego: Academic.

Davison, W. P. (1983). The third-person effect in communication. *Public Opinion Quarterly, 47,* 1–15.

Dworkin, A. (1974). *Woman hating.* New York: E. P. Dutton.

Dyer, W. W. (1976). *Your erroneous zones.* New York: Avon Books.

Eidelson, R. J., & Epstein, N. (1982). Cognition and relationship maladjustment: Development of a measure of dysfunctional relationship beliefs. *Journal of Consulting and Clinical Psychology, 50,* 715–720.

Epstein, N., & Eidelson, R. J. (1981). Unrealistic beliefs of clinical couples: Their relationship to expectations, goals and satisfaction. *The American Journal of Family Therapy, 9*(4), 13–22.

Fink, A. S., & Galician, M.-L. (1996). *Love or marriage: Television soap opera usage and the construction and cultivation of viewers' attitudes about romantic relationships.* Paper presented at the annual meeting of The Organization for the Study of Communication, Language, and Gender, Monterey Bay, CA.

Galician, M.-L. (1995, October). *The romanticization of love in the mass media: A comparison of the relationship among unrealistic romantic expectations, ideal role models, heterosexual coupleship satisfaction, and mass media usage of Baby Boomers and Generation Xers.* Paper presented at the annual meeting of The Organization for the Study of Communication, Language, and Gender, Minneapolis/St. Paul, MN.

Galician, M.-L. (1997, February). *The romanticization of love in the mass media: The relationship of mass communication media usage, unrealistic romantic expectations, coupleship dissatisfactions of Baby Boomer and Generation X males and females.* Paper presented at the annual meeting of the Western States Communication Association, Monterey Bay, CA.

Gerbner, G., Gross, L., Morgan, M., & Signorielli, N. (1986). Living with television: The dynamics of the cultivation process. In J. Bryant & D. Zillmann (Eds.), *Perspectives on media effects* (pp. 17–40). Hillsdale, NJ: Lawrence Erlbaum.

Greenberg, B. S., Abelman, R., & Neuendorf, K. (1981). Sex on the soap operas: Afternoon delight. *Journal of Communication, 31*(3), 83–89.

Krutnik, F. (1990). The faint aroma of performing seals: The "nervous" romance of the comedy of the sexes. *The Velvet Light Trap, 26,* 57–72.

Laner, M. R., & Russell, J. N. (1994). Course content and change in students: Are marital expectations altered by marriage education? *Teaching Sociology, 22,* 10–18.

Laner, M. R., & Russell, J. N. (1995). Marital expectations and level of premarital involvement: Does marriage education make a difference? *Teaching Sociology, 23,* 1–7.

Lowery, S. A., & DeFleur, M. L. (1983). *Milestones in mass communication research.* New York: Longman.

Lowry, D. T., Love, G., & Kirby, M. (1981). Sex on the soap operas: Patterns of intimacy. *Journal of Communication, 31*(3), 90–96.

Perse, E. M. (1986). Soap opera viewing patterns of college students and cultivation. *Journal of Broadcasting & Electronic Media, 30,* 175–193.

Perse, E. M., & Rubin, A. M. (1988). Audience activity and satisfaction with favorite television soap operas. *Journalism Quarterly, 65,* 368–375.

Petty, R. E., & Cacioppo, J. T. (1986). The elaboration likelihood model of persuasion, In L. Berkowitz (Ed.), *Advances in experimental social psychology* (pp. 123–205). Hillsdale, NJ: Erlbaum.

Potter, W. J., & Chang, I. C. (1990). Television exposure measures and cultivation hypothesis. *Journal of Broadcasting and Electronic Media, 34,* 313–333.

Press, A., & Strathman, T. (1993). Work, family, and social class in television images of women: Prime-time television and the construction of postfeminism. *Women and Language, 16*(2), 7–15.

Rubin, A.M. (1985). Uses of daytime television soap operas by college students. *Journal of Broadcasting & Electronic Media, 29,* 241–258.

Schwartz, P. (1994). *Peer marriage: How love between equals really works.* New York: Free Press.

Segrin, C., & Nabi, R. L. (2002). Does television viewing cultivate unrealistic expectations about marriage? *Journal of Communication, 52*(2), 247–263.

Shah, D. V., Faber, R. J., & Youn, S. (1999). Susceptibility and severity: Perceptual dimensions underlying the third-person effect. *Communication Research, 26*(2), 240–267.

Shapiro, J., & Kroeger, L. (1991). Is life just a romantic novel? The relationship between attitudes about intimate relationships and the popular media. *American Journal of Family Therapy, 19*(3), 226–236.

Shapiro, J., Kroeger, L., & Warren, J. (n.d.). Get a life: Media, peer, and family influences on adolescents' attitudes about intimate relationships. Unpublished manuscript.

Signorielli, N. (1991). Adolescents and ambivalence toward marriage: A cultivation analysis. *Youth and Society, 23,* 121–149.

Spanier, G. (1976). Measuring dyadic adjustment: New scales for assessing the quality of marriage and similar dyads. *Journal of Marriage and the Family, 38,* 15–28.

Sparks, G. G. (2002). *Mass effects research: A basic overview.* Belmont, CA: Wadsworth.

Sternberg, R. J. (1998). *Cupid's arrow: The course of love through time.* New York: Cambridge University Press.

Tan, A. S. (1985). *Mass communication theories and research* (2nd ed.). New York: John Wiley & Sons.

Toner, S. J. (1988). Television and the American imagination: Notions of romance. *Journal of Popular Culture, 22*(3), 1.

Wilson, S. L. R. (1995). *Mass media/mass culture: An introduction* (3rd ed.). McGraw-Hill.

Zimbardo, P. G., Ebbesen, E. B., & Maslach, C. (1977). *Influencing attitudes and changing behavior.* Reading, MA: Addison-Wesley.

6

STRATEGIES & SKILLS OF MEDIA LITERACY

Tools for Media Analysis & Criticism

Media literacy is not so much a finite body of knowledge but rather a skill, a process, a way of thinking that, like reading comprehension, is always evolving. To become media literate is not to memorize facts or statistics about the media, but rather to raise the right questions about what you are watching, reading or listening to. At the heart of media literacy is the principle of inquiry.
— Elizabeth Thoman, "Mission Statement," *Media&Values*

Criticism, at its best, is informed talk about matters of importance.
— Philip Wander & Steven Jenkins,
"Rhetoric, Society, and the Critical Response"

In Part II, we'll apply the background information from the five foundations of Part I to *dis*-illusion the major mass media myths about sex, love, and romance. Using media literacy strategies and skills, we'll analyze and criticize actual mass media portrayals in terms of four of the foundational areas: unrealistic ideals, realistic models, mass media narrative techniques, and mass media effects. This fifth and final foundational chapter of Part I clarifies the strategies and skills of media literacy and specifies the analysis and criticism approach that we'll follow — Dr. Galician's Seven-Step *Dis*-illusioning Directions.

WHAT IS "MEDIA LITERACY"?

Some Definitions

Media literacy is an international movement, so many useful definitions have been offered:

> Media literacy seeks to empower citizenship, to transform citizens' passive relationship to media into an active, critical engagement capable of challenging the traditions and structures of a privatized, commercial media culture, and thereby find new avenues of citizen speech and discourse.

— Wally Bowen, Citizens for Media Literacy, Asheville, NC, 1996

Media literacy empowers people to be both critical thinkers and creative producers of an increasingly wide range of messages using image, language, and sound. It is the skillful application of literacy skills to media and technology messages. As communication technologies transform society, they impact our understanding of ourselves, our communities, and our diverse cultures, making media literacy an essential life skill for the 21st century.

— The Alliance for a Media Literate America (AMLA),
AMLA Website <www.nmec.org>, November 1, 2001

Media Literacy is an informed, critical understanding of the mass media. It involves an examination of the techniques, technologies and institutions that are involved in media production, the ability to critically analyze media messages and a recognition of the role that audiences play in making meaning from those messages.

— Rick Shepherd, "Why Teach Media Literacy," *Teach Magazine*,
Quadrant Educational Media Services, Oct./Nov. 1993

Media Literacy is concerned with helping students develop an informed and critical understanding of the nature of mass media, the techniques used by them, and the impact of these techniques. More specifically, it is education that aims to increase students' understanding and enjoyment of how the media work, how they produce meaning, how they are organized, and how they construct reality. Media literacy also aims to provide students with the ability to create media products.

— Barry Duncan, et al., *Media Literacy Resource Guide,*
Ontario (Canada) Ministry of Education, 1989

[Media Literacy] moves from merely recognizing and comprehending information to higher order critical-thinking skills implicit in questioning, analyzing and evaluating that information.

— David Considine, *Telemedium: The Journal for Media Literacy, 41* (2), 1994

The *Journal of Communication* devoted a special issue to media literacy. In his "Editor's Notes," Alan Rubin — a noted mass communication scholar and a former editor also of the *Journal of Broadcasting & Electronic Media* — cited the definitions of several other media scholars and organizations. Here's his own:

Media literacy, then, is about understanding the sources and technologies of communication, the codes that are used, the messages that are produced, and the selection, interpretation, and impact of those messages. (1998, p. 3)

The Importance of Media Literacy

Today's information, entertainment, and persuasion industries communicate to us through a powerful combination of words, images and sounds. In our global village, no one is beyond their influence. Therefore, we need to develop a wider set of skills to help us better understand the messages we receive, and we need to learn how to design and distribute our own messages. Being literate in a media age requires critical thinking skills that empower us in our personal, public, and professional lives.

Does Media Literacy Mean "Media Bashing" or "Media Censorship"?

While media literacy does raise critical questions about the impact of media and technology, it's *not an anti-media movement*. Rather, it represents a coalition of concerned individuals and organizations, including parents, educators, faith-based groups, healthcare providers, and citizen and consumer groups seeking a more enlightened way of understanding our media environment. In fact, some media organizations themselves are active participants in media literacy groups. AMLA, the Alliance for a Media Literate America (formerly the Partnership for Media Education), lists many of them on their website <www.nmec.org>.

And it's *not a media censorship movement*. Media literacy pioneer Elizabeth Thoman (2001) explained:

> Media no longer just influence our culture. They are our culture. Media's pivotal role in our global culture is why media censorship will never work. What's needed, instead, is a major rethinking of media's role in all of our lives.

Media literacy is a realistic practice, so it's not about seeking perfection or purity from the mass media. As media literacy expert James Potter (1998) noted in the first edition of his highly acclaimed book, *Media Literacy:* "A key to media literacy is not to engage in the impossible quest for truthful or objective messages. They don't exist" (p. 9).

Elizabeth Thoman on the Skills & Strategies of Media Literacy

For 25 years, Elizabeth Thoman, a Roman Catholic nun, has been a leader in the media education movement she pioneered in the United States. In 1977 she founded *Media&Values* magazine to raise a critical voice on issues of media and society. As the founder and current president of the Center for Media Literacy in Los Angeles, she created the first generation of curriculum resources for teaching about media in the United States, developed a national distribution clearinghouse for teaching resources in the field (now on the Internet), and founded the Felton Media Literacy Scholars Program, a leadership development and teacher training program in Southern California. She's also the secretary of AMLA.

As one of our nation's leading voices for media literacy, Thoman — a graduate of the Annenberg School for Communication at the University of Southern California — has testified before Congress, attended White House conferences, keynoted numerous conventions, and been interviewed extensively by the press.

In "Skills & Strategies for Media Education," a comprehensive document on the Center for Media Literacy's website <www.medialit.org>, she outlined the core principles and key components of media literacy. The next section provides a synopsis.

In answer to "What is media literacy?," Thoman (2001) explained:

> Just what it sounds like: the ability to interpret and create personal meaning from the hundreds, even thousands of verbal and visual symbols we take in everyday through television, radio, computers, newspapers, and magazines, and of course advertising. It's the ability to choose and select, the ability to challenge and question, the ability to be conscious about what's going on around you and not be passive and therefore, vulnerable.

The goal is to help people become literate in all media forms "so that they control the interpretation of what they see or hear rather than letting the interpretation control them" (Thoman, 2001).

Five Important Ideas About Media Messages

In "Five Important Ideas to Teach Your Kids about TV" published in Thoman's *Media&Values,* Jay Davis (1990) compiled several seminal documents from media educators in England and Canada (pioneering nations in the movement). These five ideas — which are central to our study of media portrayals of sex, love, and romance — have endured as the Center for Media Literacy's "five ideas that everyone should know about media messages, whether the message comes packaged as a TV sitcom, a computer game, a music video, a magazine ad, or a movie in the theatre" (Thoman, 2001):

> 1. All media messages are "constructed." What happens is that whatever is "constructed" by just a few people then becomes "the way it is" for the rest of us. But as the audience, we don't get to see or hear the words, pictures or arrangements that were rejected.

Note that in addition to reminding us that *media construct our social reality,* Thoman is advising us to consider not only what's *in* media messages but also what might be left *out.* Note also that information is *not* knowledge — and information is socially constructed.

> 2. Media messages are constructed using a creative language with its own rules. Each form of communication has its own creative language: scary music heightens fear, camera close-ups convey intimacy, big headlines signal significance. Understanding the system of media language increases our appreciation and enjoyment of media experiences, as well as helps us to be less susceptible to manipulation.

Like McLuhan, Thoman believes that *the medium is the message.* As you saw in Chapter 4, each medium has its own unique aesthetic, codes, and conventions, and each medium's content is closely related to its form — so, for example, newspapers present the world to us in a very different way from the way television does.

> 3. Different people experience the same media message differently. Because of each individual's age, upbringing, and education, no two people see the same movie or hear the same song on the radio. We may not be conscious of it but [all] of us, even toddlers, are constantly trying to "make sense" of what we see, hear, or read. The more questions we can ask about what we are experiencing around us, the more alert we can be about accepting or rejecting messages.

Thoman's point also relates to our earlier discussion regarding selective exposure, selective perception, and selective retention of mass mediated messages. In fact, the **"reception theory"** school of media criticism (also called **"textual analysis"**) suggests that messages are not just in the text but also in us as receivers who interpret the messages and "negotiate meaning."

> 4. Media are primarily businesses driven by a profit motive. Newspapers lay out their pages with ads first; the space remaining is devoted to news. Likewise, we all know that commercials are part and parcel of most TV watching. What many people do not know is that what's really being sold through television is not only the advertised products to the audience but also the audience to the advertisers! The real purpose of programs we watch on commercial TV, whether news or entertainment, is not just to entertain us but rather to create an audience (and put them in a receptive mood) so that they can sell time to sponsors to advertise their products

in commercials. Sponsors pay for the time based on the number of people the station predicts will be watching. Sponsors also target their advertising message to specific kinds of viewers — for example, women 20–35 who spend money on the advertised products or children 2–7 who influence their parent's spending. Most media are provided to us by private, global corporations with something to sell rather than by caring organizations with something to tell.

Most mass media are indeed commercial entities — commercially driven, with commercial implications. We shouldn't be fooled into thinking otherwise. Of course, on the other hand, if commercially sponsored media suddenly became commercial-free and we as consumers had to underwrite their actual cost (rather than just paying a small portion through subscriptions and admission tickets), we'd find the prices beyond most of our budgets. (One point Thoman doesn't make here is that because the media are commercially oriented, we as consumers have great power we don't often use consciously or actively. We'll discuss the role of consumer power and activism later in this chapter.)

> 5. Media have embedded values and points of view. Media, because they are constructed, carry a subtext of who and what is important at least to the person or persons creating the construction. Media are also storytellers (even commercials tell a quick and simple story), and stories require characters, settings, and a plot that has a beginning, middle and end. The choice of a character's age, gender, or race mixed in with the lifestyles, attitudes, and behaviors that are portrayed, the selection of a setting (urban? rural? affluent? poor?), and the actions and reactions in the plot are just some of the ways that values become "embedded" in a TV show, movie, or ad. It's important to learn how to "read" all kinds of media messages in order to discover the points of view that are embedded in them. Only then can we judge whether to accept or reject these messages.

For our purpose, this is perhaps the most crucial of the five "ideas." While some imbedded values might be worthy of our adoption, what we *don't* want is to have them seductively slipped down our backs without our knowledge or permission. Don't forget the *illusion of personal invulnerability* and the *third-person effect* (Chapter 5). And remember also that we're most likely to be receptive to the embedded values when we're just using media for enjoyment (when our guard is down). Once we're in a hypnotic state, it's harder for us to wake ourselves up from the trance and escape the power of the messages' suggestions.

Five Basic Questions About Media Messages

From the five ideas above, Thoman and her colleagues devised five basic questions that can be asked about any media message:
1.   Who created this message and why are they sending it?
2.   What techniques are being used to attract my attention?
3.   What lifestyles, values and points of view are represented in the message?
4.   How might different people understand this message differently from me?
5.   What is omitted from this message?

We should ask these questions about any mediated message — whether entertainment or news or advertising. Thoman (2001) cautioned:

> While getting "caught up" in a storytelling experience has been the essence of entertainment since our ancestors told tales around the fire, the relentless pace of entertainment media today requires that at least once in a while, we should stop and look, really look, at how a media message is put together and the many meanings that can derive from it.

Action Learning (The Empowerment Spiral)

To guide this questioning, Thoman (2001) recommended several models, including the Action Learning model, which she described as excellent for "uncorking a spiral of inquiry that leads to increased comprehension, greater critical thinking, and ability to make informed judgments." Based on the work of the late Brazilian educator **Paolo Freire**, Action Learning can be summarized as a four-step "empowerment" process — Awareness, Analysis, Reflection, and Action:

- In the **Awareness** step, you participate in some activity (like counting the number of violent incidents in a children's cartoon) that leads to the insight: "Oh! I never thought of that before."

- The next step, **Analysis**, you take time to figure out "how" an issue came to be. Core questioning and close analysis are two techniques used in this step to better understand the complexity of the selected media topic. Production experiences could also help you understand "how" and "what" happens in the exchange between media producers and their audiences.

- In the **Reflection** step, you look deeper to ask "So what?" or "What ought we to do?" about the identified media issue. You might want to also consider philosophical or religious tenets, ethical values, or democratic principles that are accepted as guides for individual and collective decision-making.

- Finally, the **Action** step gives you an opportunity to formulate constructive actions that will lead to changing your own media choices and viewing habits as well as working for change locally, nationally, or globally.

We'll incorporate these empowerment processes as we conduct our seven-step *dis*illusioning of unrealistic portrayals of sex, love, and romance in the mass media.

AMLA: Alliance for a Media Literate America

Another national media literacy organization Thoman helped establish is the Alliance for a Media Literate America (founded in 1997 as the Partnership for Media Education) — a meeting ground for both educators and practitioners. On June 23, 2001, the organization issued its Founding Declaration (AMLA, 2001), which sheds more light on the concept of media literacy:

> *Whereas the explosion of new communication technologies has made media literacy skills essential for life in the 21st century, and*
>
> *Whereas we are living through a technological revolution that is transforming our society, changing the way we understand ourselves and our communities, as well as the way we work, communicate, live, teach and learn, and*
>
> *Whereas, media technologies are accessible to individuals in unprecedented numbers, and*
>
> *Whereas democratic citizenship in our media-saturated culture requires that all Americans be able to analyze what we see and hear, as well as what we read, and*
>
> *Whereas the inclusion of media literacy in state education standards has underscored the need for appropriate training and support for educators, and there is an urgent need to disseminate the growing number of effective strategies developed by teachers across the country who have incorporated media literacy into their classrooms, and*
>
> *Whereas medical, social service, and justice system professionals have identified media literacy as a vital tool in the promotion of public health, prevention, and wellness, and*
>
> *Whereas media literacy skills enable people to use the full range of communication technologies for creative expression, and personal and professional growth, and*
>
> *Whereas the ability to produce media significantly enhances people's ability to communicate, as*

well as to understand media messages, and media makers, both professional and community based, have considerable expertise to share, and

Whereas media literacy can benefit from opportunities for practitioners from different fields and perspectives to meet to exchange ideas, experiences, and expertise, and

Whereas opportunities for respectful dialogue are essential to the expansion of media literacy in the United States, and

Whereas, a national organization is uniquely able to harness the collective passion and energy of its members to fuel the growth of media literacy, and link the thousands of heretofore isolated media literacy practitioners and projects across the country into a vibrant support network, and

Whereas a national coalition of practitioners can advocate for media literacy in ways that are more powerful and influential than any individual, project, or institution can achieve alone,

We, therefore, this day of June 23, 2001, create the Alliance for a Media Literate America as a national membership organization dedicated to the promotion of media literacy education that encourages hope rather than cynicism, participation rather than passivity, probing discussion rather than rhetorical attacks, healthy skepticism rather than suspicion, and inclusion rather than exclusion. As we celebrate our accomplishments and learn from our challenges, we will broaden our field, our dialogues, our visibility, and our practice.

Media Literacy Resources

For in-depth details about media literacy, here are several excellent books devoted to the topic:

Potter, W. J. (2001). *Media literacy* (2nd ed.). Thousand Oaks, CA: Sage.

Silverblatt, A. (1995). *Media literacy: Keys to interpreting media messages.* Westport, CT: Praeger.

Silverblatt, A., & Enright Eliceriri, E. M. (1997). *Dictionary of media literacy.* Westport, CT: Greenwood.

Silverblatt, A., Ferry, J., & Finan, B. (1999). *Approaches to media literacy: A handbook.* Armonk, NY: M.E. Sharpe.

In addition, you might find these websites informative:

Alliance for a Media Literate America
www.nmec.org

Center for Media Education
www.cme.org

Center for Media Literacy
www. medialiteracy.org

Media Education Foundation
www.mediaed.org

Media Literacy Clearinghouse
www.med.sc.edu:1081/

Three Ways Consumers & Critics "Read" Media "Texts"

In media literacy (and in cultural critical theory), media — including the *nonprint* media —are often discussed as "texts" with "readers" (consumers) who have essentially three ways to interpret the meaning of the texts: **preferred** (also called dominant), **negotiated**, or **oppositional** (also called resistive).

Because the mass media are commercial entities, they tend to reflect the predominant ideology within a culture from which they themselves benefit. According to Silverblatt, Ferry, and Finan (1999), "This ideology assumes a disarming 'naturalness' within a text, which makes it particularly effective in promoting the prevailing ideology. Media presentations begin with unquestioned assumptions about the correctness of this order" (p. 4). In other words, most mass media portrayals are *hegemonic*.

Like viewing a painting, reading a mass media text is an interpretative act. Audiences can interpret media messages in a variety of ways, but the text usually "invites" or even "dictates" a *preferred* or *dominant reading* that supports the prevailing ideology. The audience tends to prefer the implied meaning or subtext because the primary figure in the presentation clearly leads us in the direction of the media communicator's perspective.

All media presentations offer a preferred reading, but they're all also open to alternative interpretations. In an *oppositional* or *resistive reading,* the reader assumes the perspective of a sub-culture at odds with the dominant culture. A third reading, the *negotiated reading,* is situated between the preferred and oppositional readings; that is, the reader questions parts of the content of the text but not its basic underlying dominant ideology (Vande Berg, Wenner, & Gronbeck, 1998, pp. 242, 251 n4).

Because unrealistic portrayals of sex, love, and romance are the focus of our media analysis and criticism, *we'll seek and report the oppositional/resistive reading* after identifying and describing the preferred reading. We'll use rational models of romantic love as the benchmark for our questioning of both the specific content and the underlying ideology of the preferred reading. We'll also seek to understand why the general public usually accepts the preferred reading of these irrational portrayals rather than resisting and opposing them.

WHAT IS THE *DIS*-ILLUSIONING PROCESS?

Dis-illusion comes only to the illusioned. One cannot be dis-illusioned of what one never put faith in.

—Dorothy Thompson, *The Courage to Be Happy*

In Part II, we'll apply the five foundations to conduct our analysis and criticism of a variety of **mass media manifestations** — actual media examples of unrealistic portrayals that illustrate and reinforce myths and stereotypes of sex, love, and romance. The remainder of this chapter tells you precisely how to do that. The steps are clarified in detail.[1]

Critics do not simply offer their personal opinions. Instead, they follow a systematic process. From the great variety of media analysis and criticism methods and approaches, I've synthesized the common core components and added some specific strategies and skills of media literacy to create the Seven-Step *Dis*-Illusioning Directions, which we will follow for our analysis and criticism of unrealistic media portrayals. The seven steps are:

---

[1]The specific instructions are provided as a basis from which to build your own work. Your instructor or editor might have different requirements. A sample worksheet (Appendix A) and an 8-page sample analysis and criticism (Appendix B) will also help you.

1. Detection (finding/identifying)

2. Description (illustrating/exemplifying)

3. Deconstruction (analyzing)

4. Diagnosis (evaluating/criticizing)

5. Design (reconstructing/reframing)

6. Debriefing (reconsidering/remedying)

7. Dissemination (publishing/broadcasting).

The section entitled "What Are Analysis & Criticism?" in Chapter 1 discussed the basics of media analysis and criticism. You might want to review that section now.

The heart of analysis and criticism is, obviously, the analysis (examination of the specific parts of a mass media manifestation) and the criticism (judgments and evaluations based on your analysis). Too frequently, however, formal media criticism follows a model that goes only as far as Step 4 (Diagnosis) of the seven-step method I've devised for *dis*-illusioning myths and stereotypes. The "extra" steps (5, 6, and 7) incorporate the *Reflection* and *Action* elements of a more dynamic plan — Action Learning's Empowerment Spiral (Awareness, Analysis, Reflection, and Action), which I consider to be crucial to our work.

Details of the Seven-Step *Dis*-illusioning Directions

The *dis*-illusioning process is a process of *"dis*-covery." As such, it's creative and stimulating — and FUN! The following pages provide a detailed explanation of the Seven-Step *Dis*-illusioning Directions:

STEP 1. DETECTION (finding/identifying)

What is it?
Where is it?

• Find a portrayal of sex, love, and romance that is a mass media manifestation of one of the myths from the *Quiz*. This unrealistic portrayal can be either an entire work (such as a movie or TV series or magazine) or a segment of it (such as a specific scene from a movie or an episode of a TV series or a specific magazine article or advertisement).

• Identify the manifestation by citing the complete title of the work, the date, and the mass medium. Also provide other additional markers necessary to help someone else locate it easily — such as author, page numbers, network or station, performers, approximate time in a visual presentations, etc.

STEP 2. DESCRIPTION (illustrating/exemplifying)

What's it all about?

• Describe the manifestation briefly but in sufficient detail to illustrate the key aspects of the portrayal and its context for those who have not "read" your "text."

• Tell who created this message — and why. (You must research this. If you cannot find documentation, clarify that you are *assuming* what the creator intended.)

• Note which mass communication function or purpose (entertainment, news/information, or persuasion) is the *primary* one. If applicable, further specify the genre (such as romantic comedy, country song, testimonial ad, etc.).

STEP 3. DECONSTRUCTION (analyzing)

What unrealistic ideals, myth, stereotypes, and/or illusions underlie this portrayal?
What is omitted from this message?
What embedded values, points of view, and lifestyles are represented in the
portrayal?

* Specify whether this manifestation includes other myths and stereotypes in addition to the primary one stated in the title of your analysis and criticism.[2] If applicable, note the link of the myth(s) in this portrayal to the myths discussed in Chapter 2.

* Give sufficient evidence to support why you believe the manifestation is linked to any specific myth(s)/stereotype(s).

* Provide specific examples — of both the content (message) and the form (medium) — that support your interpretation, which should be clearly stated early in the analysis. Examine the elements — such as plot and character and mass media narrative devices (discussed in Chapter 4) — to elaborate on the messages (meanings) you find.

* Explain what significant omissions distance the portrayal from reality.

* Include the commentary and research of others (with full citation) to further document your interpretation.

STEP 4. DIAGNOSIS (evaluating/criticizing)

Based on your analysis in Step 3, what is your judgment or evaluation of this
unrealistic portrayal?
Are "readers" of this media "text" likely to adopt the viewpoint of the creators of the
message? (If so, why would readers be more likely to adopt this "preferred" reading
rather than a "resistive" one?)
How might different people understand this message differently?
What are some possible effects (cognitive, affective, and behavioral) of this portrayal
on "readers" of this "text"?
Do these impacts appear intentional or not?

* Carefully explain the meaning and possible interpretations of the media text. (First summarize the preferred reading, and then offer your oppositional reading.)

* Compare the portrayal against the rational models to offer your evaluation of the merit of the portrayal, including whether or not you judge it to be potentially harmful.

* Suggest why readers of this text would be more likely to adopt the "preferred" reading rather than an "oppositional" ("resistive") one.

* Use appropriate mass media effects theories and research (including case studies) to suggest how audience members might experience the portrayal. (You might even conduct some small-scale audience research yourself.)

* Cite expert sources to support your judgment of the portrayal. You can also cite those that disagree with your argument, of course.

   Note: Your criticism must be well supported by clear explanations — with examples — of how you reached your diagnosis. (Remember: Criticism is not merely your off-hand personal opinion.)

---

[2] For example, as detailed in the 8-page sample analysis and criticism in Appendix B, the *primary* mythic theme in *As Good As It Gets* is #7 (Beast-to-a-Prince), but the romantic pairing of the 30-something actress with the 60-something actor illustrates Myth #6, the easy dismissal of the vastly differing lifestyles and values systems of these two characters illustrates Myth #9, and the "happy" ending — that even a pathologically disturbed man can complete a woman's needs and fulfill her dreams — illustrates Myth #10. If several myths are equally dominant, include all of them in your title and main argument.

STEP 5. DESIGN (reconstructing/reframing)

What's a more realistic reconstruction of this portrayal?

- Offer specific ideas and recommendations for reframing the portrayal more realistically.

- Tie your own reconstruction to the theories and models of healthy rational relationships described in Chapter 3 and summarized as the 12 *Prescriptions™.*

- Create your alternate design so that it's congruent with the framework of the manifestation.

- Explain why your reconstruction is likely or unlikely to be used.

- Describe any related actual mass media reconstructions (i.e., existing mass media manifestations of realistic constructive models).[3]

STEP 6. DEBRIEFING[4] (reconsidering/remedying)

What impact has your critical analysis had on you personally?
Did you ever believe the underlying myth or stereotype?
Have your own views changed or been reinforced? How?
Have you been harmed by this irrational portrayal or similar ones? How?
What do you think and how do you feel about that?
Despite your dis-illusioning, do you still enjoy this portrayal? Why?[5]

- Reflect carefully and explain any impact this unrealistic portrayal (or others like it) have had on you or anyone you know.

- Describe any personal "consciousness-raising" you experienced in the process of *dis*-illusioning this portrayal, including why you might nevertheless enjoy this portrayal.

    Note: This step is a crucial bridge from knowledge and even feelings to ameliorative action that expresses and demonstrates self-empowerment and even leadership.

---

[3]These are rare in the mass media. I've included one in 11 of the 12 chapters of Part II, as a "nomination" for my annual *Dr. FUN's Realistic Romance™ Awards,* which honor portrayals that follow one or more of the *Prescriptions™* rather than the myths and stereotypes of the *Quiz.*

[4]"**Debriefing**" is a term from the research methodology lexicon. It's a mandatory part of ethically conducted research that uses human subjects. In a debriefing session, researchers should meet with all human subjects who participated in the study to thoroughly explain any previously undisclosed aspects. The purpose is to limit or eliminate any potential harm these participants might experience as a result of either deceptive or nondeceptive techniques that were necessary to avoid bias in gathering the research data or in producing the intended results of an experiment. One of the goals of debriefing after research deception is to remove any confusion or defuse any tension that might have been generated by the deception. Debriefing "should be thorough enough to remove any lasting effects that might have been created by the experimental manipulation or by any other aspect of the experiment" (Wimmer & Dominick, 2000, p. 72). Subjects' questions should be answered.

I chose "debriefing" as the term for Step 6 *because* of its rich meaning in this other context. You might have experienced media deception without realizing it until now, so I want *you* to debrief *yourself — to limit or eliminate any potential harm* caused by the influence of these illusions. I want you to help yourself *to remove any confusion or defuse any tension that might have been generated by the deception.*

[5]Oftentimes someone who completes a formal *dis*-illusioning admits to nevertheless still enjoying the portrayal. This is an important point to ponder if you feel this way. It's ironic but understandable — like the *Stockholm Syndrome,* a term that describes the psychological phenomenon whereby, as a survival mechanism, kidnap victims delusionally come to "love" their captor. (This syndrome is also sometimes used to describe the behavior of battered partners.) In a sense, we've been "kidnapped" by the mass media characters and themes that have seduced us. It's hard and even threatening to change our long-held views. But we must fearlessly interrogate our own views to fully understand why we hold these irrational portrayals so dear. Then we can make a conscious decision about our enjoyment of them. (As mentioned, metaphoric appreciation of some of them can actually be healthy and productive.)

STEP 7. DISSEMINATION (publishing/broadcasting)

Are you motivated to act constructively as a media consumer or creator to share your insights with others?

What resistive tactics[6] have you employed or will you employ?

• Describe your advocacy action plan and timetable for implementation.

• Specify the activities you intend to undertake — from contacting those responsible for this portrayal to publishing or broadcasting your "discoveries."

• Clarify which actions are personal, public, and professional.

Documentation

Each of the seven steps starts with a "D." You'll notice that *another* "D" — documentation — is important *throughout* all seven steps. Be sure to use specific examples and to cite credible sources to document and support your arguments and analyses. For proper citation of these sources in your text and in your bibliography (or list of references), consult a style manual.

All cited sources should be properly attributed in the text and listed in a final *References* section at the end. A recognized scholarly style manual will detail this process as well as offer guidelines for format items such as headers and pagination. Usage questions are also answered in these manuals.

Two widely used styles manuals for term papers and scholarly research submissions are the *Publication Manual of the American Psychological Association* for APA style or the *MLA Handbook for Writers of Research Papers* for MLA (Modern Language Association) style. Newspapers usually prefer the *Associated Press Stylebook and Libel Manual* for AP style. (The Seven-Step *Dis*-Illusioning Directions are intended for extended media analysis and criticism; however, with adjustment, the steps could be used in shortened form to create media "reviews" for newspapers and magazines as well as broadcast outlets.)

Worksheets

A good way to start your analysis and criticism — whether written or oral — is by reviewing your selected media manifestation and jotting down some notes using the worksheet at the end of each chapter of Part II.[7] Each chapter's worksheet is preprinted with that chapter's myth and *Prescription*™ to jumpstart your analysis. You can tear these worksheets out of this book for easier use. (A sample completed worksheet is in Appendix A.) The worksheets also serve as a checklist to make sure you've included everything necessary to complete a formal analysis and criticism. As you fill in your worksheet, you'll find that you have an excellent basis for a formal presentation.

---

[6]Among the "Action" strategies in Freire's empowerment model are discussing media content with friends, colleagues, and children; exercising critical choices in personal use of media; writing letters to editors and other media managers; meeting with media creators and senders; boycotting advertisers or media products; promoting the adoption of media literacy instruction in preschool, elementary, secondary, and higher education; joining media literacy organizations. To this list, I add publishing your formal media analysis and criticism (in print or electronic forms) and, if you're a professional media communicator (now or in the future), creating and promoting more sensitive portrayals.

[7]Chapter 18 has no worksheet, as Myth #12 is actually a statement about the other 11 myths.

Sample of a Formal Media Analysis & Criticism Following the 7-Step Process and Using a Worksheet

As noted, Appendix B offers you an 8-page sample of an analysis and criticism of the portrayal of Mass Media Myth #7 (The love of a good and faithful true woman can change a man from a "beast" into a "prince.") as manifested in the 1997 movie *As Good As It Gets*. The paper is developed from the worksheet in Appendix A.

Notice that I call it a *sample* (an entity that is representative of a class; a specimen) — *not a model* (one serving as an example to be imitated or compared). Use your worksheets to create your *own* analyses and criticisms rather than merely imitating the sample worksheet and the analysis and criticism. In other words, there's a framework that must be followed, but within that framework you should exercise originality. Of course, be sure to follow all directions provided by your instructor or editor for preparing and submitting your work.

Format Recommendations

While the *content* is the most important aspect of your analysis and criticism, the *form* counts, too. (Remember: *The medium is the message!*) Errors in spelling, punctuation, grammar, and syntax reduce the value of your work.

The sample demonstrates not only the content of an analysis and criticism but also a suggested format. Here are some general format recommendations:

Title Page. Use a title page or cover sheet. Cite the entire myth and its number as part of your title, which should also include the title and date of your mass media manifestation as well as its medium. (Repeat the title at the top of the first page of your paper.)

Thesis. State your thesis — either as a statement or a question — at the beginning of your critical analysis (before Step 1). Your thesis is your position or argument, the major point you're going to make in the critical analysis: in other words, your particular insight, interpretation, and evaluation. (Note: Critical analyses often start with one or two compelling introductory paragraphs to get our attention, in which case your thesis statement comes right after that.)

Main Headings and Subheadings. Use the seven steps as your main headings — in their numerical order (1-7), preceded by a heading entitled "Thesis" for your thesis. You'll note from the sample that *within each of the seven steps* you can present the bulleted information from the worksheet in whatever order flows best in your particular presentation. This order may vary a bit with each different portrayal you *dis*-illusion as well as with the presentation form (written or oral). Include the worksheet's bulleted headings as subheadings in your presentation — in the order that you actually use them in your analysis and criticism, of course.

Analysis & Criticism of *Realistic* Portrayals of Sex, Love, & Romance

You can also use the seven-step process to critically review *realistic* portrayals of sex, love, and romance in the mass media. Unfortunately, such manifestations are rare, particularly in the more popular media genres. Nevertheless, we should seek them and inform others about them. That's why each year on Valentine's Day, when I announce *Dr. FUN's Stupid Cupid Awards* for unrealistic portrayals that mirror each of the 12 *Quiz* myths and stereotypes, I also honor at least one healthy mass media manifestation of each of the 12 *Prescriptions™* with a *Realistic Romance™ Award*. A "Nomination" for a portrayal of a constructive model of coupleship is similar to a Design (Step 5). Here's how they're different:

- in a Design, you reframe or reconstruct an existing mythic or stereotypic portrayal in the mass media to demonstrate a healthier portrayal that matches the Prescriptions™

- in a Nomination, you identify and honor an existing example and clarify how it illustrates the Rx.

Caution: Don't allow mass-mediated *countertypes* to seduce you into thinking that they are models of healthy, realistic relationships. As discussed earlier, most countertypes are stereotypes that present only surface correctives rather than genuine remedies. At first glance, countertypes seem to portray a productive alternative to the myth or stereotype, but on closer analysis you'll find that countertypes are usually as irrational and unjust as the originating stereotypes they purport to replace. (See Chapter 12 for an extended examination of countertypes of the individual elements of Mass Media Myth #6.)

SUMMARY

As an international movement, media literacy has many useful definitions. Because no one is beyond the considerable influence of the mass media, we need to develop a set of skills to help us better understand the mediated messages we receive and to design and distribute our own messages. Being literate in a media age requires critical thinking skills that empower us in our personal, public, and professional lives. While media literacy does raise critical questions about the impact of media and technology, it's not an anti-media or pro-censorship movement.

A pioneer in the media education movement is the Center for Media Literacy's Elizabeth Thoman. "Five ideas that everyone should know about media messages" are: (1) All media messages are "constructed"; (2) Media messages are constructed using a creative language with its own rules; (3) Different people experience the same media message differently; (4) Media are primarily businesses driven by a profit motive; and (5) Media have embedded values and points of view. Five basic questions that can be asked about any media message are (1) Who created this message and why are they sending it? (2) What techniques are being used to attract my attention? (3) What lifestyles, values and points of view are represented in the message? (4) How might different people understand this message differently from me? (5) What is omitted from this message?

The Action Learning model, based on the work of Paolo Freire, is a four-step "empowerment" process for media literacy: Awareness, Analysis, Reflection, and Action. In media literacy (and in cultural critical theory), media — including the nonprint media — are often discussed as "texts" with "readers" who have essentially three ways to interpret the meaning of the texts: preferred (reflecting the dominant ideology), negotiated (resisting a portion of the message but not the entire text or its basic ideology), or oppositional (resisting the dominant ideology).

Media critics do not simply offer their personal opinions. From the variety of methods for media analysis and criticism, one that incorporates many of their common features is the *Seven-Step* Dis-*illusioning Directions* (Detection-Description-Deconstruction-Diagnosis-Design-Debriefing-Dissemination), a system of media literacy strategies and skills that we will use to conduct our analysis and criticism of unrealistic portrayals of sex, love, and romance in the mass media. This *dis*-illusioning process is a process of "dis-covery." As such it's creative and stimulating — and FUN!

A detailed explanation of each of the seven steps is provided, along with format recommendations. Within the specified framework, there's room for originality, which is encouraged.

SOURCES CITED

AMLA founding document. (2001, 12 June). Retrieved December 15, 2001 from AMLA: The Alliance for a Media Literate America: http://www.nmec.org/declaration.html

Potter, W. J. (1998). *Media literacy*. Thousand Oaks, CA: Sage.

Rubin. A. (1998). Editor's note: Media literacy. *Journal of Communication, 48*(1), 3–4.

Silverblatt, A., Ferry, J., & Finan, B.(1999). *Approaches to media literacy: A handbook*. Armonk, NY: M.E. Sharpe.

Thoman, E. (2001). Mission statement, *Media&Values*. Retrieved December 14, 2001 from The Center for Media Literacy: http://www.medialit.org

Thoman, E. (2001). Skills & strategies for media education: A pioneering media literacy leader outlines the core principles and key components of this new educational agenda. Retrieved December 14, 2001 from The Center for Media Literacy: http://www.medialit.org

Thompson, D. (1957). *The courage to be happy*. Boston: Houghton Mifflin

Vande Berg, L. R., Wenner, L. A., & Gronbeck, B. E. (1998). *Critical approaches to television*. Boston: Houghton Mifflin.

Wander, P., & Jenkins, S. (1972). Rhetoric, society, and the critical response. *Quarterly Journal of Speech, 58*, 441–450.

PART II

Applications of Analysis & Criticism of Sex, Love, & Romance in the Mass Media

---

The challenge of modernity is to live without illusions and without becoming disillusioned.

—Antonio Gramsci, Italian intellectual and politician

Part II focuses on applications of the five foundations of Part I, with each of the 12 chapters of Part II concentrating on analysis and criticism of one of the 12 major mass-mediated myths and stereotypes about sex, love, and romance synthesized as *Dr. FUN's Mass Media Love Quiz*. In each chapter, we'll examine specific mass media manifestations of related unrealistic portrayals not only in entertainment content but also in the news and advertising of a wide variety of media: books, newspapers, magazines, comic books, movies and animated features, radio and popular music, television and music videos, and the internet.

To *dis*-illusion these myths and stereotypes, we will follow the *Seven-Step Dis-illusioning Directions,* detailed in Chapter 6. Guiding our criticisms and reconstructions of the 12 myths are corresponding recommendations for healthy, realistic coupleship (rarely presented by the mass media). These recommendations from the social psychology and therapeutic literature (discussed in Chapter 3) are synthesized as the 12 *Dr. Galician's Prescriptions™ for Getting Real About Romance.*

Each chapter follows the same format, described below. First, however, I want you to know a little more about the research basis of the *Quiz* — around which Part II is built — and the function of the *Prescriptions™*.

THE RESEARCH BASIS OF *DR. FUN'S MASS MEDIA LOVE QUIZ* & *DR. GALICIAN'S PRESCRIPTIONS™*

Development of the *Quiz*

As I mentioned in the Preface and in Chapter 1, in 1995 I was invited to appear on one of ABC-TV's national network shows to talk about my research of how mass media portrayals affect both sexes' romantic love expectations and satisfactions.

To more easily and quickly communicate my complex scholarly studies to a national television audience and to help viewers assess their "romantic realism," I created my *Dr. FUN's Mass Media Love Quiz.*

When I created the *Quiz* for the 1995 ABC-TV show, it was an 8-item instrument with the major mass mediated myths and stereotypes that my research had uncovered at that point. Based on my continuing research, I later added the additional four items that now complete the 12-item *Quiz.*

The 12 myths in the *Quiz* are numbered in logical order, from the simple (#1) to the more complex (#12). Several are interrelated, as discussed in the relevant chapters of *Part II.* Here's an overview:

> Myth #1 naturally connects to Myth #2 and #3: If someone is cosmically predestined for you (#1), you'll fall in love the minute you spot each other (#2), and you'll be able to "read" each other easily (#3). These three myths flow into the perfect, easy sexual relations of Myth #4. The ideal woman for these activities (models and centerfolds — a standard to which many men are now held as well) is described in Myth #5, which begins the delineation of role assignments detailed in Myth #6 (male superiority).

> From this traditional role assignment, it's an easy step to the Myth #7 roles from the Karpman Drama Triangle that this beautiful (#5) and subordinate woman (#6) can play in passive-aggressive fashion with any beasts who need to be fixed. (Of course, the sex roles in Myth #7 are sometimes reversed.) Continuing with the Drama Triangle predictions, it's easy to see how couples can engage in battle-mode behavior (#8). (Myth #8 can be viewed as the other side of Myth #2: Both assert that the "proof" of love is unbridled passion.)

> Many of the mis-matchings captioned by these myths are contained in the concept of Myth #9, a more complex myth about the supremacy of love, even in the face of different and opposing values. (For example, if you're preordained, what power would different values have? Further, relationships with unequal power distributions, as in Myth #6, frequently relate to values differences.) In a rational evaluation, of course, it's apparent that people with different values frequently try to change each other (#7) and wind up fighting dysfunctionally (#8).

> Finally, the culminating Myth #10 essentially encompasses all nine of the earlier ones. Myth #11 adds a note about specific real people — actors and actresses — who serve as media influencers for their many fans in portrayals that enact many of the first 10 myths both in dramatic performances as characters and in their highly reported personal lives. And the final myth — Myth #12 — is perhaps the most damaging myth of all: If we're unaware of the influence of the other 11 myths, we're more likely to fall under their power.

Purpose of the Quiz

Although the origin of my *Quiz* was television's need for simplification, I've since used it successfully as both a practical and stimulating teaching tool and a constructive research instrument, as have others. It formed the core of my in-depth personal interviews with males and females from 3 years of age to 103 years old as well as with media producers, relationship experts, and marital therapists. Students in my classes and audience members at my programs have enjoyed taking the *Quiz* and using the results to better understand how the mass media work in their own lives and in the lives of other media consumers.

It's important to understand that — for the individual taking the *Quiz* — there are no "right" or "wrong" answers. You either agree or disagree with each of the 12 statements. I always say, "Don't worry: No one will grade you!" I'm not making a joke when I say this, because the purpose of the *Quiz* is **heuristic**, which means:

> Of, relating to, or constituting an educational method in which learning takes place through discoveries that result from investigations made by the student.

In other words, the *Quiz* is really a starting point for individuals and couples to begin to assess their own views and to begin to explore how mass mediated portrayals contribute to these views.

Remember also that myths and stereotypes are *not necessarily or entirely false.* The problem with them is that they are usually atypical rather than the norm, so they're poor and even dangerous as models for our real-life thoughts, feelings, or behaviors. They're better understood *metaphorically,* in which case they're not apt to be as potentially harmful and can even be beneficial. (For example, in the Jungian sense of personality integration, we might better understand the "Beauty and the Beast" myth as a metaphor for integrating our *own* "good" and "bad" sides, rather than trying to change lovers we think are beastly or "bad" while presuming ourselves to be saintly and "good."

Further, while myths and stereotypes are sometimes applicable within their originating culture and their own time, they're usually not transposable to our own modern day. *They don't necessarily describe 21st century relationships.* Some of these 12 major mass media myths go back to themes in classical mythology and evolutionary biology; for example, the One and Only Perfect Partner (based on Plato's three sexes/hermaphrodite fable), Love at First Sight (Cupid's Arrow/cross-cultural metaphor), The Love of the Beautiful (equated with the transformational power of the Good, as described by Plato and virtually all cultures), Me-Tarzan/You-Jane (primitive protection needs and resource provision); Barriers and Battles, including the so-called Battle of the Sexes (tests of love related to resources and sexual access), and Heroes and Love. *Are such ancient themes and behaviors a good basis for us in the 21st century?*

Finally, remember also that as with all stereotypes, these myths diminish the personhood of others and ourselves, often socializing us without our knowledge and consent. It's important to be aware of the consequences of adopting each of these myths.

As you use the *Quiz,* keep its purpose and these distinctions in mind. And be aware that not everyone answers the items honestly and that some people genuinely "agree" or "disagree" in their mind though their actual related behavior might be just the opposite. As noted earlier, it's "education" vs. "enculturation."

Development of the *Prescriptions™*

The *Quiz* focuses attention on unrealistic media portrayals. However, in and of itself, it's an incomplete basis for following the Seven-Step *Dis*-illusioning Directions. To conduct a complete analysis and criticism, it's crucial to compare the unrealistic portrayals against a standard that offers a healthy alternative. That's why each of the 12 mass media myths about love in the *Quiz* has a related antidote from *Dr. Galician's Prescriptions™ for Getting Real About Romance,* which are based on the rational models discussed in Chapter 3, my research and personal experience, and the advice of other experts, including my husband, Dr. David Natharius. The *Prescriptions™* encapsulate the realistic relationship models that constitute the benchmarks for our analysis and criticism of media portrayals of sex, love, and romance. They're also helpful as you seek to identify any media manifestations that *are* constructive and as you develop your own ideas for *reframing* the unrealistic portrayals (Step 5). Of course, the *Prescriptions™* are also useful as guidelines for real-life romantic relationships.

FORMAT OF THE 12 CHAPTERS IN PART II

Each chapter focuses on one myth and follows the same format to *dis*-illusion specific mass media manifestations of that myth.

- First, you'll read two or three research-based **case studies** of real people (with fictional names to protect privacy) who — once upon a time — believed this myth and, as a result, did *not* live very happily-ever-after, and you'll think about whether or not you relate to those situations.

- The next section presents **additional research and commentary** directly related to the chapter's myth, including a statistical summary of the responses of male and female college students like you to that chapter's *Quiz* item as well as relevant details from my study of Generation Xers and Baby Boomers.

- Each chapter then centers on *dis*-**illusioning this myth** as exemplified in specific manifestations in various media. (The majority of the examples in this book derive from the electronic media and magazines, as a wider spectrum of readers are familiar with them.) Our analysis and criticism will follow the Seven-Step *Dis*-illusioning Directions,[1] either in whole or in part.

- To help you get started on your own analysis and criticism, each chapter offers a list of **additional mass media manifestations** of the chapter's myth. They're categorized by medium. You can use these examples, but you should also develop your own list.

- A **worksheet** that provides a template for you is at the end of Chapters 7–17. The worksheets also serve as a checklist to make sure you've included everything necessary to begin a formal analysis and criticism. You can tear these worksheets out of this book for easier use. A **sample completed worksheet** is in Appendix A, and an 8-page **sample formal analysis and criticism** developed from the sample worksheet is in Appendix B.

- A boxed *Dis-illusion Digest* in each chapter provides a summary.

Following Chapter 18, the Epilogue offers some final thoughts about the influence of unrealistic portrayals of sex, love, and romance in the mass media and advocates your continuing analysis and criticism of them — personally, publicly, and professionally.

---

[1]For a detailed explanation of the seven steps, see Chapter 6. As discussed earlier, the heart of analysis and criticism is the *analysis* (examination of the specific parts of a mass media manifestation) and the *criticism* (judgments and evaluations based on your analysis). Accordingly, the *dis*-illusionings of each myth in Part II focus on these two steps. In addition, *Designs* (reframings) of some of these unrealistic portrayals are suggested, and some *Debriefings* from the comments of actual students and seminar attendees are shared. Some chapters include nominations for *Dr. FUN's Realistic Romance™ Awards,* which honor existing mass media portrayals that offer realistic, healthy models. For the complete list of annual winners of these awards (one for each of the *Prescriptions™*) as well as the complete list of *Dr. FUN's Stupid Cupid Awards* (one for each myth), visit my websites: www.RealisticRomance.com or www.asu.edu/cronkite/faculty/galician/drfun/. I welcome *your* nominations.

7

DR. FUN'S MASS MEDIA LOVE QUIZ
MYTH #1

Your perfect partner is
cosmically predestined, so nothing/nobody
can ultimately separate you.

Dr. Galician's Prescription™ #1
R_x: CONSIDER COUNTLESS CANDIDATES.

*[H]uman nature was originally one and we were a whole, and the desire and
pursuit of the whole is called love.*
> — "Aristophanes," Plato, *The Republic*

I was born to love and be the wife of this man.
> — Julia Roberts ("Hollywood's highest-paid female star"),
> speaking of her new husband, cameraman Danny Moder

Here's a story of a real person[1] who — once upon a time — believed this myth
and, as a result, did *not* live very happily-ever-after.

[Ella, twenty-something female university student]

Ever since I was a wee child, I bore this fond love for Disney movies. My absolute
favorite was *Cinderella*. My closets were full of costumes from dance recitals, so I'd
play dress-up, pulling up my long blond hair just like Cinderella at the Ball. I'd
peek out the window, pretending that my prince was just around the corner. Although I've outgrown my ballet costumes, I still believe in this thought for the
most part. I truly do believe that my perfect partner is predestined for me, but I feel
that there are circumstances that keep us from realizing that bond. For example,
my perfect partner might live in Nicaragua, and I might never meet him before I
die. I understand that my thoughts might seem influenced by the media and have
a very deluded, ridiculous outlook on life, but why should I believe otherwise?
Shouldn't I yearn for perfection?

---

[1]Names have been changed to protect individuals' privacy.

Here's another true story:

[Andrew, twenty-something male university student]

My own life kinda followed the storyline of *My Best Friend's Wedding*. In this romantic comedy, Julia Roberts' best friend, Dermot Mulroney, is about to get married to Cameron Diaz. When Julia hears of this, she is determined to break up this wedding. At this point, Julia becomes jealous and sees her future falling apart. She's heart-broken 'cuz she felt that Dermot was meant for her. She flies to Chicago with hopes of stealing him back. She will do anything in order to be with her Dermot, whether it means trying to embarrass Cameron or trying to convince Dermot that Cameron is not for him. Julia soon realizes that no matter what she does, she can't be with her dream mate.

This relationship matches a previous one of mine. I thought Bonnie Braids was my perfect mate. Bonnie and I grew up together — went to grade school, junior high, and high school together. I enjoyed her company and I definitely wanted to be with her forever. We dated a lot throughout our high school years but towards the end I could tell our relationship was slipping. It seemed like she always wanted to be the center of attention with a football or basketball player or another popular male. Even though I'm a good guy, I couldn't compete in this category. As much as it hurt my soul, I realized there was no future with Bonnie, and we parted as friends.

ADDITIONAL RESEARCH & COMMENTARY
RELATED TO THIS MASS MEDIA MYTH

This myth originated in ancient times with the Platonic ideal: Somewhere is your other missing half, cruelly separated from you by the jealous gods of classical antiquity. But you know that you're living in the 21st century. And you're a human capable of changing and improving your "destiny" rather than irrationally letting it enslave you.

In a Rutgers University National Marriage Project study of 1,003 young adults ages 20 to 29 — "The State of Our Unions: The Social Health of Marriage in America 2001" — an overwhelming majority (94%) of the never-married singles had a romantic, unrealistic view of marriage that included staying single until they found a "perfect" mate, evidenced by their agreement with the statement: "When you marry you want your spouse to be your soul mate, first and foremost" (Whitehead & Popenoe, 2001). "It really provides a very unrealistic view of what marriage really is," said sociologist David Popenoe, one of the study's lead authors (as cited in Jackson, 2001, p. E1).

Media critics have suggested that television is partly responsible for these widely held irrational viewpoints among young men and women:

The vast majority of TV writers are young and single, and it's an axiom of writing that it's easier to write about what you know. Also, television is mostly about simple concepts and conflicts. Perpetual dating in search of true love is the simplest of plots to exploit. That's why TV often is more about singles in fruitless searches for perfect mates. (Jackson, 2001, p. E8)

Male and Female University Students' Responses to This *Quiz* Item

College men and women respond with basically the same Agree/Disagree percentage to the question of whether there's a predestined perfect partner out there for you (so you can't really be separated): Only about one quarter of both sexes agree with this myth, with women only slightly more likely than men to agree. Approximately 75% of both sexes disagree.

Thus, these writers both perpetuate and simplify cultural myths for less than altruistic or even artistic purposes.

"TV will never be a good place to look for love lessons," argues Greg Godek, author of *1001 Ways to Be Romantic* (Jackson, 2001, p. E8). And Rob Davis, president of Mate-Search International, offers evidence of how television portrayals of romantic relationships specifically affect what his clients want in a mate: "Female clients want to hold out for their soul mate" (Jackson, 2001, p. E8). They witness the almost cosmically predestined and long-awaited union of "soul mates" Chandler and Monica on the highly popular *Friends,* and that's what these women (and a good number of men) want, too.

DIS-ILLUSIONING THIS MYTH

Perfectly Predestined — But Passionless in New York

Two popular romantic comedies released in 2001 — *Serendipity* and *Kate and Leopold* — glorified Myth #1. Incurable romantics might have enjoyed the reinforcement of the notion that magical signs will show us who's "meant" for us (so *we* don't have to use our heads or hearts), but there's actually very little of the passion component of romance in either of these two sappy films about the power of fated love.

Serendipity

Serendipity — whose very title signals its intent — is constructed so completely on this myth that the preferred reading is explicit, if not blatant. Kate Beckinsale and John Cusack play characters who meet as customers at a New York City department store glove counter one Christmas. Each has a romantic partner, but they can't escape their love-at-first-sight connection. Cusack's character (Jonathan Trager) wants to pursue the connection immediately, but Beckinsale's dotty persona (Sara Thomas) believes if they're fated to meet again and be together, then they will. To test her theory, she writes her name and contact info in a book and sells it, and she instructs him to write his name and number on a $5 bill that she puts into circulation. They part, get engaged to others, and think of each other now and then. On the eve of his formal wedding at the Waldorf Astoria, Jonathan decides he must find Sara — even though he knows only her first name. (Oh, and she's moved. But not to worry.) In a series of events that defy logic and border on the annoying (Yes: Sara gets the $5 bill, and Jonathan's fiancee gives him *the* book on the eve of their wedding!), they finally find each other and, in celebration of their fated union, dump their respective fiances. (Jonathan's almost-bride is notified only a few hours before the lavish ceremony.)

What's left out? Aside from the ridiculous plot devices that rely on incredible coincidences, we're shown nothing of the jilted fiances, both of whom are decent, attractive individuals who deserve better treatment. The resistive reading finds nothing decent or attractive in the relationship of Jonathan and Sara, who know nothing about each other, yet they throw over their current partners in the unmotivated hope of finding something better.

By any rational model, the jilted ones are definitely the winners here. Unfortunately, such themes — set in a glamorous New York dressed up for Christmas — can create longings for similarly magical signs to confirm what healthy people couples already know. As one of my students put it in the Debriefing section of an analysis and criticism:

> The personal harm that I experienced from this myth is the possibility that sub-consciously I continue to hold out for the magical reunion between me and my soul mate that I believed would eventually occur — as long as I have "faith," of course. By doing so, I am not allowing myself to experience the relationships I develop to the fullest degree possible. Subconscious limitations do not allow an individual to be in the correct mind frame necessary to develop the basis of a healthy relationship.

Kate and Leopold

In *Kate and Leopold*, the meant-to-be lovers are separated by a century and a quarter. Kate (Meg Ryan) is a successful New York City advertising executive of our time who can't find the love she craves until 19th century Leopold (Hugh Jackman), an impoverished but brilliant British aristocrat, comes into her life and utterly charms her. Is it an *accident* or is it *fate* that Leopold find himself suddenly transported through a time warp from the New York of 1876, where he's come to choose a wealthy American bride who can support him? (The way between past and present is by jumping into the river from the girders of the Brooklyn Bridge.)

The subtext of this movie is that there's apparently not a single appropriate dating partner for this world-weary woman in all of Manhattan. But it wouldn't matter if there were, because Kate's photograph is on display in Leopold's 19th century New York digs, where — back again in *his* time (via another jump off the bridge) — he's just about to make the fateful marriage proposal. So, dashing from the banquet where she's been awarded a major promotion, Kate dashes to the bridge, jumps, and arrives in the past just in time for Leopold to choose her. (Where their financial support will come from is omitted from this nonsensical narrative. Yes, it's a fantasy — but even within that genre, the vital plot points should hold together.)

In her review of this movie in *Entertainment Weekly,* Alice King (2002) offered an appropriate oppositional reading:

> Call me a killjoy, but there's something insidious about a romantic fantasy — however frothy fun — that requires a character to give up her real life to find happiness. ... Ultimately, the 'modern' woman makes a decision that would cause any therapist to blanch. (p. 77)

The preferred reading of this film is similar to that of *The Little Mermaid,* who must renounce her very being — or at least the lower half of herself, as well as her family and friends — to be accepted in the world of her prince. And in the original story, it's all in vain: She dies when her fickle prince takes a human wife — a more realistic metaphor about relationships between people of widely opposing values (see Chapter 15). The only difference between the two characters is that Ariel leaps *out* of the sea, while Kate jumps *into* it. This message is hardly empowering for the young girls who watch the Disney feature and identify with the attractive mer-woman or for the career women who watch Meg Ryan jump from the Brooklyn Bridge at the end of the adult film. (Let's hope Kate's dramatic suicidal manoeuver — which the lighting, camera angles, music, and even the dialog encourage us to believe is a *courageous* act — isn't imitated by young women who are dissatisfied with the men available in the 21st century!)

Dr. FUN's Realistic Romance™ Awards Nomination: *Castaway*

One of my students who *dis*-illusioned the manifestation of this myth in the 1997 movie *Grosse Pointe Blank* — in which John Cusack plays a character who is fatefully reunited with his high school sweetheart (Minnie Driver) after a ten-year separation — pointed out in Step 5 that a far more realistic portrayal of a similar situation is presented in *Castaway* (2000). When Tom Hanks' character returns to his hometown after having been stranded all by himself on an island for several years, he finds that his fiancee (played by Helen Hunt) understandably presumed that he was dead and went on with her life — including getting married and having a child. This is especially difficult for him, because the major part of his psychological survival strategy on the island had been envisioning her and believing that she was waiting for him. Nevertheless, after he gets over the initial shock, the two have a warm conversation. Ultimately, he, too, finds someone.

I like this presentation because it doesn't play on the one-and-only fantasy. And the narrative doesn't resort to demonizing either of the lovers who are no longer romantic partners. As the *Prescription™* for this myth says, there are many appropriate candidates.

Additional Mass Media Manifestations of This Myth to *Dis*-illusion

Movies

Bridget Jones's Diary
Brigadoon
Cinderella
Fools Rush In
Grosse Pointe Blank
Only You
Sleepless in Seattle
Sliding Doors
Snow White & the Seven Dwarfs
What Dreams May Come
When Harry Met Sally
Women on Top

Recorded Music

You Are My Destiny
You Were Meant for Me

Television

Dharma & Greg
Friends
Sex and the City

DIS-ILLUSION DIGEST

Dr. FUN's Mass Media Love Quiz Myth #1

YOUR PERFECT PARTNER IS COSMICALLY PREDESTINED, SO NOTHING/NOBODY CAN ULTIMATELY SEPARATE YOU.

A partner who is "perfect" would be less than fully human, but — as we know — mass media myths glorify the unrealistically ideal. While you're waiting for your one-and-only Mr. or Ms. "Right," your blinders prevent you from seeing a whole spectrum of appropriate candidates who could make an excellent match. ("Appropriate" is actually a more *appropriate* term than "right.") Of course, waiting for "destiny" and its magical signs is easier than taking responsibility for your own life and love by doing your own work and trusting your own judgments.

Dr. Galician's Prescription™ #1

CONSIDER COUNTLESS CANDIDATES.

SOURCES CITED

Jackson, T. (2001, July 14). TV marriages twist reality, study says. *Arizona Republic,* p. E1, E8.

King, A. (2002, June 14). *Kate and Leopold* [Review of the film *Kate and Leopold*]. *Entertainment Weekly,* p. 77.

Plato. (1960). *The Republic and other works* (B. Jowett, Trans.). Garden City, NY: Dolphin. (Original work published circa 385 B.C.E.)

Whitehead, B.D., & Popenoe, D. (2001). Who wants to marry a soul mate?: New survey findings on young adults' attitudes about love and marriage. *The state of our unions: The social health of marriage in America 2001.* Retrieved July 14, 2001 from http://www.marriage.rutgers.edu

WORKSHEET FOR MASS MEDIA MYTH #1

(See Chapter 6 for details of *Dr. Galician's Seven-Step* Dis-illusioning Directions.)

Your perfect partner is cosmically predestined, so nothing/nobody can ultimately separate you.

R$_x$: CONSIDER COUNTLESS CANDIDATES.

Title of Your Analysis & Criticism

Your Thesis

STEP 1. DETECTION (finding/identifying)

Identification (title, date, and medium, with "markers")

Entire work/specific segment

STEP 2. DESCRIPTION (illustrating/exemplifying)

Detailed description

Creator; creator's purpose

Function/purpose (entertainment/news and information/persuasion) and genre

STEP 3. DECONSTRUCTION (analyzing)

Underlying myths/stereotypes (primary/secondary)

Evidence for linking myths/stereotypes; specific examples of content (message) and form (medium) that represent embedded values

Significant omissions

Cited commentary/research

STEP 4. DIAGNOSIS (evaluating/criticizing)

Meaning and possible interpretations (preferred and oppositional)

Comparison with rational models

Possible effects (harm)

Expert citations

Judgment/evaluation

STEP 5. DESIGN (reconstructing/reframing)

Realistic reframing

Related theories and rational models

Likelihood of use

Existing reconstructions

STEP 6. DEBRIEFING (reconsidering/remedying)

Personal impact of *dis*-illusioning; comparison of personal belief before/after, including enjoyment

Personal harm from myth

STEP 7. DISSEMINATION (publishing/broadcasting)

Advocacy action plan

Timetable of specific activities (personal/public/professional)

8

DR. FUN'S MASS MEDIA LOVE QUIZ
MYTH #2

There's such a thing as "love at first sight."

Dr. Galician's Prescription™ #2
R_x: CONSULT YOUR CALENDAR AND COUNT CAREFULLY.

· *Just one look, that's all it took.*
> — Gregory Carroll & Doris Payne, *Just One Look*

Quick loving a woman means quick not loving a woman.
> — A Yoruba (African) proverb

Here's a story of a real person[1] who — once upon a time — believed this myth and, as a result, did *not* live very happily-ever-after.

[Wendy, twenty-something female university student]

Every day I wake up and think to myself, "Today is the day" — the day I'll see the man of my dreams from afar and with just one glance we'll fall madly in love. That'll be the start to my fairytale romance and life. Then I wake up and remember that I don't live on a movie or TV set. I am such a hopeless romantic that it scares me. I want to believe that all it takes is just one glance and that is it: He is mine forever. I cannot tell you how many times I have looked at a guy and started to plan our future. This guy could be a homicidal maniac, but there is just something about him ....

Here's another true story:

[Brent, 22-year-old male university student]

When I was the ripe age of 17, I met a girl named Gloriana at an out-of-state sports meet. I always felt that when love came, I'd know it immediately. And this was it. We fell in love the moment we looked at each other. The minute I got home, I spilled my heart out on paper and mailed my letter "with a lick cuz a kiss don't stick." I was love struck. I felt sick to my stomach. We spent a fortune talking long distance on the phone every night for hours. Then she came to visit. The moment

---

[1]Names have been changed to protect individuals' privacy.

127

she walked through the door, it all fell apart. I realized that it was illusion at first sight, not love. I didn't even know who this person was! After a few days, I discovered I didn't even *like* her.

I was always under the impression that love is like it is in the movies: slow motion, everything fading away, love that lasts forever. In my great disappointment with Gloriana, I realized that love is an evolution, not a movie scene.

ADDITIONAL RESEARCH & COMMENTARY
RELATED TO THIS MASS MEDIA MYTH

It's easy to understand the university students' responses to this *Quiz* item. As we saw in Chapter 2, the myth of Cupid's arrow appears in many different cultures at many different times. It describes something archetypal. It's not to be dismissed lightly after millennia of enculturation. Add to that the timeless and yet so *un*timely template for so many of our unwritten rules for "wooing and being wooed" — the 12th century courtly love traditions "that permeate our novels, films, music, and psyches" (as the publisher reminds readers on the jacket of medieval scholar Andrea Hopkins' *The Book of Courtly Love: The Passionate Code of the Troubadours*). And as Hopkins herself explained: "Courtly love — is always at first sight" (1994, p. 17). Remember, too, that these codes of chivalric love were completely *idealized* models that forbade actual *physical* contact because they were constructed to deal with the emptiness of aristocratic loveless marriages. If anything, we've perverted this "chaste" concept.

> **Male and Female University Students' Responses to This *Quiz* Item**
>
> On the question of whether there's such a thing as "love at first sight," men and women respond with basically the same Agree/Disagree percentage: About half of both sexes agree, and the other half disagree. The point is that half of all these male and female students *do* say they believe in this myth.

To better understand the *physical* aspect of this experience of being pierced by Cupid's arrow, we need to look again at the evolutionary psychology theory that primitive men needed to be visually oriented to be good hunters and protectors. It's true that love at first sight (and even at repeated sight) is usually a physical experience that we perceive and describe as "beyond our control." Larry Hart and Richard Rodgers expressed this sensation in their classic song — *Bewitched, Bothered, & Bewildered* (recorded by artists as diverse as Frank Sinatra and Sinead O'Connor).

Of course, music is itself a powerful mass-mediated motivator, and moving songs have "bewitched" generations of media consumers, imprinting this dramatic depiction in our psyches — from our normal erotic feelings — reinforcing or creating the perverted expectation that we *must* feel like this or it just isn't "love." Thus, *love* is maneuvered beyond reason and choice — and beyond our own responsibility. As "Wendy" and "Brent" reported in their stories at the beginning of this chapter — and as countless of us say without consciously considering the impact of our language on our thoughts, feelings, and behaviors — they *fell* in love.

Why are we *falling* in love? *Fall* means "To undergo conquest or capture, especially as the result of an armed attack; To drop wounded or dead, especially in battle; To experience defeat or ruin; To lessen in amount or degree." If love is so wonderful, why aren't we *rising* to the occasion? Or *being uplifted?* Or *growing?* Of course, *falling* has come also to signify "To give in to temptation; sin; To lose one's chastity."

Sternberg's Triangular Theory of Love model is useful here. The physical arousal that can indeed occur at our first sight of certain individuals we find attractive is best characterized not as *love* but as *lust*. It's the passion component of the triangle. But sex (passion) alone is merely "infatuated love." (It's not even as evolved as "romantic love," which combines two of the three foundational components — passion + intimacy.) Infatuated love is indeed our hormones screaming and shoving. As such, most experts agree it's a poor basis for long-term close relationships — although it can certainly ignite the spark.

However, this kind of infatuated love is what the mass media most frequently model. (The other media-legitimized model is "*hate* at first sight," which we know will turn into love by the end of the narration. Like *love* at first sight, this "reversed" form represents merely the emotional component, as we'll discuss in Chapter 14.) But it's easy to understand *why* the popular culture perpetuates this model. Just consider the devices of mass media narration detailed in Chapter 4. Sex sells. Emotion sells. Excitement sells. And they're far easier to portray (and simpler for audiences to follow) than the more cerebral and time-intensive processes of love.

What's dangerous is that these narratives reinforce and create unrealistic expectations.

The sad truth is that unlike in the mass media, most experiences of "love at first sight" are short-lived. Fun flings at best. Bitter disappointments at worst. As the clever Cole Porter so aptly put it in his popular song *Just One of Those Things* (1935) — a perfect example of a realistic reframing (Step 5. Design) that *does* exist in the mass media:

> If we'd thought a bit of the end of it
> When we started painting the town,
> We'd have been aware that our love affair
> Was too hot not to cool down.

DIS-ILLUSIONING THIS MYTH

Songs & Scenes About Cupid's Slings & Arrows

Falling in Love Again

"Falling in love" as a concept removes all personal responsibility for our actions. In addition to countless novels and movies that foster this concept, popular songs have reiterated this myth. Another great songwriting team (Sammy Lerner and Frederick Hollander) capsulized this unhealthy concept and 28-year-old Marlene Dietrich promoted it in Josef von Sternberg's classic film *The Blue Angel*[2] (1930), Germany's first movie with sound, filmed simultaneously in English and in German:

> Falling in love again
> Never wanted to

---

[2]This cinema landmark — filled with mass media myths, stereotypes, and archetypes that form a straight line from the Furies to Freud — catapulted the young actress to international stardom, and this elemental song later became her "signature" theme.

What am I to do?
Can't help it.

Dietrich's femme fatale character thus conveniently absolves herself of all personal responsibility for her amorous actions. In another stanza, the men in her life are also described as powerless in the face of passion ("like moths around a flame"), likewise conveniently absolving her "victims" of responsibility. Sadly, it's dehumanizingly *dis*empowering for all of them.

Mass Media Devices

Music in movie and television portrayals of this myth can further reinforce the myth by setting the tone and convincing us of the rightness and majesty of such moments. In addition, camera techniques usually help convey the preferred reading by lingering on the lovers or zooming in and out either very quickly or very slowly, making time stand still and underscoring the dramatic intensity of the moment. These techniques indicate how we should react to the narrative, thus reinforcing the preferred reading. They distract us from opposing mythic and stereotypic portrayals and make it difficult for us to resist their unrealistic and unhealthy ideologies.

To get a sense of these techniques and their power in reinforcing the love-at-first-sight myth, it's interesting to compare various screen treatments of the moment that Romeo first sees Juliet. (Sight and sound devices are impressively combined in Baz Luhrmann's offbeat 1996 depiction — *William Shakespeare's Romeo + Juliet* — set in California's Verona Beach and starring Leonard DiCaprio and Clare Danes. In his 2001 Academy Award®-nominated *Moulin Rouge*, Luhrmann satirizes these techniques in the scene early in the film when Christian, the idealistic writer played by Ewan McGregor, first sees the gorgeous courtesan Satine, portrayed by Nicole Kidman in an Oscar®-nominated performance.) Remember that Romeo's already in love with love when he goes to the ball. He's pining for Rosaline. But the minute he sees Juliet he completely forgets his former love. Blame it on blind Cupid.

Dr. FUN's Realistic Romance™ Awards Nomination: Just One of Those Things

As noted above, I like the way Cole Porter's classic song, *Just One of Those Things* (1935) expressed the realistic consequence of this myth. In fact, the verse of this song includes the lyric:

As Juliet cried, in her Romeo's ear,
"Romeo, why not face the fact, my dear?"

As the title indicates, Porter is a bit cynical, but he's accurate about the research-based results of most "too hot not to cool down" sudden attractions. He even provides great and gracious departure dialog, suggesting the possibility of a continuing friendship ("Here's hoping we meet now and then.") while acknowledging wisely that it was "great fun" — but "just one of those things."

Additional Mass Media Manifestations of This Myth to *Dis-illusion*

Books

Gone with the Wind
Romeo & Juliet

Movies

Bed of Roses
Cinderella, Snow White, etc.
City of Angels
Coming to America
Footloose
The French Lieutenant's Woman
Moulin Rouge
Notting Hill
Out of Sight
Romeo & Juliet
South Pacific
Serendipity
Titanic
Wayne's World
The Wedding Planner
West Side Story

Recorded Music

Bewitched, Bothered, & Bewildered
I Love You
I Saw Her Standing There
Just One Look (That's All It Took)
Lady in Red
Love at First Sight
Love in the Library

Television

90210
Dharma & Greg
Family Matters
Full House
Mad About You
Melrose Place
Saved by the Bell
Sex and the City

DIS-ILLUSION DIGEST

Dr. FUN's Mass Media Love Quiz Myth #2

THERE'S SUCH A THING AS "LOVE AT FIRST SIGHT."

There's attraction at first sight, but real love takes real time. Too many movies and TV shows give us the opposite idea. But they have only two hours or less to spin their tales. Popular songs have about three minutes. And advertisers have only 30 seconds. Physical attraction can grow into lasting love, but realistic romance is based on the test of time not the emotion of the moment. Long-lasting love is indeed a "choice" — not something we "fall" into because of blind Cupid.

Dr. Galician's Prescription™ #2

CONSULT YOUR CALENDAR AND COUNT CAREFULLY.

SOURCES CITED

Hopkins, A. (1994). *The book of courtly love: The passionate code of the troubadours.* New York: HarperSan Francisco.

Sternberg, R. J. (1988). Triangulating love. In R. J. Sternberg & M. L. Barnes (Eds.), *The psychology of love* (pp. 119–138). New Haven, CT: Yale University Press.

WORKSHEET FOR MASS MEDIA MYTH #2

(See Chapter 6 for details of *Dr. Galician's Seven-Step* Dis-illusioning Directions.)

There's such a thing as "love at first sight."

R_x: CONSULT your CALENDAR and COUNT CAREFULLY.

Title of Your Analysis & Criticism

Your Thesis

STEP 1. DETECTION (finding/identifying)

Identification (title, date, and medium, with "markers")

Entire work/specific segment

STEP 2. DESCRIPTION (illustrating/exemplifying)

Detailed description

Creator; creator's purpose

Function/purpose (entertainment/news and information/persuasion) and genre

STEP 3. DECONSTRUCTION (analyzing)

Underlying myths/stereotypes (primary/secondary)

Evidence for linking myths/stereotypes; specific examples of content (message) and form (medium) that represent embedded values

Significant omissions

Cited commentary/research

STEP 4. DIAGNOSIS (evaluating/criticizing)

Meaning and possible interpretations (preferred and oppositional)

Comparison with rational models

Possible effects (harm)

Expert citations

Judgment/evaluation

STEP 5. DESIGN (reconstructing/reframing)

Realistic reframing

Related theories and rational models

Likelihood of use

Existing reconstructions

STEP 6. DEBRIEFING (reconsidering/remedying)

Personal impact of *dis*-illusioning; comparison of personal belief before/after, including enjoyment

Personal harm from myth

STEP 7. DISSEMINATION (publishing/broadcasting)

Advocacy action plan

Timetable of specific activities (personal/public/professional)

9

DR. FUN'S MASS MEDIA LOVE QUIZ MYTH #3

Your true soul mate should KNOW what you're thinking or feeling (without your having to tell).

Dr. Galician's Prescription™ #3
Rx: COMMUNICATE COURAGEOUSLY.

Not a word need be spoken (in our language of love).
— Popular rock lyric

17. People who have a close relationship can sense each other's needs as if they read each other's minds.
32. People who love each other know exactly what each other's thoughts are without a word ever being said.
37. If you have to ask your partner for something, it shows that s/he was not "tuned into" your needs.
— Three items of the Relationship Belief Inventory (RBI),
agreement with which indicates irrational thinking
and unrealistic expectations (Eidelson & Epstein, 1982)

Here's a story of a real person[1] who — once upon a time — believed this myth and, as a result, did *not* live very happily-ever-after.

[Jason, 21-year-old male college student]

Through movies and television I've become accustomed to seeing how mass media "couples" act and react to each other. They always know how to say the most unbelievably romantic thing at the right time. They also have some weird form of telepathy where they're always thinking the same thing and know the other person's viewpoint. These kinds of portrayals have made my own current real relationship needlessly difficult sometimes.

---

[1]Names have been changed to protect individuals' privacy.

135

Because I'm so used to the couples in the media who immediately know when their significant other is upset and immediately accommodate them, I often expect my real girlfriend to intuitively know when I've had a bad day. Sometimes I get mad when she doesn't. She gets upset with me when I don't pay enough attention to her and "know" what she's thinking and feeling. The media have led us to believe that there's a sixth sense that stems from love.

But in real life, there's no dramatic music or close-ups that tell your partner, *"Pay attention. What I'm about to say is really important and I need extra help through this."*

Here's another true story:

[Judy, 18-year-old female high school student]

I always fantasized about a picture-perfect relationship like on TV — where each partner knows what the other is feeling and thinking without communicating. Last year I was going out with a very nice guy, but he needed communication to know what was going on. This was disappointing to me! I felt if we were right for each other, he'd know my style and my tastes. He tried to buy me gifts to make me happy, but they were always the wrong style or color. When prom time came, I wanted lilies. I got roses. That was it! I broke up with him that night.

Finally:

[Babette, 49-year-old divorced mother]

I grew up watching *Dick Van Dyke* and *I Love Lucy.* From these shows I acquired the belief that when two people are close enough to be married, they both automatically know what the other needs, thinks, and wants. Throughout my real marriage, I got really angry with my husband because he didn't meet my needs as magically as I'd come to expect from TV. Of course, now I realize that TV lied. And now I'm divorced. I also know now that a good marriage is all about good communication.

ADDITIONAL RESEARCH & COMMENTARY RELATED TO THIS MASS MEDIA MYTH

In my broader survey of two different age cohorts, Generation Xers of both sexes scored higher than their Baby Boomer counterparts on the "mind-reading" dysfunction (expecting mind-reading in partners). (In fact, Generation Xers were more unrealistic on all five beliefs measured by Eidelson and Epstein's Relationship Belief Inventory [RBI]; see Chapter 3 for a description of the five beliefs.) This could be a function of maturation rather than an actual age-cohort difference. In other words, it might be that as individuals experience longer-term relationships, their views become more realistic through "on-the-job training" or real-world exposure. Generation Xers were also heavier consumers of mass media than Baby Boomers, so it might be that the Xers' beliefs were still more heavily influenced by the mass media. Xers' greater belief in mind-reading also was tied to their heavier use of television, as well as of movies and magazines. That's where we see couples who do read each other's minds.

In general, men of both age cohorts in my study were more unrealistic in their beliefs than were women of both age cohorts. This matches my findings about university students who take the *Quiz*.

Male and Female University Students' Responses to This *Quiz* Item

Slightly more than half of the men as well as half of the women say they believe that your soul mate should be a mind-reader.

As you learned in Chapter 3, Epstein and Eidelson aren't the only experts who hold that this mind-reading expectation is irrational and dysfunctional. Review the advice of Lazarus and the other experts who recommend learning *good communication skills,* including asking for what you want.

I can also share with you my own "case study." Although I've always been quite outspoken in most other areas of my life, when it came to romance I'd always been afraid to speak my mind. (That's what happens when you're using media-inspired fantasy scripts and wearing masks.) I hoped and prayed my partners would just magically know what I was thinking and feeling — just like in the movies and books I loved. Fortunately, I finally realized that reluctance to be completely open and honest with my romantic partners stemmed from my fear of being told "no." My irrational line of thinking was: If I didn't say what I wanted, I couldn't be refused. I also was fearful of hurting my partners' feelings. And I expected that "if they *really* loved me, they'd *know* without my having to tell." One of the most important strategies I employed once I stopped wanting my own love life to be like a movie or a novel was simply to summon the *courage* to ask my partner for what I want and openly share what I don't want, rather than expecting him to read my mind. And believe me, it did take courage. (It also takes a partner who *wants* to hear what you really mean.)

One of the things that separates top salespeople from unsuccessful ones is that top salespeople "ask for the order." Many less successful sellers are good at presenting the product and talking about it. But they stop short of actually *asking* the customer to *buy* it. Their reason is similar to mine: The fear of rejection. But great salespeople know that after a few rejections they'll finally get an order. So they keep on asking for those orders and even welcoming the rejections along the pathway to the affirmations. By moving to their straightforward request for a sale, they're also better able to clarify objections, which they then can remove once they're on the table.

It's like that for real couples, too. Sternberg's intimacy component — one of the three major building blocks of consummate love — is itself an amalgam of close feelings based on enhanced communication and open sharing.

But for some people (and for media narratives), the smooth relationship that results from dropping the mind-reading expectation seems too predictable and less exciting. Of course, it's less exciting: There's so much less conflict! And there's so much less drama. That's why *conflict,* as we've seen, is a major necessity for mass media narrative — not just for entertainment forms but also for persuasion (problem-solution: You have a problem, they have a solution; You have no problem, they have stuff they can't sell) and even for the news (for which conflict is the major ingredient).

The mind-reading dysfunction is one of the most destructive in love relationships (and indeed in any interpersonal relationships). Fortunately, it's one of the easiest to replace. Wouldn't it be great if we saw that modeled more in the mass media?

DIS-ILLUSIONING THIS MYTH

They Just Don't Get It:
What Women Want & *Dr. T and the Women*

The mind-reading dysfunction — a staple of romance novels — is portrayed far more often in the print media than in the electronic media because it's difficult to visualize this mental process. However, two films released in 2000 — *What Women Want* and *Dr. T and the Women* — purport to represent images of men who are able to read women's minds. Nevertheless, a closer reading reveals that these portrayals offer convoluted subtexts that satirize this myth while reinforcing the rescue myths (#6 and #7).

According to gender communication and visual media scholar David Natharius (2002):

> When the subtexts of these films are examined, we can see that the represented men have no greater understanding of women than countless numbers of male characters in dozens of preceding films dealing with relational conflict issues between women and men. In essence, these two films still suggest that men are not "getting it." (p. 5)

What Women Want

In this popular romantic comedy, a freak electrical accident enables avowed male chauvinist Nick Marshall (played by Mel Gibson) — a divorced advertising agency executive — to literally hear what women are thinking. Keeping his sudden mind-reading ability a secret, he uses it to manipulate the women in his life, including his co-workers, his daughter, and his new boss, Darcy Maguire (Helen Hunt), who has gotten the job he wanted for himself. Nick has always thought of himself as a hyper-masculinized lady's man, but he learns from the women's uncensored thoughts that they actually hold him in low regard. Suddenly, for the first time in his life, he begins to listen. He develops empathy. He knows what women want. Or does he?

With his secret power, he sabotages Darcy — simultaneously wooing her and stealing her ideas until she is fired. But by then he realizes that she has not just a great body but also a great mind and spirit, and so he quickly gets her reinstated at work and then runs to her apartment and up the stairs to confess and seek forgiveness. Her first reaction is to dismiss him from both her professional and private lives, but as he turns to leave, she runs after him to "rescue him" from himself, providing us with the happy ending's fade-out kiss.

As Natharius notes:

> When the subtext of the film is examined, we can see that Nick can be added to a long list of male characters in movies who suddenly, for whatever reason, have an epiphany and decide that they are going to change their life for a woman. (p. 7)

Dr. T and the Women

Another of those characters on that list is the title character (played by Richard Gere) in *Dr. T and the Women*. This movie presents a *countertype* to the mind-reading mythology, because Dr. Sullivan Travis — a successful and busy Dallas gynecologist who seems to have a great rapport with his patients — is actually just another clueless male chauvinist when it comes to the women in his personal life.

Ironically, both Nick and Dr. T can also be added to the list of film characters who run up the stairs of Helen Hunt's apartment in that climactic life-changing moment. Additionally, *Dr. T* provides a fascinating reframing of Myth #6 (in that stairway scene), which we'll examine in Chapter 12.

It's unfortunate that portrayals of productive communication skills are rarely presented. Appealing characters who model "courageous communication" might be a positive influence for both males and females. Instead we're usually shown one extreme or the other: mystical mind-reading or total cluelessness. But, as we've discussed, open communication would eradicate most of the conflict that is the dramatic necessity of media narrative.

Dr. FUN's Realistic Romance™ Awards Nomination: West & Peske's Reconstruction of *Romeo and Juliet*

One of the most humorous but healthy reframings of this myth is *"Romeo and Juliet* (Or, When You Assume You Make an ASS out of U and ME)," one of the many classic romances effectively parodied in Beverly West and Nancy Peske's *Frankly Scarlett, I Do Give a Damn!* In this version, the lovers survive because Romeo remembers that Juliet has warned him not to assume. Heeding this advice when he enters the tomb, he hesitates before killing himself in order to join what appears to be his dead wife. Of course, she's only in a drug-induced sleep, from which she is about to awake.

Here's a sampling of the reframed oration he delivers:

Waaaaaait a minute.
Perhaps I am falling prey
to the impetuous romanticism
about which Juliet warned me.
Hasn't she always told me
that when you *assume,*
you make an *ass* out of *u* and *me?* (1996, p. 45)

Instead, he decides to "take some time out" and "make a few inquiries as to the true nature of these seemingly tragic events."

Here's a rational model we can all follow.

Additional Mass Media Manifestations of This Myth to *Dis*-illusion

Books

Great Expectations
Most romance novels

Movies

Ghost
Love Story
Princess Bride
Titanic
What Women Want

Recorded Music

Killing Me Softly
More Than Words
Not a Word Need Be Spoken
  (in Our Language of Love)
The Promise
You Were Meant for Me

Television

90210
Cosby Show
Dick Van Dyke
Friends
I Love Lucy
Mad About You
Party of Five

DIS-ILLUSION DIGEST

Dr. FUN's Mass Media Love Quiz Myth #3
YOUR TRUE SOUL MATE SHOULD KNOW
WHAT YOU'RE THINKING OR FEELING
(WITHOUT YOUR HAVING TO TELL).

Mind-readers function only in circuses — and romance novels, which feed our fantasy of having a perfect relationship without really working at it. "Never having to say you're sorry" *Love Story* fantasy that is foolish, disrespectful, and, ultimately, counterproductive. Realistically romantic partners learn about each other by daring to be open and honest about what they want.

Dr. Galician's Prescription™ #3
COMMUNICATE COURAGEOUSLY.

SOURCES CITED

Eidelson, R. J., & Epstein, N. (1982). Cognition and relationship maladjustment: Development of a measure of dysfunctional relationship beliefs. *Journal of Consulting and Clinical Psychology, 50,* 715–720.

Galician, M.-L. (1995, October). *The romanticization of love in the mass media: A comparison of the relationship among unrealistic romantic expectations, ideal role models, heterosexual coupleship satisfaction, and mass media usage of Baby Boomers and Generation Xers.* Paper presented at the annual meeting of The Organization for the Study of Communication, Language, and Gender, Minneapolis/St. Paul, MN.

Galician, M.-L. (1997, February). *The romanticization of love in the mass media: The relationship of mass communication media usage, unrealistic romantic expectations, coupleship dissatisfactions of Baby Boomer and Generation X males and females.* Paper presented at the annual meeting of the Western States Communication Association, Monterey Bay, CA.

Lazarus, A.A. (1985). *Marital myths: Two dozen mistaken beliefs that can ruin a marriage or make a bad one worse.* San Luis Obispo, CA: Impact.

Natharius, D. (2002, March). *Now that men know what women want, are men getting what they want?* Paper presented at the annual meeting of the Western States Communication Association, Long Beach, CA.

Sternberg, R. J. (1988). Triangulating love. In R. J. Sternberg & M. L. Barnes (Eds.), *The psychology of love* (pp. 119–138). New Haven, CT: Yale University Press.

West, B., & Peske, N. (1996) *Frankly Scarlett, I do give a damn! Classic romances retold.* New York: HarperCollins.

WORKSHEET FOR MASS MEDIA MYTH #3

(See Chapter 6 for details of *Dr. Galician's Seven-Step* Dis-*illusioning Directions.*)

Your true soul mate should KNOW what you're thinking or feeling (without your having to tell).

R$_x$: COMMUNICATE COURAGEOUSLY.

Title of Your Analysis & Criticism

Your Thesis

STEP 1. DETECTION (finding/identifying)

Identification (title, date, and medium, with "markers")

Entire work/specific segment

STEP 2. DESCRIPTION (illustrating/exemplifying)

Detailed description

Creator; creator's purpose

Function/purpose (entertainment/news and information/persuasion) and genre

STEP 3. DECONSTRUCTION (analyzing)

Underlying myths/stereotypes (primary/secondary)

Evidence for linking myths/stereotypes; specific examples of content (message) and form (medium) that represent embedded values

Significant omissions

Cited commentary/research

STEP 4. DIAGNOSIS (evaluating/criticizing)

Meaning and possible interpretations (preferred and oppositional)

Comparison with rational models

Possible effects (harm)

Expert citations

Judgment/evaluation

STEP 5. DESIGN (reconstructing/reframing)

Realistic reframing

Related theories and rational models

Likelihood of use

Existing reconstructions

STEP 6. DEBRIEFING (reconsidering/remedying)

Personal impact of *dis*-illusioning; comparison of personal belief before/after, including enjoyment

Personal harm from myth

STEP 7. DISSEMINATION (publishing/broadcasting)

Advocacy action plan

Timetable of specific activities (personal/public/professional)

10

DR. FUN'S MASS MEDIA LOVE QUIZ MYTH #4

If your partner is truly meant for you, sex is easy and wonderful.

Dr. Galician's Prescription™ #4
R$_X$: CONCENTRATE ON COMMITMENT AND CONSTANCY.

Sexual Healing is good for me
Makes me feel so fine, it's such a rush ...
> — Marvin Gaye, David Ritz, and Odell Brown, *Sexual Healing*

Here's a story of a real person[1] who — once upon a time — believed this myth and, as a result, did *not* live very happily-ever-after.

[Christy, 27-year-old female bartender]

The mass media portrays sex as being this wonderful romantic thing that's always perfect. Nothing ever goes wrong. There's always flowers or candlelight or both. The very first time I had sex it was nothing like on television. The whole experience was uncomfortable, scary, and not very enjoyable. And this was with someone I'd dated for four years — so I find it hard to believe that everything could be so great the first time like it always is on TV! In reality, it takes time to get used to each other before sex can become really wonderful and easy.

And from a man's point of view:

[Todd, male 25-year-old in a long-term relationship]

I'd been with other girls, but Liz was the first one I really cared about and imagined a future with, so with her I waited. Because I wanted everything to be "like in the movies" the first time we had sex, I planned a very romantic evening with music and champagne and the works. But when it came time to "do the deed," I froze. It was embarrassing. I was just so nervous about everything being perfect that I think I scared myself. Fortunately, we've come a long way since then. But even now, sex isn't always "easy and wonderful" — even though I know Liz is the one for me. Take it from a guy who knows and who's honest!

---

[1]Names have been changed to protect individuals' privacy.

ADDITIONAL RESEARCH & COMMENTARY
RELATED TO THIS MASS MEDIA MYTH

**Male and Female University Students'
Responses to This *Quiz* Item**

On *this* item of whether sex should be easy and wonderful if your partner's meant for you, men and women — as a group — tend to respond quite differently. Approximately two thirds of the men say they agree, but nearly two thirds of the women *dis*agree. In other words, the majority of the two sexes held opposing beliefs about this myth.

These male university students who took the *Quiz* mirror the ones in my survey of Boomers and Xers. In that study, males were especially different from females in terms of the dysfunctional belief of "Sexual Perfectionism," which includes feeling responsible for the sexual success of a relationship. Apparently, this aspect of romance remains, stereotypically, a traditionally male domain despite decades of "sexual equality." Ironically, researchers note that this belief can actually *inhibit* sexual performance, as illustrated in the experience of "Todd" in the story above. And also ironically, Xer men have more unrealistic sexual expectations than Boomer men. Likewise, Xer women are more unrealistic than Boomer women. These views tend to be tied directly to Xers' heavier use of movies and magazines.

But where do these views come from? One of my students who worked on HBO's popular and raunchy latenight *Real Sex* told me that some of the unusual sex acts and conversations were real but others were scripted — and some of the "couples" weren't even real couples. It seems that a lot of selective editing goes into this production with the somewhat deceptive title. Another sleazy, supposedly spontaneous "reality" show — *Temptation Island* — was similarly scripted.

The rash of "reality" dating shows on television in the last few years demonstrates (a) how desperate contestants are for relationships — even those in which they and their potential dates are debased and discounted as nothing more than a sex object, (b) how desperate audiences are to watch other people make fools of themselves in a variety of ill-advised sexual situations, and (c) how desperate networks are for viewers and ratings. (Many of my students confess that they watch these shows to learn "what *not* to do" and to laugh at the inept and often pathetic contestants.) Ironically, despite their visual and vocal envelope-pushing in terms of explicit sexuality, the whole genre actually smacks of the flesh-peddling and mail-order brides of bygone eras. It's burlesque. And it's all about cheap thrills via cheap to produce programming. "Real love take real time," and real programming required real producers and writers who take the time to create a lasting show.

We all get some unrealistic ideas about sex (as well as love and romance) from the mass media — particularly from magazines like *Playboy, Maxim, Cosmo,* and even *Seventeen;* romantic novels and movies; TV soap operas; and pornography. In *Sex in America,* de Rougemont (1964, pp. 303–304) argued that "the means of eroticism" are the mass media. As we examine their methods more closely, we seek to resist and oppose mythology and stereotypes as a basis for actual behavior because they're generally counterproductive, dehumanizing, and even dangerous.

Describing "false love," Katz and Liu (1998) pointed out that we mistakenly say "making love" when we mean "nothing more than having sex" (p. 48). Similarly, I'm always amazed when people in real life and in the media euphemistically describe a sexual episode with a relative stranger as "intimacy" — when in reality there's nothing *intimate* about being objectified (with no sense of commitment or true coupleship) as a piece of meat or body parts.

This is not to suggest that sex is not a *part* of love. As noted earlier, Sternberg's Triangular Theory of Love includes sex (passion) as one of the three primary components of the triangle. But passion alone is merely "infatuated love" — a poor basis for long-term close relationships.

Some people fear that if we know more about sexuality from a realistic viewpoint, we'll lose the excitement and romance that come from the "mystery." But there's no excitement and romance about rising numbers of unwanted pregnancies and life-threatening sexually transmitted diseases. Yet the "sex is wonderful and easy" theme rarely includes any cautions about such consequences. In analysis and criticism of the mass media, remember that it's often as important to see *what's left out* of the mediated messages as to study *what's in* them.

DIS-ILLUSIONING THIS MYTH

Depictions of sex in all media — from romance novels to television to movies — are becoming more and more graphic. Nothing seems to be left to the imagination. Couples meet, fall in love (or at least in lust), and without exchanging last names they exchange body fluids — and sometimes deadly diseases, though these are rarely depicted as a consequence.

Music or Sex?

Combined with their pulsating rhythms and mood-inducing musical patterns, popular song lyrics can have a great impact on listeners, who tend to be young. One of my students *dis*-illusioned Britney Spears' *I'm a Slave 4 You.* She pointed out that the moaning and heavy breathing on the track encourages almost animalistic sexual behavior. In the same way that Myth #2 excuses passion's lack of control, the lyric of this song explains: "I'm a slave for you, I cannot hold it. I cannot control it."

Although the artist herself typically appears provocatively clad as a sex goddess, she claims that the song is about "being a slave for *music*" and not for sex. However, every one of the people my student informally surveyed as part of her analysis and criticism said the song was about *sex*, not music. The majority said they'd feel less inhibited about having a promiscuous affair after hearing this song as compared to a more traditionally romantic song.

As with all movements that reach the extreme, a backlash usually sets in. And now it looks as if a move away from such explicitness might have begun. An Associated Press story recently reported that a "new crop of female singer-songwriters is challenging the notion that you have to bare your navel and cavort in tight clothes to be sexy and successful in pop music" (Moody, 2002, p. E3) (see Chapter 11). The article calls these artists "the anti-Britneys," and quotes one of them — 17-year-old Avril Lavigne, whose debut disc, *Let's Go,* went gold in one month: "I'm just saying I don't want to sell sex. I feel that's lame and low. I've got so much more to say."

Magazines: Manuals for Easy, Wonderful Sex?

If this backlash is coming, it's not reflected in most popular magazines. Magazines are often considered cultural barometers. In today's climate, women's magazines have become as explicit as those targeted to men. Sometimes the covers of *Cosmo* and *Playboy* are nearly indistinguishable, with sex promoted as an elixir. As we've discussed, sex sells, and it helps these magazines entice readers to look inside to see the advertising that supports these publications.

Another student analyzed just one issue of *Cosmo* (February 2002) and found that 9 articles were about easy and wonderful sex. One article — "Your Guy's Body: 4 Secret Pleasure Trails Every Man Has" — advised readers to follow "*Cosmo's* Map to Male Pleasure" to ensure that your man would never leave you. Illustrated with photographs of a gorgeous naked man, the preferred reading is that making sex easy and wonderful enough equates to a meant-to-be relationship. The magazine's focus on sex suggests that sex is the most important and affirming aspect of a relationship, yet it is only *one* of the three key elements of Sternberg's Triangular Theory of Love.

Of course, the men and women pictured in these magazines invariably look like models and centerfolds rather than normal people. We'll examine this aspect of popular magazines more closely in Chapter 11.

Dr. FUN's *Realistic Romance™ Awards* Nomination: *The Light*

One of my students recommended the positive elements of the song *The Light* from the 2000 album *Like Water for Chocolate* by the hip hop artist Common (formerly known as Common Sense). In one part of the song, the artist directly addresses and counters Myth #4 (as well as Myth #6):

> I know the sex ain't gon' keep you, but as my equal
> is how I must treat you.

In another part of the rap, he further reframes Myth #4 and instead offers its *Prescription™*:

> Few understand the union of woman and man
> And sex and a tingle is where they assume that it land.
> But that's fly by night ...
> ...
> Let's stick to understandin' and we won't fall.

I applaud the courage of this artist — who is anything *but* "common" in his unusual, healthy approach to love. *Common Sense* was indeed a well-deserved and appropriate name for him. I hope that his influence with hip hop fans will encourage young people to think about realistic romance alternatives.

Additional Mass Media Manifestations of This Myth to *Dis*-illusion

Books

Most action thrillers
Most pornography
Most romance novels

Magazines

Cosmo
Playboy

Movies

Dirty Dancing
Ghost
Most porn or "adult" films
The Tall Guy
Titanic
Top Gun

Recorded Music

I'll Make Love to You
Let's Get It On
Sexual Healing

Television

90210
Days of Our Lives
  (and most soap operas)
Dharma & Greg
Friends
General Hospital
Mad About You
Melrose Place
Party of Five

DIS-ILLUSION DIGEST

Dr. FUN's Mass Media Love Quiz Myth #4

IF YOUR PARTNER IS TRULY MEANT FOR YOU, SEX IS EASY AND WONDERFUL.

As with all intimacy, genuinely good sex takes time, trust, and togetherness. In real life (unlike in the pages of *Playboy* and *Cosmo* or the music videos of seductive singers), sex is only one of three essential elements of love. Without the other components, it's mere infatuation, which is fleeting and lacking in commitment or communication.

Dr. Galician's Prescription™ #4

CONCENTRATE ON COMMITMENT AND CONSTANCY.

SOURCES CITED

de Rougemont, D. (1964). The rising tide of Eros. In H.A. Grunwald (Ed.), *Sex in America.* New York: Bantam Books.

Galician, M.-L. (1995, October). *The romanticization of love in the mass media: A comparison of the relationship among unrealistic romantic expectations, ideal role models, heterosexual coupleship satisfaction, and mass media usage of Baby Boomers and Generation Xers.* Paper presented at the annual meeting of The Organization for the Study of Communication, Language, and Gender, Minneapolis/St. Paul, MN.

Galician, M.-L. (1997, February). *The romanticization of love in the mass media: The relationship of mass communication media usage, unrealistic romantic expectations, coupleship dissatisfactions of Baby Boomer and Generation X males and females.* Paper presented at the annual meeting of the Western States Communication Association, Monterey Bay, CA.

Katz, S. J., & Liu, A. E. (1988). *False love and other romantic illusions.* New York: Pocket Books.

Moody, N. M. (2002, July 28.) Earthly anti-Britneys are dulling Spears' edge. *Arizona Republic*, p. E3.

Sternberg, R. J. (1988). Triangulating love. In R. J. Sternberg & M. L. Barnes (Eds.), *The psychology of love* (pp. 119–138). New Haven, CT: Yale University Press.

WORKSHEET FOR MASS MEDIA MYTH #4
(See Chapter 6 for details of *Dr. Galician's Seven-Step* Dis-*illusioning Directions.*)

If your partner is truly meant for you, sex is easy and wonderful.

R$_x$: CONCENTRATE on COMMITMENT and CONSTANCY.

Title of Your Analysis & Criticism

Your Thesis

STEP 1. DETECTION (finding/identifying)

Identification (title, date, and medium, with "markers")

Entire work/specific segment

STEP 2. DESCRIPTION (illustrating/exemplifying)

Detailed description

Creator; creator's purpose

Function/purpose (entertainment/news and information/persuasion) and genre

STEP 3. DECONSTRUCTION (analyzing)

Underlying myths/stereotypes (primary/secondary)

Evidence for linking myths/stereotypes; specific examples of content (message) and form (medium) that represent embedded values

Significant omissions

Cited commentary/research

STEP 4. DIAGNOSIS (evaluating/criticizing)

Meaning and possible interpretations (preferred and oppositional)

Comparison with rational models

Possible effects (harm)

Expert citations

Judgment/evaluation

STEP 5. DESIGN (reconstructing/reframing)

Realistic reframing

Related theories and rational models

Likelihood of use

Existing reconstructions

STEP 6. DEBRIEFING (reconsidering/remedying)

Personal impact of *dis*-illusioning; comparison of personal belief before/after, including enjoyment

Personal harm from myth

STEP 7. DISSEMINATION (publishing/broadcasting)

Advocacy action plan

Timetable of specific activities (personal/public/professional)

11

DR. FUN'S MASS MEDIA LOVE QUIZ MYTH #5

To attract and keep a man, a woman should look like a model or a centerfold.

Dr. Galician's Prescription™ #5
R_x: CHERISH COMPLETENESS IN COMPANIONS
(NOT JUST THE COVER).

B student; C cup.
> — Listed by an Arizona teenager as part of his
> "Perfect Girl Criteria" (as cited by Amanda Kingsbury in
> "Get Real: Media Myths May Mold Love and Romance
> into Unrealistic Goals," *The Tribune*)

I think women are looking for too much of the GQ thing. And I'm just an old Marlboro Man.
> — Fenton M. Love of Virginia, cited in the same article

Here's a story of a real person[1] who — once upon a time — believed this myth and, as a result, did *not* live very happily-ever-after.

[Greg, 25-year-old single male musician]

When I was a kid I was infatuated with superstar Janet Jackson: She could sing and dance and had a body to die for. I never missed her television appearances, which I'd scrutinize for her outfits and her hair. She always looked flawless. When I started dating in high school, I'd compare my girlfriends to Janet. I'd tell them what to wear and how to fix their hair to look like her.

But when I met Lisa things changed. After dating for quite a while, we moved in together. I didn't like to see my beauty queen in her scruffy pajamas and slippers. Even worse, I hated her messy hair, puffy face, and stinky breath in the morning.

---

[1]Names have been changed to protect individuals' privacy.

Finally it dawned on me that her great personality and genuine love were more important than looking like a superstar all the time. After all, models, centerfolds, and superstars use great computer tricks and camera angles to help them look better than they are. It also dawned on me that I'm no Tyson Beckford in the morning either.

Even more dangerous:

[Becky, 31-year-old divorced female, executive secretary]

Ever since I was a teenager, my room was always decorated with hundreds of pictures of women from magazines like *Teen* and *Seventeen*. These were the girls I idolized and was constantly striving to be like. I had to restrict myself to an incredibly tight diet. Some days, my only meal would be an apple. The problem was that I was constantly reinforced with these impossible ideals. I had boyfriends at my house and guys calling me all the time. I was on the royal court at my high school. All this attention made me feel important, so I worked even harder to retain my model-like figure. It became an obsession.

When I got older, my teen magazines were replaced by *Glamour* and *Cosmo.* To look more like the models in these pages, I had fake breasts installed as well as numerous liposuctions. After a disastrous marriage to a bodybuilder, I divorced and took stock of myself. It's taken a long time to recover from this myth, but I'm lucky to have survived. A lot of people completely ruin their health and actually die from all this.

ADDITIONAL RESEARCH & COMMENTARY
RELATED TO THIS MASS MEDIA MYTH

Here's another one of those items where the *Quiz* responses tend to reflect our own personal P.C. — what we'd *like* to believe we believe. In other words, our behaviors might not match our beliefs. We're more influenced by the mass media than we might acknowledge. Rob Davis, president of Mate-Search International, recently told a newspaper reporter what his clients want in a mate:

> **Male and Female University Students' Responses to This *Quiz* Item**
>
> Very few men or women agree that a woman should look like a model or centerfold to attract and hold a man, but *within* those small percentages men are far more likely to agree (around 15% — compared with only around 3% of the women).

They all want the same person with the perfect body, the perfect personality, people with no flaws. They see these people on *Sex in the City,* and they actually believe this stuff exists. They are living in Disneyland. (as cited in Jackson, 2001, p. E8)

Evolutionary psychology theorizes that primitive males needed to be *visually oriented* to be good hunters and protectors and that certain primitive female body characteristics might have signaled the all-important survival-of-the-species factors — health and fertility. But that's all decidedly primeval.

Unfortunately, as Kenrick and his colleagues found (see Chapter 5), unrealistic *Playboy*-style pictures of attractive women can have attitudinal and behavioral effects on men and on their real-life relationships. Real women can't measure up to these seemingly real fantasies.

Ironically, women impose these same or even more rigid standards upon themselves — "assisting in their own oppression," according to cultural critics. In *The Beauty Myth: How Images of Beauty Are Used Against Women*, Naomi Wolf (1992) wrote extensively about the psychological and physical damage that results from these false ideals and the unrealistic, impossible standards encultrated by our society and promulgated primarily by the mass media. She argued that women's insecurities are heightened by these media images and then exploited by the diet, cosmetic, and plastic surgery industries. For decades, Jean Kilbourne has written books and produced videos that show how advertising focused on beauty and sex has been "Killing Us Softly." In my studies, women who were heavier users of fashion and fitness magazines had more unrealistic expectations of sex, love, and romance.

And it's not just women and girls who are held to an irrational standard of beauty. Men and boys, too, are increasingly being depicted in idealized ways — from the traditional macho body-builder to the newer feminized male physique.

Countless normal males and females irrationally attempt to ape models who are 20% under normal healthy weight, who devote full-time to their appearance, and who appear in digitally enhanced specially lit settings in which all imperfections are artificially removed. And while we'd never admit that these are also the standards against which we measure potential romantic partners, those of us who wish to be honest with ourselves at least must assess the role of this mediated myth in our lives.

For example, on the popular NBC-TV series *Ed,* the title character relentlessly pursued blond skinny "Carol" (who completely ignored Ed because she was devoting her full romantic attention to the emotional abuse heaped on her by her obnoxious "boyfriend"). Ed spent a lot of time crying on the shoulder of his longtime gal-pal "Molly." Molly is loyal, funny, thoughtful, pretty, smart, grounded, but maybe 25 to 40 pounds over the current McBealesque *media* norm for a *leading* lady love-interest — so *obviously* Ed couldn't even consider a relationship with this character who was clearly a better choice in every way. The possibility of such a relationship wasn't even a subtext.

*DIS-*ILLUSIONING THIS MYTH

Magazines: The Place for Models & Centerfolds

A great variety of men's and women's magazine promote an ideal of beauty that is unattainable by most normal people. (It used to be that this idea was a standard only women had to meet, but increasingly men are being subjected to the same unrealistic standards of attractiveness, as evidenced by male models and articles that instigate dissatisfaction with the self.) These magazines thrive on creating problems for which their advertisers provide solutions.

There's nothing wrong with trying to improve our appearance and enhance our health. In fact, those are worthy goals. However, when the standards are actually far beyond the norm, we must stop and interrogate the media messages that undermine our self-esteem. We must remember that the men and women who appear in these publications might look quite different in person. To use them as an ideal doesn't make sense.

In examining a wide range of these fashion and health and fitness magazines, I've found that there's very little difference between the covers of the men's and women's magazines. *Playboy* and *Maxim* are nearly identical to the covers of *Cosmo:* half-naked babes displaying cleavage and navels. Women haven't come a long way at all if we're still trying ape an adolescent male fantasy or copy the look of celebrities.

And it's unfair to plant these unrealistic expectations in male readers. As one young man reported in the debriefing section of his *dis*-illusioning: "I understand the problems with Myth #5, but at the same time it's hard not to want a girl who looks like the girls on the cover of *Maxim*."

What's distressing about the appeals used by these publications is that despite their pretense at offering healthy concepts for physical and emotional improvement, they ultimately reduce male-female relationships to appearance and sexuality. And they rob individuals of their personhood when they dispense advice with the implication that it will work on everyone.

Prerequisites for Princesshood: *Coming to America*

In the 1988 comedy *Coming to America*, Eddie Murphy plays handsome Prince Akeem, sole heir to the throne of the African kingdom of Zamunda, where royal marriages are prearranged. At his 21st birthday celebration, he must marry a woman who has been trained all her life to please him. As heralds begin their fanfares to announce the bride-to-be (whom Akeem has never seen) and as the crowds part to make room for her entrance, a beautifully attired but heavy-set woman pushes forward and faces the prince. He turns to his friend (played by Arsenio Hall) in disbelief and disappointment. But just as he's about to despair, this woman is shown to be merely an assistant to the real future princess, who is then brought forward.

The real soon-to-be princess is slim and pretty. Prince Akeem is relieved. (Sadly, most movie watchers are, too.) Even though he's not spoken a word to the weightier woman, he has instantly dismissed her as a candidate. She could be the most interesting, gracious, and sweet-tempered person in his kingdom, but how would he ever know? (Interestingly, he also rejects the slimmer model because she's a vacuous beauty with no sense of self. Instead, he goes off to America to find a bride — eventually landing another beautiful slim woman who has a little more spunk.) The preferred reading is clear: To be a princess in Zamunda, at any rate, a woman must look like a model or centerfold.

One of my students presented a reframing (Step 5. Design) in which Akeem and his American girlfriend realize that their different cultures and lifestyles would be *too* different. They promise to remain friends, and Akeem invites her and her family to visit him. He goes back home to Zamunda and renews his acquaintance with his heavy-set countrywoman, with whom he has much in common. After a suitable courtship period, she becomes his bride.

Convoluted Countertype: *Shallow Hal*

In the Farrelly brothers' *Shallow Hal* (2001), comedic Jack Black is Hal Larsen, a shallow man who is unattractive both physically and emotionally, but who nevertheless will date only "babes." After motivator Tony Robbins (playing himself) plants a suggestion in Hal's mind, he suddenly sees people in terms of their inner beauty. As a result, he falls for the morbidly obese Rosemary (Gwyneth Paltrow in a rubber "fat suit"), whom he perceives as the stick-thin actress actually appears.

The movie is driven by the mistaken images Hal has — as when he can't understand why people in a restaurant laugh when Rosemary's chair collapses under her or when she wolfs multiple milkshakes in one sitting. Are *we* supposed to laugh, as did many people in the theatre where I saw this movie? If we do, we should be ashamed of ourselves, as should the Farrellys for passing off this mean-spirited piece as a feel-good look-for-what's-inside-the-person statement, which it's not — even though Hal finally sees. It's a convoluted countertype that reinforces a variety of unhealthy myths.

In the first place, this woman is not just heavy, she's hardly able to walk. A person who is so obese that she breaks chairs and empties the water from public swimming pools when she dives in clearly needs medical attention. (Her parents are wealthy. Why don't they help her? At this rate she'll be dead soon. And she's a public menace — as when children *in* that swimming pool are tossed about onto the deck.)

But this issue is never addressed. Because we *know* it's really gorgeous Gwyneth under the rubber, we're mindlessly led to feel she's a worthy candidate for the grudging commitment this jerk finally offers when he understands and sees her as the overweight person she really is. And, he *is* a jerk who, ironically, is not deserving of the kind and generous person that Rosemary is. Yes, he mitigates his crude attitudes and behavior somewhat during his time with her (see Myth #7). But we've been there and seen that all too many times to care about his slight rehabilitation.

In the second place, why is the starved-looking Paltrow posited as the paragon of beauty that Hal sees when he looks at Rosemary? Aside from the fact that this shape is equally unnatural, shouldn't Hal see Rosemary as she really is and accept her because she's such a great person (if indeed that's the point of this romantic comedy that isn't very funny and isn't successful as a satire)? When he finally does at the end, it's not believable and or satisfying.

In the third place, if the Farrellys really wanted to say something about our obsession with looks, why not make Hal a *hunk* who falls for someone who isn't a babe? Why do unattractive women in movies and TV shows always have to content themselves and even be grateful when a physically unattractive and morally reprehensible loser like Hal gives them the time of day? *Let's have a kind and loving Brad Pitt fall for Rosemary.*

But more to the point, let's have Brad Pitt fall for a Rosemary who might be only 25 to 40 pounds over model and centerfold weight — in other words, closer to a real woman of normal weight.

The gross abnormality of Rosemary's physical form (coupled with the abnormal model-thin form of the Rosemary of Hal's "Hal-lucinations") makes the story a fairy tale or fable rather than a narrative of more universal real-life application. We might easily buy the high-toned concept of accepting others for their insides rather than for their outsides, but we're not shown anything realistic enough to motivate us to make the huge leap from concept to practice. Because of the hypocrisy of this parody, we can comfortably continue our own.

Who's *Shallow Hal* after all? Maybe he's all of us.

A Sensitive Exploration of This Myth:
The Heartbreak Kid

An intriguing film that explores this myth in more depth and with more realism than most Hollywood vehicles is director Elaine May's 1972 *The Heartbreak Kid* (written by Neil Simon). In this poignant film that clothes many truths in great humor, Charles Grodin plays a honeymooner whose new bride (Jeannie Berlin, May's daughter) is not unattractive but is not a model or centerfold by any means.

When he meets a woman who *does* measure up to that ideal (cool blonde Cybill Shepherd, with her actual modeling days not long behind her), he falls instantly in love with her, divorces his wife before they leave their honeymoon resort, and pursues his dream girl to her hometown thousands of miles away. Her parents can't stand him (They know about his short-lived marriage.), and she's hesitant to give up her college football hero boyfriends for this very average-looking older guy. But he's so relentless in his obsession with his Venus that he eventually convinces her to marry him. Her parents even attend the formal wedding.

Here's the realistic ending and the tragicomedic twist: At the reception, the groom is moping around in much the same way as he was at his earlier wedding at the beginning of the picture. And it's clear that now that he's got his prize, he's still not content. As Lazarus pointed out, we can't expect to be happy by using a partner as "emotional oxygen" (see also Myth #10).

Dr. FUN's Realistic Romance™ Awards Nomination: "Cinder Elephant"

A delightful, non-idealistic reframing of this myth in the *Cinderella* story appears in the short story collection *A Wolf at the Door and Other Retold Fairy Tales* (2001; edited by Ellen Datlow and Terri Windling). According to the back cover of this book aimed at adolescent readers, "These are not your mother's fairy tales." The title character in "Cinder Elephant" isn't helpless or petite. Caldecott-winning author Jane Yolen explains:

> "Cinder Elephant" has more to do with the fact that I wear a size nine and a half shoe and went from rompers to a size twelve dress with no intervening steps than any deep love for Cinderella. I hated the Disney *Cinderella* with a passion. All those mice. All those birds. The birds in "Cinder Elephant" are a satire on those twittery bluebirds. (p. 29)

Yolen's story begins:

> There was once a lovely big girl who lived with her father in a large house near the king's park. ...And though she was bigger than most, the girl had a sweet face, a loving heart, a kind disposition, and big feet.

Elly (Eleanor), who has unkind skinny stepsisters, is a bird-watcher. The birds make her an outfit of feathers so she can go the ball. And, using twigs and grass, they make her a pair of slippers that are the same size as the author's. The birds think Elly looks beautiful, but the narrator acknowledges, "Actually she looked like a big fat hen sitting on a nest."

But thoughtful Prince Junior is also a bird-watcher. He's amazed at this lovely giant hen, whom he gently pursues. The two share a love of sports. And even though his father admonishes him that "princes marry swans — not hens," Prince Junior searches all over with her "grass slipper" (which dropped off her foot when she was suddenly blown aloft by her feathery gown) until he finds his "dear hen."

I think the moral of Yolen's tale is brilliant: "If you love a waist, you waste a love" (p. 28).

Additional Mass Media Manifestations of This Myth to *Dis*-illusion

Books

Beauty books

Magazines

Allure
Cosmo
Glamour
GQ
Maxim
Playboy
Seventeen
Shape
Teen
Teen People
YM
Vogue

Movies

America's Sweethearts
Beautiful Girls
Circle of Friends
First Wives Club
Mannequin
The Mirror Has Two Faces
Miss Congeniality
Most Disney animated features
Princess Diaries
The Truth About Cats & Dogs

Recorded Music

Baby Got Back
Britney Spears' videos
The Girl That I Marry
The Most Beautiful Girl
* in the World*
Venus

Television

90210
Ally McBeal
Baywatch
Ed
Seinfeld
Sex and the City

DIS-ILLUSION DIGEST

Dr. FUN's Mass Media Love Quiz Myth #5

TO ATTRACT AND KEEP A MAN,
A WOMAN SHOULD LOOK LIKE A MODEL OR A CENTERFOLD.

Real love doesn't superficially turn a person into an object. Nevertheless, even though they might not realize it, many men subconsciously use actresses, models, and centerfolds as a standard for their own real-life partners, who cannot help disappointing them (unless they, too, have the surgical and photographic enhancements that pop culture icons get). What's worse is that even women's magazines reinforce unhealthy body images. On TV and in the movies, it's either "*Babe*Watch" (as I call it!) at one extreme or "Ally-McBeal-*Please*-Give-This-Poor-Girl-A-Meal" at the other end. Sadly, males, too, are increasingly under pressure to measure up to an unrealistic physical standard that's either hypermasculine or feminized.

Dr. Galician's Prescription™ #5

CHERISH COMPLETENESS IN COMPANIONS
(NOT JUST THE COVER).

SOURCES CITED

Galician, M.-L. (1995, October). *The romanticization of love in the mass media: A comparison of the relationship among unrealistic romantic expectations, ideal role models, heterosexual coupleship satisfaction, and mass media usage of Baby Boomers and Generation Xers.* Paper presented at the annual meeting of The Organization for the Study of Communication, Language, and Gender, Minneapolis/St. Paul, MN.

Galician, M.-L. (1997, February). *The romanticization of love in the mass media: The relationship of mass communication media usage, unrealistic romantic expectations, coupleship dissatisfactions of Baby Boomer and Generation X males and females.* Paper presented at the annual meeting of the Western States Communication Association, Monterey Bay, CA.

Jackson, T. (2001, July 14). TV marriages twist reality, study says. *Arizona Republic,* p. E1, E8.

Kingsbury, A. (1999, March 23). Get real: Media myths may mold love and romance into unrealistic goals. *The Tribune* [Scottsdale/Mesa/Tempe & Chandler, AZ], pp. D1, D6.

Lazarus, A. A. (1985). *Marital myths: Two dozen mistaken beliefs that can ruin a marriage or make a bad one worse.* San Luis Obispo, CA: Impact.

Wolf, N. (1992). *The beauty myth: How images of beauty are used against women.* New York: Doubleday.

WORKSHEET FOR MASS MEDIA MYTH #5
(See Chapter 6 for details of *Dr. Galician's Seven-Step* Dis-*illusioning Directions.*)

To attract and keep a man, a woman should look like a model or a centerfold.

R_x: CHERISH COMPLETENESS in COMPANIONS (not just the COVER).

Title of Your Analysis & Criticism

Your Thesis

STEP 1. DETECTION (finding/identifying)

Identification (title, date, and medium, with "markers")

Entire work/specific segment

STEP 2. DESCRIPTION (illustrating/exemplifying)

Detailed description

Creator; creator's purpose

Function/purpose (entertainment/news and information/persuasion) and genre

STEP 3. DECONSTRUCTION (analyzing)

Underlying myths/stereotypes (primary/secondary)

Evidence for linking myths/stereotypes; specific examples of content (message) and form (medium) that represent embedded values

Significant omissions

Cited commentary/research

STEP 4. DIAGNOSIS (evaluating/criticizing)

Meaning and possible interpretations (preferred and oppositional)

Comparison with rational models

Possible effects (harm)

Expert citations

Judgment/evaluation

STEP 5. DESIGN (reconstructing/reframing)

Realistic reframing

Related theories and rational models

Likelihood of use

Existing reconstructions

STEP 6. DEBRIEFING (reconsidering/remedying)

Personal impact of *dis*-illusioning; comparison of personal belief before/after, including enjoyment

Personal harm from myth

STEP 7. DISSEMINATION (publishing/broadcasting)

Advocacy action plan

Timetable of specific activities (personal/public/professional)

12

DR. FUN'S MASS MEDIA LOVE QUIZ MYTH #6

The man should *NOT* be shorter, weaker, younger, poorer, or less successful than the woman.

Dr. Galician's Prescription™ #6
R$_x$: CREATE COEQUALITY; COOPERATE.

Well, I can wear heels now.

— Nicole Kidman, discussing her split from
Tom Cruise on *Late Night with David Letterman*

Here's a story of a real person[1] who — once upon a time — believed this myth and, as a result, did *not* live very happily-ever-after.

[Joanna, 19-year-old female college student]

At 5'10", I'm pretty tall for a female. It was great in high school when I played volleyball — but not so great when it comes to dating. It's very rare that I see a woman who's taller than a man in movies. Camera angles and props seem to trick us into believing that even some short actors are tall. I'm afraid those images have infiltrated my thought process. Even though I know that height isn't the more important thing in a relationship, I just feel more secure dating a guy who's even taller than I am. I hate leaning down to kiss a boy, too. It feels like I'm kissing a little kid.

An older male perspective:

[Franklin, 63-year-old retired male professor in Iowa]

I thought I'd never find a mate because I was always the shortest boy in school. When my friends started flirting with girls, I was too intimidated — especially when I saw movies like *Casablanca* and *A Streetcar Named Desire,* with strong tall male stars who overpowered the women. Fortunately, I finally had a growth spurt in high school and later married my 5'1" college sweetheart. But those movie images haunted me for a long time.

---

[1]Names have been changed to protect individuals' privacy.

Here's a response to another part of the myth:

[Robin, 19-year-old female student]

I love country songs, and I want the life that all country stars sing about: The couple meets when they're young, the man fights for the woman, he wins, they marry, and he takes care of her forever. She supports him mentally, and he supports her physically and monetarily. I know this will never happen, but in my dreams I want that mass media myth. Oh, if only all my dreams would come true!

ADDITIONAL RESEARCH & COMMENTARY RELATED TO THIS MASS MEDIA MYTH

Like the university students who have taken the *Quiz*, the majority of Baby Boomers as well as of Generation Xers in my survey said the man and woman are "fairly equal in dominance" in their own relationships. Interestingly, the proportion of Boomers was larger (60%, compared with 52% for Xers), whereas twice as many Xers (20% compared with 10% for Boomers) said the woman is dominant; 30% of both age cohorts said the man is dominant.

> **Male and Female University Students' Responses to This *Quiz* Item**
>
> By a 4:1 ratio (80% disagree/20% agree) both sexes deny they believe in male-female inequality in relationships. Men are only slightly more likely to agree with this myth of the need for male superiority in romantic relationships.

However, in my in-depth interviews, I found that these are often "head-not-heart" responses. In other words, the respondents believed or would like to believe in equality and equity, but their actual behavior doesn't always match their stated beliefs and in many cases actually contradicts what they say. We might call these kinds of responses mere "lip service." But the contradiction goes further than that. It relates to the education/enculturation divide. We don't always do what we know is right or even what's good for us. As the case studies above illustrate (and they're not atypical), our habits and our socialization keep us from enacting certain behaviors. And the hegemonic media reinforce the beliefs we don't like to acknowledge we hold.

My survey of Boomers and Xers found that both men and women retained this outdated hegemonic *male-superiority/female-dependency* myth. I thought the younger Generation X age group would be more "liberated" in their male-female views, so I was surprised that it was just the opposite: The Xers were more likely than the older Boomers to believe in it. The most stereotypic view was held by heavy viewers of music videos, which tend to portray patriarchal coupleship and objectified females.

In the mass media, this stereotypic viewpoint is reinforced *even* in the so-called nonfiction nonentertainment forms like the news: A news anchor "couple" is practically always an older man with a younger woman. They're hardly ever the *same* age, much less an older woman/younger man duo. And the male is usually the dominant partner in terms of demeanor and experience. What do we learn from that *peripheral route* image during our *ritualistic* use of a medium?

In their book *Critical Approaches to Television,* media scholars Vande Berg, Wenner, and Gronbeck explain that myths can constrain us, preventing social change and promoting even violent behavior against "the other." They justify counterproductive behavior — such as male superiority over the "weaker sex" — as *naturalized.* For example, Saturday morning cartoons teach the myths of sex differences to the young. These authors maintain that one of the cultural critic's primary tasks is to "problematize and strip away such myths" (Vande Berg, Wenner, & Gronbeck, 1998, p. 294).

Relationship expert Gary Smalley claims that the "Number 1 killer (of a marriage) is communicating to your mate that you're somehow superior" (as cited in Carroll, 1999, p. D1). "There are 100,000 ways to communicate that ... Without realizing it, couples degrade and invalidate each other."

This *invalidating* is equally unfair to both sexes. Just as it's dehumanizing for women to be objectified as attractive body parts, so is it inhumane (to say nothing of cold-hearted and calculating!) to view men as a meal-ticket or security guard. Women who are looking for a knight-in-shining-armor should ask themselves what they think they need to be rescued *from!* (When I myself finally did this, I realized that what I wasn't a damsel-in-distress and what I really wanted was a *companion.)*

Unfortunately, many of us — men and women — have been powerfully seduced by the mass media to adopt irrational models. Fortunately, it's never too late to escape that trap.

Lazarus (see Chapter 3) is quite clear: Rescue fantasies are toxic — for the rescuee as well as for the rescuer. Karpman detailed the destructive rescue cycle. Sills noted that we perform a disservice to ourselves by relying on prehistoric biological motivations for mate selection in our own enlightened time. It's absurd. Moreover, it's actually the antithesis of loving respectful coupleship. Having a *partner* is incompatible with having a *master* or a *servant.*

In contrast to traditional coupleship with more stereotyped separate male-female roles that frequently lead to separate lives, peer marriage — as described and advocated by noted sociologist Pepper Schwartz (see Chapter 3) — is characterized by intense companionship, deep knowledge of the partner's personality, an inclination to negotiate and converse more than other couples, and no visible yearning for attention and affection. Schwartz has argued that peer relationships are superior because the defining principle of peer couples is deep friendship whereas the defining principles of traditional couples are idealization and hierarchy, which can destroy intimacy.

However, the media rarely normalize peer coupleship or present it as the preferred reading. These relationships — like all healthy relationships — lack the tension and conflict that feed drama, whether comedy or tragedy. Instead, "Me-Tarzan, You-Jane" couples are the norm — no matter how updated they might seem. On the rare occasions that the media *do* show a non-traditional relationship, it's usually the opposite extreme — the "woman on top" *countertype* — rather than the peer couple. This hegemonic reversal is equally mythic and marginalizing. In Smalley's terms, it's "degrading and invalidating." And it's usually reserved for comedy, underscoring the subtext that such relationships are considered ridiculous by their creators. (In fact, early preliterate societies were matriarchal, and many early myths promote the older woman-younger man model.) We'll explore some examples of these countertypes in the next section.

While it's reasonable to play Mommy or Daddy once in while to a partner who needs special coddling, taking on this permanent role (or seeking to be the "child" in a grown-up relationship) is seriously unhealthy. Remember, too, that psychologically androgynous persons exhibit more gender role flexibility, which has been shown to result in great personal adjustment and marital satisfaction (see Chapter 3). In other words, fully actualized men with well developed multifaceted human capacities can demonstrate their *anima* by playing the so-called "mommy role," and women can use their *animus* to play the "daddy role." And it doesn't have to be a comedy.

The scientific literature continues to document that males and females are far more alike than different. It's our enculturation that keeps us "otherizing" the sexes. (In psychology, this "otherizing" tendency is called the "paranoid position.") The social psychology literature and relationship experts continue to endorse reality-based peer coupleship. Yet the dehumanizing archaic stereotypic model is what the mass media continue to portray and glorify in the 21st century.

DIS-ILLUSIONING THIS MYTH

Can Superman Ever Just Be a Man?

This myth, which normalizes male superiority in relationships, dominates nearly every romance novel, every magazine illustration and ad, every television show (including every news anchor "couple") and commercial, and every romantic and action movie. There's an illuminating line in *Superman: The Movie* (1978) that interrogates this myth. Lois Lane is falling from a skyscraper. Just in time, the Man of Steel flies up to catch her.

"Don't worry, Miss. I've got you" he confidently announces — to which the startled but spunky Ms. Lane replies: "You've got *me*...; who's got *you*?"

This is a resistive question we seldom ask when confronted by any one of the innumerable mass media manifestations of this myth. But we should ask it in opposing such media themes, because they are as unfair to men as they are demeaning to women.

A Short Date: *Sex and the City* ("Politically Erect")

The bawdy award-winning HBO cable television series *Sex in the City*, which satirizes both the popular culture and romantic relationships, features four single thirty-something girlfriends who, more often than not, exemplify dysfunctional approaches to the consummate love they desperately seek in all the wrong places and in all the wrong ways. "Politically Erect," episode 32 of the show's third season (2002), offered a comedic but poignant perspective of Myth #6. The narrator, Carrie Bradshaw (Sarah Jessica Parker), is dating a powerful, rich politician even though she doesn't care for his politics. At an upscale bar, the quartet's "femme fatale" — tall, shapely sexaholic PR executive Samantha Jones (Kim Cattrall) — meets a delightful and successful man who invites her to dinner. She's thrilled until he steps off his stool and reveals himself as extremely short.

She tries to dump him, suggesting he might be better off with someone who is "Your ...your own size." "Listen, sweetheart," he retorts, "give me one hour in the sack, and you'll swear I'm the Jolly Green Giant!" After the hour, Samantha discovers that he's correct, so she gives him another chance (Myth #4).

However, a few days later, when he leaves the table for a moment during their dinner date, Samantha sees a boys' department label in the suit jacket on his chair. This is just too much for her. When she explains that this is so disturbing she's got to leave immediately, he asks: "Where do *you* shop? The big and tall whores' store?"

And now comes the moment that redeems this portrayal. Instead of getting angry, the good-hearted Samantha has a good laugh. So does her date. And Carrie's voiceover offers a potential healthy reframing: "Samantha found what she was looking for — someone who made her laugh. They dated for two weeks. Though he was short, for Samantha it was a very long relationship."

A more productive countertype, of course, would have this short gentleman portray a continuing serious love interest.

Reversals or Countertypes of This Myth

This myth's power elements — height, strength, age, wealth, success — are traditional male character necessities in the romantic narratives rampant in the mass media. As mentioned above, although the mass media rarely present peer couples, they do sometimes present the opposite extreme of traditional couples — the "woman on top" countertype. As discussed in Chapter 2, countertypes are nevertheless stereotypes, often offering merely surface correctives rather than genuine remedies and sometimes creating equally damaging stereotypes.

A few years ago, I asked students to join me in compiling a list of movie and television portrayals of sex, love, and romance that *reversed* Myth #6 by showing women who were taller, stronger, older, richer, and/or more successful than their male love interest. See "Some Reversals (Countertypes) of *Dr. FUN's Mass Media Love Quiz* Myth #6" on the next page for our list of some of these countertypes.

It Must Be Science Fiction

Let's look more closely at these examples to see why countertypes are *not* healthy reframings (Step 5. Design.) First of all, as you can see, nearly every manifestation listed is comedic or satiric. A few — such as *The Incredible Shrinking Man* and *The Attack of the 50-foot Woman* — are *science fiction* classics. Apparently, their creators found the notion of a woman more powerful than her partner so absurd that they could only envision it as a fantasy. Moreover, in both of these movies, the perversion of traditional coupleship creates a nightmare for the man because of the woman's actions. Both films offer powerful metaphors about the danger of relationships in which the woman overwhelms the man.

The Incredible Shrinking Man. The husband in *The Incredible Shrinking Man* (1957), who is reduced to living in a dollhouse when radiation poisoning causes him to shrink, is victimized by the pet cat, precipitating his descent into the huge cellar of the couple's home and his ultimate death — because his wife went out and forgot to lock the animal up. The subtext is that she can't be relied upon — even though her miniaturized husband reminded her to do it. (In the same scene, he has to remind her not to walk so heavily on the stairs or talk so loud, as the noise is now deafening to him. We hear the echoing thud of her steps as the director cuts to the poor little man with his hands on his ears, being driven crazy by his thoughtless wife. In other words, to be a good wife, she must be careful to not be heard.)

The Attack of the 50-foot Woman. We see the danger of letting a woman get the "upper hand" (literally!) in the *The Attack of the 50-foot Woman* (1958): When the wife (who has grown because of radiation contamination from an alien encounter) catches up with her two-timing husband in a sleazy bar where he is carousing with his friends and the "other woman," the giant shoves her hand through the ceiling (a counterpoint to the *Shrinking Man*'s cellar) and scoops him up. (Actually, because of the cheesy "special effects," the hand looks more like a

Some Reversals (Countertypes) of *Dr. FUN's Mass Media Love Quiz* Myth #6

SHORTER MAN/TALLER WOMAN

Movies

any Woody Allen film

any Cruise/Kidman film (*Far & Away*: She's taller, richer, *and* more educated than he is.)

Back to the Future (Fox is shorter than his girlfriend.)

Living Out Loud (Danny DeVito is shorter — and poorer and less successful — than Holly Hunter.)

Television

Ally McBeal (John is shorter than Nell.)

Days of Our Lives (Lucas is shorter than wife Nicole.)

Family Ties (Fox is shorter than real-life wife Pollen.)

Friends (Chandler is shorter than Monica.)

Golden Girls (Blanche *always* seeks younger men!)

Just Shoot Me (David Spade dates/marries a tall gorgeous model.)

Martin (He's shorter than his wife.)

Spin City (Michael J. Fox is shorter than his girlfriend.)

WEAKER MAN/STRONGER WOMAN

Movies

Cutthroat Island (Geena Davis fights to save Matthew Modine.)

Ever After: A Cinderella Story (Drew Barrymore carries prince to rescue him.)

Mighty Aphrodite (Woody is weaker.)

Red Sonja (She's often ahead of Arnold!)

Top Gun (instructor/student)

Xena (She's stronger than any man!)

Television

Third Rock (Sally is taller, stronger, more attractive than her boyfriend.)

YOUNGER MAN/OLDER WOMAN

Movies

Big (Hanks is actually a child!)

Bull Durham (Sarandon is older than Robbins — her real-life partner, too.)

The Graduate (Mrs. Robinson/Benjamin)

White Palace (Sarandon/Spader) — (one of the few countertype **dramas**)

Television

20/20 ("Barbara Walters is older than Hugh Downs.") [She's actually younger.]

Sports Center ("Roberts is older/larger than Scott.")

various anchor duos and co-hosts

POORER MAN/RICHER WOMAN

Movies

Aladdin (street rat/princess)

Cocktail (Cruise is a poor bartender; Shue is rich and successful.)

Curly Sue (rich woman/homeless man)

How Stella Got Her Groove Back (She's also older and more successful.)

A Life Less Ordinary (Rich father fires daughter's beau.)

Look Who's Talking (He's a cabbie; she's successful businesswoman.)

Overboard (She's a rich girl; he's a fish-gutter.)

Princess Bride (She's a "lady"; he's a "farmboy.")

Titanic (rich girl/poor boy)

LESS SUCCESSFUL MAN/MORE SUCCESSFUL WOMAN

Movies

Basic Instinct (Stone more successful — and outs*marts* Douglas.)

Beautiful Girls (lawyer Tracy/pianist Willy)

Big Daddy (He's out of work; she's a lawyer.)

Boomerang (Robin Givens is more successful/powerful than Eddie Murphy.)

Notting Hill (She's is a famous actress; he's "just" a bookseller.)

There's Something About Mary (She's tall, smart winner; he's short, dim-witted loser.)

Television

King of Queens (Her job is more respected than his.)

POWERLESS MAN/POWERFUL WOMAN

Movies

Mr. Mom (He's the house-husband; she works.)

Mrs. Doubtfire (He's the nanny — weak and unsuccessful as a husband.)

Television

Cheers (Sam works under Kirstie Alley.)

Full House (Becky works; Jesse minds kids at home.)

Who's the Boss (Tony works for Angela, who becomes his girlfriend.)

solid plaster claw or electronic cherrypicker onto which the husband seems to have to lift himself to *be* raised by the vengeful wife.) "She's got Harry," the shocked friends scream as they run for their lives. It's campy — but (as with most sci-fi) there's a psychosocial message nevertheless.

Carrying the Man

The woman literally carries the man in several more recent films — *Ever After: A Cinderella Story* and *Cutthroat Island*. In *Far and Away*, the carrying is figurative.

Ever After: A Cinderella Story. In *Ever After: A Cinderella Story* (1998), Drew Barrymore rescues the prince from Gypsies who agree that she can have anything she can carry. Physically strengthened from years of endless chores forced on her by her stepmother, she hoists him over her shoulder and triumphantly walks off. They share a love of books, but this emotionally weak prince is unworthy of a woman of such strong moral fiber. The ending I'd like to see has her searching for a peer who is not necessarily royal. (See *Dr. FUN's Realistic Romance™ Awards* Nomination of *Just Ella*, a *Cinderella* reframing, in Chapter 16.)

Cutthroat Island. The more comedic *Cutthroat Island* (1995)— a reversal spoof of the swashbuckling pirate genre — has 6-foot Pirate Queen/Captain Geena Davis braving villains in a daring rescue of the brainy but less physical Matthew Modine. In dialog that underscores that already obvious spoof, she advises him to follow her lead and keep up with her. He's amazed as she (or her stunt double) jumps from buildings and onto horses leading a runaway carriage. ("You're more active than most of the women I know," Modine deadpans as she hands the carriage reins to him while she beats up a bad guy whom she throws off the moving vehicle.)

But because of its extremes, this parody serves only to reinforce the underlying myth. It shows only that men can be weak and women can be as violent as men — not that couples can be equals.

Far and Away. In *Far and Away* (1992) — an epic about the plight of Irish immigrants in the 1890s — the taller, richer, and more educated landlord's daughter (portrayed by Nicole Kidman) is given her comeuppance for carrying the man (portrayed by her then-husband Tom Cruise) when he assumes the more normalized role of carrying *her* and dumping her (fully clothed) into the bathtub, where — once she is literally submerged — he shows his "power" by forcing her to admit his superiority. This is supposed to be a moment of levity in an otherwise somber film. (The Cruise character himself is brutalized in the bare-knuckle boxing ring.)

Why do we laugh at this exhibition of the worst in a relationship?

News Anchor "Couples"

Another problem created by the media barrage of this myth's stereotype of sex, love, and romance is illustrated by the list. As examples of the countertype, student frequently named news anchor duos from one of the major networks or from their hometown — mistakenly believing that an actually much *younger* woman is *older* than her male news partner. Because we're so accustomed to seeing much older men coupled with much younger woman in portrayals that have become normalized by the mass media, many people can't even accurately judge the age of these real newswomen. This misperception applies to actresses in fictional entertainment portrayals as well. Unless the women are *babies* in comparison to their male counterparts, audiences judge them to be *older* — even when they're the same age or younger. Of course, a truly older female anchor with a younger man is a rarity.

One of the Few Countertype Dramas: White Palace

White Palace (1990) is one of the few manifestations on the list that is *not* a comedy or fantasy. It's a realistic, moody drama in which a successful lawyer in his late twenties (portrayed by James Spader) falls in love with a mid-forty-ish diner waitress (Susan Sarandon). This age difference is the basis of the countertype, while class difference is the basis of the stereotype. They share a steamy sexual attraction, which builds to a genuine commitment at the end of the movie. This film is also one of the few to show a relationship *after* the courtship. They leave town and move to New York, where they start a new life together in a seedy apartment. In other words, for breaking the mythic taboo, the lawyer must give up some of his success and the woman will not be carried off into the sunset as she might have if she'd held out for a traditional older man.

Dr. FUN's Realistic Romance™ Awards Nomination: The Stairway "Rescue" Scene in Dr. T and the Women

As mentioned earlier, a climactic scene in *Dr. T and the Women* (2000) offers a manifestation of a healthy portrayal that resists this myth. In the Robert Altman film (inhabited by the usual odd assortment of Altmanesque characters), Dr. T — Dr. Sullivan Travis (Sully) — runs a successful gynecology practice. His patients adore him. But his personal life is a mess. His unhappy wife has regressed to a childlike state that requires institutionalization. His daughters are a mystery to him. And he's having an affair with his private club's golf pro, an independent younger woman played by Helen Hunt.

He finally decides to leave his practice and his family to run off somewhere "fun" with his lover. Wildly enthusiastic, he rushes to her apartment and dashes up the staircase to her bedroom[2] to tell her his plan and to assure her that she won't have to work or worry about money as *he* will take care of her.

Helen's response to the chauvinistic Sully shocks and bewilders him: "Why would I *want* that?" she asks, equally bewildered. Clearly, this admirable self-actualized woman — a candidate deserving of a peer relationship with a healthy *partner* — is not just another needy "Pretty Woman." (Remember how delighted that suddenly reformed street-walker portrayed by Julia Roberts was to be rescued at the end of the movie by *her* suddenly reformed stair-climber, also played by Gere?)

---

[2]This scene recalls the climactic stairway scene the same actress plays with Mel Gibson in *What Women Want*. And in both films, it's clear, as Natharius (2002) noted, that these men don't have a clue what that is.

Dr. FUN's Realistic Romance™ Awards Nomination:
The Thomas Crown Affair (1999 version)

Unlike the majority of the countertypes, the 1999 remake of the 1966 *Thomas Crown Affair* works as a rare existing Hollywood *reframing* of Myth #6. And it's a reframing that was successful at the box office. The romantic couple — played by Renee Russo (born in 1954) and Pierce Brosnan (only one year older, born in 1953) — are unusual in that they're the actually same age, which they're both allowed to look. As the review in *VideoHound®'s Golden Movie Retriever 2001* put it: "The forty-something duo sizzle (how fantastic to see two age-appropriate lovers for a change) ..." (Craddock, 2001, p. 956). The question we must ask is: Why is it the exception rather than the norm?

Additional Mass Media Manifestations of This Myth to *Dis*-illusion

Books

Bridges of Madison County
Rebecca
Romance novels

Comic Books

Batman
Spiderman
Superman

Magazines

Most couples in ads

Movies

Action movies (Arnold, Clint, John Wayne, Rambo, etc.)
As Good As It Gets
Batman; Superman; Spiderman
Casablanca
Entrapment
Funny Face
High Noon
The Horse Whisperer
Love in the Afternoon
The Mummy
Pretty Woman
Six Days, Seven Nights
Streetcar Named Desire
True Lies

Recorded Music

Most love songs
Most music videos
My Heart Belongs to Daddy
You Are Woman, I Am Man

Television

Couples in TV commercials
Dharma & Greg
I Dream of Jeanie
I Love Lucy
Live with Regis & Kelly
   (Former cohost was Kathy Lee, also a younger woman.)
Melrose Place
Sex and the City
TV anchor "couples" (co-hosts)

DIS-ILLUSION DIGEST

Dr. FUN's Mass Media Love Quiz Myth #6

THE MAN SHOULD **NOT** BE SHORTER, WEAKER, YOUNGER, POORER, OR LESS SUCCESSFUL THAN THE WOMAN.

Don't equate physical height and strength with moral fortitude. What women and men should look for in each other is stature and weight in terms of character. To fit the "Me-Tarzan, You-Jane" cultural stereotypes that mass media perpetuate, many leading men in movies and TV shows have to stand on boxes to appear taller than their leading ladies. Even news anchor "couples" are usually an older man–younger woman duo. These archaic images (which are ironically antithetical to real love) reinforce sexual inequality and block many potentially wonderful relationships from ever getting started. It's as unfair and dehumanizing to males as it is to females. Women today aren't damsels-in-distress and men shouldn't be forced to be their knights-in-shining-armor.

Dr. Galician's Prescription™ #6
CREATE COEQUALITY; COOPERATE.

SOURCES CITED

Carroll, D. (1999, October 12). Seminar leader zeroes in on actions that kill marriage: "Love skills" help couples to achieve intimacy. *Arizona Republic,* pp. D1–D2.]

Craddock, J. (Ed.). (2001). *VideoHound®'s golden movie retreiver 2001: The complete guide to movies on videocassette and dvd.* New York: Thompson Learning.

Galician, M.-L. (1995, October). *The romanticization of love in the mass media: A comparison of the relationship among unrealistic romantic expectations, ideal role models, heterosexual coupleship satisfaction, and mass media usage of Baby Boomers and Generation Xers.* Paper presented at the annual meeting of The Organization for the Study of Communication, Language, and Gender, Minneapolis/St. Paul, MN.

Galician, M.-L. (1997, February). *The romanticization of love in the mass media: The relationship of mass communication media usage, unrealistic romantic expectations, coupleship dissatisfactions of Baby Boomer and Generation X males and females.* Paper presented at the annual meeting of the Western States Communication Association, Monterey Bay, CA.

Karpman, S. (1968). Fairy tales and script drama analysis. *Transactional Analysis Bulletin, 7* (26), 39–43.

Lazarus, A. A. (1985). *Marital myths: Two dozen mistaken beliefs that can ruin a marriage or make a bad one worse.* San Luis Obispo, CA: Impact.

Natharius, D. (2002, March). *Now that men know what women want, are men getting what they want?* Paper presented at the annual meeting of the Western States Communication Association, Long Beach, CA.

Schwartz, P. (1994). *Peer marriage: How love between equals really works.* New York: The Free Press.

Sills, J. (1984). *How to stop looking for someone perfect and find someone to love.* New York: St. Martin's.

Vande Berg, L. R., Wenner, L. A., & Gronbeck, B. E. (1998). *Critical approaches to television.* Boston: Houghton Mifflin.

WORKSHEET FOR MASS MEDIA MYTH #6

(See Chapter 6 for details of *Dr. Galician's Seven-Step* Dis-*illusioning Directions*.)

The man should NOT be shorter, weaker, younger, poorer, or less successful than the woman.

R$_x$: CREATE COEQUALITY; COOPERATE.

Title of Your Analysis & Criticism

Your Thesis

STEP 1. DETECTION (finding/identifying)

Identification (title, date, and medium, with "markers")

Entire work/specific segment

STEP 2. DESCRIPTION (illustrating/exemplifying)

Detailed description

Creator; creator's purpose

Function/purpose (entertainment/news and information/persuasion) and genre

STEP 3. DECONSTRUCTION (analyzing)

Underlying myths/stereotypes (primary/secondary)

Evidence for linking myths/stereotypes; specific examples of content (message) and form (medium) that represent embedded values

Significant omissions

Cited commentary/research

STEP 4. DIAGNOSIS (evaluating/criticizing)

Meaning and possible interpretations (preferred and oppositional)

Comparison with rational models

Possible effects (harm)

Expert citations

Judgment/evaluation

STEP 5. DESIGN (reconstructing/reframing)

Realistic reframing

Related theories and rational models

Likelihood of use

Existing reconstructions

STEP 6. DEBRIEFING (reconsidering/remedying)

Personal impact of *dis*-illusioning; comparison of personal belief before/after, including enjoyment

Personal harm from myth

STEP 7. DISSEMINATION (publishing/broadcasting)

Advocacy action plan

Timetable of specific activities (personal/public/professional)

13

DR. FUN'S MASS MEDIA LOVE QUIZ
MYTH #7

The love of a good and faithful true woman can change a man from a "beast" into a "prince."

Dr. Galician's Prescription™ #7
R$_x$: CEASE CORRECTING AND CONTROLLING; YOU CAN'T CHANGE OTHERS (ONLY YOURSELF).

You make me want to be a better man.
> — Jack Nicholson (as Melvin) to Helen Hunt (as Carol)
in their award-winning performances in *As Good As It Gets* (1997)

Here's a story of a real person[1] who — once upon a time — believed this myth and, as a result, did *not* live very happily-ever-after.

[Stevie, 10-year-old male fifth grader]

In the movie *The Beauty and the Beast,* Belle changed the Beast into a prince because she was nice, skinny, and pretty. I'd change, too, for a girl as pretty as Belle.

Here's an older and wiser view:

[Danielle, 43-year-old female English teacher, mother of two]

Although I'd always been a kind of a "goody-goody" who avoided drugs, I was drawn to Spencer because it seemed like he needed my help. We were both college students, but he was on the "wrong track" — smoking pot, shooting heroine, partying "hard core." I thought I could help him recover. All I wanted was to be his guardian angel, the one he looked back on and thought, "Where could I be without her?" Media toyed with my mind and tricked me into believing I could change Spencer into a better person and call that love. I thought I could be like Katherine Hepburn in *The African Queen* — changing Humphrey Bogart from a crusty old guy living in a boat with no use for women into someone who stops smoking, bathes more often, and treats her the way a good woman should be treated. And all

---

[1]Names have been changed to protect individuals' privacy.

because he falls in love with her. If she could do it, why couldn't I? I found out to my sorrow that I couldn't fix Spencer the way Katherine fixed Humphrey!

And one even more disastrous true story:

[Francine, a 34-year-old female dental assistant]

Growing up, I was always attracted to the "bad boys." I liked the challenge they presented. Nice guys were a waste of time because it took only a day to figure them out. At a college fraternity party, I met Chuck, who was 23. I was just 19. He was a cocky jerk, which really attracted me, of course. He charmed me into sleeping with him, and then he didn't call for two weeks. All of a sudden, he called and sweet-talked me into sleeping with him again. Then silence. This pattern continued. I thought it could be like in the fairy tales, where I could change him and make him mine. One night I finally got upset about his running around with other women. I confronted him. My hopes for fairy tale transformations ended when he took me outside and hit me in the face — and broke my nose!

ADDITIONAL RESEARCH & COMMENTARY RELATED TO THIS MASS MEDIA MYTH

In real life — unlike in mass media narratives — people can and do change for the better, but only if and when they themselves choose to do so and make a serious, concerted effort demonstrated in long-term behavior — *not* merely because their partner is good and wonderful. We might like to think we're powerful enough to transform a wayward partner, but while we can perhaps motivate and then support those who'd like to improve, we are not magicians. (It's hard enough to make changes in ourselves. Of course, trying to change others also keeps our attention focused away from the more difficult job of our *self*-improvement.)

> **Male and Female University Students' Responses to This *Quiz* Item**
>
> Men are split nearly 50/50 on whether the love of a good and true woman can change a man from a beast to a prince (with slightly more males in agreement with this myth). More women disagree (60%) than agree (40%). So here's a myth about which the majority of the men as a group differ from the majority of women as a group.

This disturbing myth, inherent in so many ancient fables and modern-day mediated fairy tales, glorifies codependency — a dangerous model closely related to the rescue theme in the sexual stereotyping of Myth #6 as well as the mistaken belief that we are incomplete without a partner, who can fill our needs and make our dreams come true (Myth #10).

As Lazarus cautioned in his *Marital Myths,* we can't change others, so we should carefully select those who don't need much changing.

The concept of a lowlife's miraculous rehabilitation and recovery brought about by the saintly behavior of a loving romantic partner is indeed — as Disney's *Beauty and the Beast* theme song informs us — a "tale as old as time." Typically, it's a sweet young girl whose goodness contagiously influences an ogre and magically transforms him into a prince — figuratively or even literally. It could even be a sweet young dog, like Disney's *Lady* who tames not a beast but a *Tramp.* Less frequently, there's a gender role reversal, with a princely character converting a real b_ _ _ _ (rhymes with "witch") into a princess.

The classic is *Beauty and the Beast* (popularized in the chap books of Europe's early printing presses) — but the story goes back thousands of years to the earliest documented epic, *Gilgamesh* (see Chapter 2). The courtly love tradition embroidered the theme, focusing on the civilizing power the chaste idealized lady love could have on the rough knights of the time who developed genuine chivalric *courtesy.*

One of the most hazardous aspects of this myth is its perversion of the simplistic notion that someone fine and good can effect positive changes in a loved one to a more complex concept related to a great deal of domestic abuse. As noted in Chapter 2's discussion of the changing dysfunctional roles — victim, rescuer, and persecutor — in the Karpman Drama Triangle (Karpman, 1968), if the "good" person *doesn't* change the "bad" person for the better, the irrational view is that it must be because the good person just isn't good *enough.* Moreover, the bad person's behavior might even be occasioned by the good person's behavior. Therefore, the good person should try even harder.

But we're not Avis — and we should never tolerate being treated like "number two." Sadly this irrational thinking can enable a great deal of abuse that many "good" partners — men as well as women — mistakenly believe they deserve and should accept because they've been brainwashed by the mass media's pathetic portrayals.

Portrayals of this myth might be useful if we interpret them metaphorically — as archetypal depictions of the struggle of good and evil *within* oneself, with the hope that our own good side will ultimately triumph over the baser side.[2] The rational model invites us to achieve the personal wholeness and integration of the "Syzygy" (Divine Couple) and, ultimately, of the "Self," which Jung described as the prime goal of human development.

In addition to their potential great danger, a troubling aspect of most media portrayals of this myth is that the "beast" (male or female) is always depicted as a particularly mean and abusive character who should be loved because there's a tiny morsel of goodness buried somewhere in there that the "good" partner should be perceptive and patient enough to discover and tease out — thus putting the burden on the good person rather than the bad one. Astonishingly, the beast is rarely drawn as merely a physically less-than-appealing character who should be loved despite an unfortunate appearance. Unfortunately, the homely guy or the overweight girl whose inner beauty deserves to be recognized and appreciated rarely find true love and live happily after[3] — though the psychopaths too frequently do.

Most of us aren't professional therapists. Even professional therapists aren't always successful in helping abusers and other antisocial individuals change their behavior. From the simplistic and simple-minded messages in so many media narratives today, however, you'd think these mental health professionals just aren't

---

[2]Whenever Disney's Donald Duck was torn between an immoral and moral choice, his decision-making process was often visualized on the screen by the materialization of two mini-Donalds: the "bad" Donald (in devil attire) hovering over one of Donald's shoulders, shouting encouragement of the bad behavior in one of Donald's ears and competing with the "good" Donald (in angel attire) hovering over the other shoulder and, more politely but just as firmly, urging him in his other ear to take the high road.

[3]A rare exception is one of my all-time favorite movies — *The Enchanted Cottage* (1945). Dorothy McGuire and Robert Young portray a pair of outcasts whose drabness (hers) and physical disfigurement (his, a war injury) "drive them away from the society that labels them as unattractive" (as the video container explains). They come to know each other and eventually marry, spending their honeymoon in a magical English cottage where — suddenly transformed by the power of true love — they no longer see each other as the insensitive world does. Instead they see only the beauty of their souls. I admit it's a tear-jerker. (I also admit that I cry at the sentimental ending every time I view it.) And though it's a fantasy, it's far more effective and honest than *Shallow Hal's* depiction of the physical attractiveness theme (see Chapter 11).

doing their jobs properly if they're not effecting changes as miraculously as inventors' daughters (Disney's *Beauty and the Beast*) or waitresses and dogs (*As Good As It Gets*) or beautiful wives who stand by their man as he cures himself of schizophrenia by simply deciding to do so (*A Beautiful Mind*).

DIS-ILLUSIONING THIS MYTH

A Crucial Step: Debriefing *Beauty and the Beast*

A complete 8-page formal analysis and criticism of this myth — as manifested in the 1997 movie *As Good As It Gets* — is provided in Appendix B, so we'll focus here on what I consider a crucial *debriefing* of this myth in its archetypal form in Disney's *Beauty and the Beast.* A similar debriefing could be applied to other portrayals of this myth.

I myself enjoyed the stirring musical score and magical personifications in Disney's animated 1991 version of *Beauty and the Beast.* (I particularly liked "Lumiere" — a great wordplay not only on the French word for "light" but also on the name of the French movie pioneers, The Lumiere Brothers). However, I think adults whose children see this impressive and influential movie should debrief them. (Debriefing should *always* follow deceptions immediately.) The debriefing should clarify that in the real world, Belle might get the same broken nose — or worse — that "Francine" got for her efforts at trying to reform a real-life beastly individual (as described in a case study at the beginning of this chapter).

My debriefing of *Beauty and the Beast* would go something like this:

ADULT: Weren't the songs delightful?

CHILD: Yes.

ADULT: Did you like Belle?

CHILD: Yes. (Note to adult for a supplementary discussion: It's not good enough for the romantic heroine to be merely beautiful — with the typical Disney nine-inch waist — and good to the point of being a doormat. She also has to be highly intelligent, as evidenced by her passion for books.)

ADULT: What should Belle really have asked the cupboards and dishes?

CHILD: I don't know....

ADULT: How to get the heck out of that castle — because we can't change other people no matter how good we are or how beautiful we are (or how many books we read). We can encourage them and suggest better pathways to them. And we can support them in their sincere efforts at long-term demonstrated self-improvement. But when someone is so clearly abusive, he (or she) could be very dangerous. A promise made to such a Beast does NOT have to be honored! And unless the troubled person is in some sort of therapeutic program run by professionals and is showing sustained progress, we need to remove ourselves from their presence as fast as possible. This could save your life.

CHILD: But isn't that deserting a friend?

ADULT: No. Abusers are *not* your friends. Besides, there are lots of really nice people in the world who will appreciate you and treat you very nicely — particularly if you're a good person. And you don't necessarily have to be beautiful (though it's nice for you if you read a lot of books). Aren't these *nice* people far more deserving of your time and attention?

By the way, Disney's stage-play version does a better job than the movie at showing some motivated behavioral change in the Beast. And Jean Cocteau's 1946 black-and-white film classic (*La Belle et La Bete*) with French superstar Jean Marais as a different kind of beast is visually stunning and by far the finest reading of the old tale, which has many different versions. (Don't bring the children to this one!)

Dr. FUN's Realistic Romance™ Awards Nomination: 28 Days

The title *28 Days* (2000) signifies the length of the sentence Sandra Bullock's alcoholic character must serve at a rehab facility for her DUI conviction. (She got drunk at her sister's wedding and ruined it.) After going through a realistic denial phase, she digs in and determines to change her life.

It's the last scene that qualifies this film and Bullock's performance for this nomination. Back home in Manhattan after her month in rehab, she's committed to staying sober. A dinner date with her nonreformed boyfriend/former drinking buddy turns into his attempt to drag her back to the old ways. When it becomes apparent that he's not going to join in her healthy transformation, she leaves the restaurant. He follows her into the street, where he tries to persuade her to return. When that fails, he tries to offer his support.

What's so good about the ending of this scene — which is the end of the movie — is that it doesn't paint these two lovers as black-and-white cartoons. It's clear that he loves her. It's also clear that he's not as strong as she's become after her life-altering 28 days. Without recrimination and with gentleness, Bullock says "Good-bye, Jasper" and walks away. She's focused on fixing herself. She doesn't try to change him. She doesn't jump on the Drama Triangle. This wise character knows that Myth #7 works only in the movies.

Additional Mass Media Manifestations of This Myth to *Dis*-illusion

Books

Beauty and the Beast
The Frog Prince
Jane Eyre
Most romantic novels

Movies

The African Queen
American Pie
A Beautiful Mind
Cocktail
Cruel Intentions
Grease
Happy Gilmore
Jerry Maguire
Moulin Rouge

Pillow Talk
Overboard
Pretty Woman
Sound of Music
Sweet November

Recorded Music

As Long As He Needs Me
Beauty and the Beast
Stand By Your Man

Television

90210
Melrose Place
Home Improvement
Party of Five

DIS-ILLUSION DIGEST

Dr. FUN's Mass Media Love Quiz Myth #7

THE LOVE OF A GOOD AND FAITHFUL TRUE WOMAN CAN CHANGE A MAN FROM A "BEAST" INTO A "PRINCE."

Children who see *Beauty and the Beast* should be warned that Belle's attempts to reform her captor would be most unwise in real life. We cannot change others — especially not abusive "heroes" (or "heroines") who have some good inside if only their partner can be "good enough" to bring it out. (And if the beastly individual — male or female — *doesn't* change, it's made to seem that it's because the good partner just isn't being "good" *enough!*) This fallacy, which scripts unhealthy roles for both the fixer and the fixee, underlies domestic violence.

Dr. Galician's Prescription™ #7

CEASE CORRECTING AND CONTROLLING; YOU CAN'T CHANGE OTHERS (ONLY YOURSELF).

SOURCES CITED

Karpman, S. (1968). Fairy tales and script drama analysis. *Transactional Analysis Bulletin, 7* (26), 39–43.

Lazarus, A.A. (1985). *Marital myths: Two dozen mistaken beliefs that can ruin a marriage or make a bad one worse.* San Luis Obispo, CA: Impact.

WORKSHEET FOR MASS MEDIA MYTH #7

(See Chapter 6 for details of *Dr. Galician's Seven-Step* Dis-illusioning Directions.)

The love of a good and faithful true woman can change a man from a "beast" into a "prince."

R_x: CEASE CORRECTING and CONTROLLING; you CAN'T CHANGE others (only yourself).

Title of Your Analysis & Criticism

Your Thesis

STEP 1. DETECTION (finding/identifying)

Identification (title, date, and medium, with "markers")

Entire work/specific segment

STEP 2. DESCRIPTION (illustrating/exemplifying)

Detailed description

Creator; creator's purpose

Function/purpose (entertainment/news and information/persuasion) and genre

STEP 3. DECONSTRUCTION (analyzing)

Underlying myths/stereotypes (primary/secondary)

Evidence for linking myths/stereotypes; specific examples of content (message) and form (medium) that represent embedded values

Significant omissions

Cited commentary/research

STEP 4. DIAGNOSIS (evaluating/criticizing)

Meaning and possible interpretations (preferred and oppositional)

Comparison with rational models

Possible effects (harm)

Expert citations

Judgment/evaluation

STEP 5. DESIGN (reconstructing/reframing)

Realistic reframing

Related theories and rational models

Likelihood of use

Existing reconstructions

STEP 6. DEBRIEFING (reconsidering/remedying)

Personal impact of *dis*-illusioning; comparison of personal belief before/after, including enjoyment

Personal harm from myth

STEP 7. DISSEMINATION (publishing/broadcasting)

Advocacy action plan

Time table of specific activities (personal/public/professional)

14

DR. FUN'S MASS MEDIA LOVE QUIZ MYTH #8

Bickering and fighting a lot mean that a man and a woman really love each other passionately.

Dr. Galician's Prescription™ #8
R_x: COURTESY COUNTS: CONSTANT CONFLICTS CREATE CHAOS.

For aught that I could ever read
Could ever hear by tale or history
The course of true love never did run smooth.
> —William Shakespeare, *A Midsummer Night's Dream*

Here's a story of a real person[1] who —once upon a time —believed this myth and, as a result, did *not* live very happily-ever-after.

[Sara, twenty-something university student, female]

I was greatly influenced by *When Harry Met Sally*. I thought that it was okay, if not perfectly normal, for couples to fight like that. When I first met my boyfriend Tom I was under the false assumption that Sally's behavior was the "right" way to act. I was cold and sharp with him. I thought this would show my true feelings and he would know how much I cared. I even told my friends that I couldn't stand him, thinking that all this would make him like me more. I would pick apart things that he did that I disagreed with. I assumed that all the heated arguments we had meant that there was a lot of passion and chemistry between us. I wanted to be like Sally in the end and get my best friend to be the love of my life....

Here's another one:

[Serena, 19-year-old female college student]

As I watched the movie *Speechless*, I knew that despite Geena Davis and Michael Keaton's constant bickering, they would fall in love. That's the way it always happens in novels and movies: The man and woman meet, fight, and fall in love. Fighting makes their attraction stronger and all the more perfect when they finally

---

[1]Names have been changed to protect individuals' privacy.

185

end up together. Ted and I fought from the beginning. The perfect formula for love, right? We fought about what movie to see, what party to go to, where to go for breakfast/lunch/dinner. Everything. But I mistook this constant bickering for a form of true love. I thought, "We fight because we love each other. We make each other angry enough to fight, so we must have strong feelings for one another. If we never fought, it would mean we lacked true passion for one another."

It never occurred to me that if we didn't fight constantly, it might be the sign of a *healthy* relationship! So anytime I felt insecure or "unloved" I'd find something to fight over. Ted's willingness to fight back reassured me that fighting was getting us nowhere. I don't know exactly what happened, but I wanted more from the relationship — something more than the bickering and fighting. Ted, of course, couldn't understand this. He resorted to fighting with me about the way I'd "changed"! I admit that I had to fight the urge to fight back! Instead, I ended the relationship. Now I'm in a very *healthy* relationship with someone else: We don't fight; we disagree and argue, which is fine. I realize now that fighting was the only bond that Ted and I shared.

A male viewpoint:

[Darren, 20-ish male college student]

The classic sitcom *Cheers* is one of my all-time favorites. Like Sam and Diane, I was in a rocky relationship, except ours wasn't peppered with great one-liners. Nevertheless, I thought that constant fighting was how an exciting couple communicated their intense feelings for each other, like in *Cheers*. Turns out constant fighting is part of relationships — dysfunctional ones! We broke up, but first we wasted a lot of time and energy trying to live up to what looked so exciting and romantic on television.

ADDITIONAL RESEARCH & COMMENTARY RELATED TO THIS MASS MEDIA MYTH

This myth is so pervasive in mediated portrayals of romantic love that it's almost a tradition of the romantic genre, whether print or electronic. And in real life many couples misinterpret their own parallel too-frequent conflict as a sign of interest and involvement in each other and in the relationship, as did "Sara," "Serena," and "Darren" along with many others I've interviewed and observed. One of my research participants reported:

> **Male and Female University Students' Responses to This *Quiz* Item**
>
> Nearly all the respondents (around 90%) of both sexes say they disagree with the notion that bickering and fighting mean that a man and a woman really love each other passionately. Slightly more men than women say they agree with this myth.

I found myself irrationally slapping my best friend/fiancé because of the media images I've seen — such as in *Indiana Jones and the Temple of Doom*. The heroine Willie constantly argues with Dr. Jones and even slaps him, but by the end of this tale, they love each other despite the bickering, fighting, and even the physical assault. Movies like this send out the wrong signals, telling couples it's O.K. and even kinda cute to fight all the time, and that it's a sign of love.

Like Willie, Sally of *When Harry Met Sally* slaps Harry's face in a pivotal and memorable scene in which they argue in a hotel kitchen at a New Year's Eve party. In real life, such actions are likely to result in the man returning the woman's slap — and physical violence can escalate. These are not comic behaviors, and they shouldn't be offered as the solution to conflict.

Don't confuse unhealthy dramatic bickering and fighting with healthy respectful disagreement, which is a sign of the open communication and safety of the intimacy component of love. However, experts don't view constant conflict as a sign of passion but as a danger signal that accurately predicts the high likelihood of the failure of a coupleship.

Northwestern University Medical School psychiatry professor Richard Carroll (as cited in Bertagnoli, 2001) has called conflict resolution "the most important survival tool a couple has" (p. E1). Researcher-therapist John Gottman and his colleagues have found that satisfied married couples had five positive interactions to every one negative interaction whereas couples who are very dissatisfied with their relationships typically engage in more negative interactions than positive (Gottman, 1994). Verbally complimenting and encouraging one another is what works best, not sparring.

On the other hand, some people confuse the heightened emotions engendered by fighting with the heightened emotions of passion. (Remember the *misattribution of arousal* theory discussed in Chapter 3.) Also, for some people, chaos is more exciting than peaceful normalized interaction. Perhaps that's why the mating rituals of the more primitive and physical Klingons in *Star Trek* — a series rife with mythical themes, many of which are inspiring, others of which are satiric — include biting and fighting like some animal species on Earth (and not unlike the rituals of the ancient *Kama Sutra*).

Sociobiologists have theorized that early female behavior of playing hard to get could have signaled great desirability, tested individual male willingness to invest resources, and communicated a promise of fidelity (Buss, 1994). But that's a theory of primitive behavior that's not appropriate in the 21st century.

Nevertheless, one reason we see the formulaic and utterly predictable "battle of the sexes" so widely depicted in 21st century media is that conflict is a dramatic necessity — even (and especially) for the news. We know that conflict sells. We know that sex sells. How hard do you think it is to sell a combination of these two appealing and exciting factors?

DIS-ILLUSIONING THIS MYTH

William Shakespeare and Jane Austen wrote clever bantering and bickering dialog for their romantic characters that was amusing and also served to diffuse or replace their sexual tension. But at a certain point in the plot, the verbal sparring gave way to peaceful resolution that seemed motivated. In more modern media, these battles of the sexes have become disturbingly nastier and dangerously more physical. Often, manifestations of this myth are linked to differences in values (Myth #9). As pathetic as these demonstrations are, they're usually shorthand for a kind of convolution of Myth #2 (love at first sight), with the instant "hate at first sight" signaling an equivalent fated passion (Myth #1) that we know will be resolved by the end of the romance novel, movie, or television show.

When Is Enough Really Enough? *The Mexican*

A recent movie takes this myth to the extreme. In *The Mexican* (2001) Brad Pitt portrays Jerry, the boyfriend of Julia Roberts' character Sam. They're ready to leave for Las Vegas to commit to a new life together. However, to settle his long-term debt to the mob and save his skin, Jerry must complete one last job: Retrieving a legendary gun called "The Mexican." (An early clue to the subtext here is that, according to its legend, the gun is cursed by the spirit of a Juliet-like individual whom not even death could separate from her "Romeo.")

As the weapon is in Mexico, this job conflicts with the couple's planned trip. Sam — apparently oblivious of the consequences to Jerry if he fails to obey the gangsters' orders — threatens to end their relationship if he goes to Mexico. Although he promised to go to Las Vegas after completing his mob assignment, this argument escalates into a major battle (underscored with battle music) that ends with Sam flying into a tantrum and throwing Jerry's belongings out of their second story window.

He goes to Mexico and she heads for Vegas alone, but she's captured and made a hostage by a mob henchman (HBO *Sopranos* star James Gandolfini) as insurance for Jerry's return with the goods. Sam even complains about Jerry to her captor.

Near the end of the movie, the couple is finally reunited at an airport in Mexico, where they immediately commence their non-productive disagreements, consisting mainly of blaming and name-calling. Alternately, they refuse to communicate at all. Sam is understandably upset that Jerry has just shot and killed the kidnapper, who had become her friend and romantic advisor. (Why hasn't Jerry's "profession" bothered her until now?) It appears this combative couple is finally ready to call it quits.

Sam leaves Jerry to board a plane to return home. Dramatic melancholy music begins and rises — suggesting that Sam is gone forever. In fact, this is not a particularly sad ending in rational terms, but it's certainly not a Hollywood ending. So something miraculous (and utterly unmotivated) happens: The sad music halts, and Sam suddenly appears from behind a luggage cart.

> "I'm gonna ask you a question," she says to Jerry, holding back the tears. "It's a good one, so think about it."

> They move closer to each other, exchanging earnest looks.

> "If two people love each other, but they just can't seem to get it together, when do you get to that point of 'enough is enough'?"

> "Never," he answers almost immediately — pausing long enough only for the requisite slow zoom-in and apparently ignoring Sam's advice yet again.

After a dramatic pause, they embrace. The camera zooms out, and we know they will stay together, continuing their never-resolved arguments until the bitter end.

This movie easily earns a nomination for *Dr. FUN's Stupid Cupid Awards.* Its sudden "happy" ending makes no sense whatsoever in terms of character development — although ironically it describes many dysfunctional relationships. Sadly, the preferred reading reinforces the irrational thinking that keeps real people stuck in these destructive kinds of relationships.

Why might some readers of this mass media text accept the preferred reading (that these people really love each other because they stay together despite their dreadful behavior to each other)? And how could anyone believe that such "passionate" behavior signifies that they love each other?

For many of us, the desire to believe the message encapsulated in the next chapter's myth (#9) — all you need is love — is so great that we want to see it depicted in the mass media and in real life, whatever the consequences. It's disturbing that such influential superstars appear in this movie, which could persuade certain vulnerable people to accept the unhealthy and dangerous behavior normalized by this film.

In mass media mythology, enough is never enough. In the real world, these abusive relationships often end when one partner seriously batters or even kills the other.

Dr. FUN's Realistic Romance™ Awards Nomination: *The Light*

This song — from the *Like Water for Chocolate* album (2000) by the hip hop artist Common (formerly known as Common Sense) — was nominated as a powerful reframing of Myth #4 (Chapter 10). It also speaks wisely to Myth #8:

> Yo, yo, check it: It's important, we communicate
> And tune the fate of this union, to the right pitch.
> I never call you my bitch or even my boo —
> There's so much in a name and so much more in you.

It's a pity that characters like *The Mexican*'s Sam and Jerry don't take this musical advice to heart.

Additional Mass Media Manifestations of This Myth to *Dis*-illusion

Books

Much Ado About Nothing
Price and Prejudice
Wuthering Heights

Movies

Addicted to Love
As Good As It Gets
Bridget Jones's Diary
Cutting Edge
Far & Away
Gone with the Wind
Indiana Jones
    & The Temple of Doom
The Marrying Man
Most Tracy-Hepburn
    and Hudson-Day movies
One Fine Day
Only You
The Quiet Man
Romancing the Stone
Speechless

Taming of the Shrew
When Harry Met Sally
You've Got Mail!

Recorded Music

Anything You Can Do
    (I Can Do Better)
I Hate You Then I Love You

Television

90210
Cheers
Ed
Friends
I Love Lucy
Jeffersons
Mad About You
Married with Children
Martin
Melrose Place
Moonlighting
Saved by the Bell

DIS-ILLUSION DIGEST

Dr. FUN's Mass Media Love Quiz Myth #8

BICKERING AND FIGHTING A LOT MEAN THAT
A MAN AND A WOMAN REALLY LOVE EACH OTHER PASSIONATELY.

Almost invariably in mass media, a male and female who take an instant strong dislike to each other will (eventually) discover that they're "made for each other" — despite their continual contests that sometimes even become dangerously physical. Respectful disagreement is healthy, but these constant combatants need conflict-resolution training. Don't confuse fighting with passion: Love is about peace, not war.

Dr. Galician's Prescription™ #8

COURTESY COUNTS: CONSTANT CONFLICTS CREATE CHAOS.

SOURCES CITED

Bertagnoli, L. (2001, July 11). Expert tells engaged pairs to talk tough. *Arizona Republic,* p. E1.

Buss, D. M. (1994). *The evolution of desire: Strategies of human mating.* New York: Basic Books.

Carroll, D. (1999, October 12). Seminar leader zeroes in on actions that kill marriage: "Love skills" help couples to achieve intimacy. *Arizona Republic,* pp. D1–D2.]

Gottman, J. M. (1994). *Why marriages succeed or fail.* New York: Simon & Schuster.

Shakespeare, W. (n.d.). *A midsummer night's dream.* In W. G. Clark & W. A. Wright (Eds.), The complete works of William Shakespeare: Vol. I (pp. 125–145). Garden City, NY: Nelson Doubleday.

WORKSHEET FOR MASS MEDIA MYTH #8

(See Chapter 6 for details of *Dr. Galician's Seven-Step* Dis-illusioning Directions.)

Bickering and fighting a lot mean that a man and a woman really love each other passionately.

Rₓ: COURTESY COUNTS: CONSTANT CONFLICTS CREATE CHAOS.

Title of Your Analysis & Criticism

Your Thesis

STEP 1. DETECTION (finding/identifying)

Identification (title, date, and medium, with "markers")

Entire work/specific segment

STEP 2. DESCRIPTION (illustrating/exemplifying)

Detailed description

Creator; creator's purpose

Function/purpose (entertainment/news and information/persuasion) and genre

STEP 3. DECONSTRUCTION (analyzing)

Underlying myths/stereotypes (primary/secondary)

Evidence for linking myths/stereotypes; specific examples of content (message) and form (medium) that represent embedded values

Significant omissions

Cited commentary/research

STEP 4. DIAGNOSIS (evaluating/criticizing)

Meaning and possible interpretations (preferred and oppositional)

Comparison with rational models

Possible effects (harm)

Expert citations

Judgment/evaluation

STEP 5. DESIGN (reconstructing/reframing)

Realistic reframing

Related theories and rational models

Likelihood of use

Existing reconstructions

STEP 6. DEBRIEFING (reconsidering/remedying)

Personal impact of *dis*-illusioning; comparison of personal belief before/after, including enjoyment

Personal harm from myth

STEP 7. DISSEMINATION (publishing/broadcasting)

Advocacy action plan

Timetable of specific activities (personal/public/professional)

15

DR. FUN'S MASS MEDIA LOVE QUIZ
MYTH #9

All you really need is love,
so it doesn't matter if you and your lover
have very different values.

Dr. Galician's Prescription™ #9
R_x: CRAVE COMMON CORE-VALUES.

All you need is love (All together, now!)
All you need is love. (Everybody!)
All you need is love, love.
Love is all you need (love is all you need).
>   — John Lennon and Paul McCartney, *All You Need Is Love*

Here's a story of a real person[1] who — once upon a time — believed this myth and, as a result, did *not* live very happily-ever-after.

[Bettina, 20-something female college student]

Tony and Angela made it work on *Who's the Boss?* Molly Ringwald and Judd Nelson heated up the screen with *The Breakfast Club.* Even Dewey and Gail from *Scream* seemed to be happy. So I thought Billy and I could make it, too, After all, we loved each other, despite our very different values and lifestyles. He smoked, and the mere smell revolts me. He got Fs; I got As. He wanted to be a mechanic; I was going to own NBC. You name it, and our preferences were exactly opposite. Try sitting in a car while I'm trying to play Garth Brooks and Billy's blaring White Zombie.

After three months of inhaling second-hand smoke and watching him avoid the simplest tasks while I acted like Superwoman, I'd had enough. Forget all my TV friends who make it look so easy to bridge the values gap. You need more than love to make things work. You need a few common values and goals.

Here's a similar case:

---

[1]Names have been changed to protect individuals' privacy.

[Angela, 25-year-old female lawyer]

"Opposites attract," I insisted when everyone (including my family) told me my marriage to Zach wouldn't work. I was a law school graduate; he was a drop-out. I was ambitious; he had no goals. When we divorced after 6 months, I wondered what made me think I could have had a successful marriage with someone like Zach. It hit me that I'd been brainwashed by movies that showed couples whose great love overcame the barriers of their totally different backgrounds and values: *Pretty Woman, Romeo and Juliet, Titanic, Mad Love, Notting Hill.* But what works in the movies doesn't work in real life.

ADDITIONAL RESEARCH & COMMENTARY
RELATED TO THIS MASS MEDIA MYTH

Many participants in my research have cited differences in lifestyles, in religious beliefs, and in goals as well as disparities in financial and educational levels as impassable barriers to what seemed at first to be potentially successful coupleships. In real life, they lament, it's just not like in novels or movies — where *opposites attract* and *love conquers all.* Lazarus (1985) advised: Although short-term flings with people who are very different can be quite exciting, and *some* difference can be enriching and stimulating, *long-term relationships usually flourish when similarity rather than dissimilarity prevails.*

> **Male and Female University Students' Responses to This *Quiz* Item**
>
> While the majority of men (around 70%) and women (88%) say they disagree with the idea that all you need is love (so it doesn't matter if you have very different values), a large minority of men (almost a third) *do* agree with this myth whereas only a small minority of women (around 12%) agree with it.

But just look at the message of some popular culture cinematic blockbusters: From *Romeo and Juliet* to *Pretty Woman* to *Titanic* to *Something About Mary,* we're encouraged to believe that two people with vastly different values and lifestyles will easily function as a couple. Love will blur their differences. In *R&J* and *Titanic,* it's easy: These folks don't live past the courtship stage, in which different values are easy to overlook. And *Pretty Woman* and *Something About Mary* both end "on the street where you live" (that is, where the woman lives). We never see these couples actually *living* a real life together.

Can you imagine a real-life dinner party mixing the on-the-street friends of the *Pretty Woman* hooker with her millionaire Wall Street boyfriend's polo set? If you recall, no genuine transformation took place in either Richard Gere's character or Julia Roberts'. She goes back to her life with her drug-abusing friends, and he remains a wound-up workaholic. (But why would we expect this movie to present a more realistic model, when those aren't even Julia's real legs? They belong to a body double.) Or how about a medical society luncheon attended by *Something's* Dr. Mary and her dopey (albeit sweet) Ted?

The literature is very clear about the importance of shared interests and values. Antoine de Saint-Exupery (who wrote *The Little Prince*) said it more poetically: "Life has taught us that love does not consist of gazing at each other but in looking outward together in the same direction."

When romantic partners share values, mutual respect naturally flows. When they don't, it's hard for them to respect where the other one is spending time and money. It's confusing and hurtful when what's important to one isn't to the other. Resentments can build — as one partner or the other begins to wear masks and play roles that are inauthentic. Again, think of how difficult it would be for *Pretty*

Woman's or *Mary*'s partners to be "themselves" at gatherings with the friends and family of their partner.

What's also important in realistic romance is appreciating and enjoying each other's friends. If you dislike the majority of your partner's friends, that's a red-flag that should signal the need for examination of your partner's appropriateness for you (or your readiness for romance).

Of course, making sure that your values are congruent requires that you know what your values are rather than looking to a partner to lead you and supply you with a sense of direction and morality. In short, it requires you to be unconflicted in your own life. In the annals of mental health and successful coupleship, this can make for exciting reading. However, in dramatic terms, this can be rather boring. So the media rarely portray it.

Remember the one acknowledged drawback of the peer couples in Schwartz's (1994) research? They are so attuned — so much like a brother and sister — that they sometimes lack the tension and mystery that *lust* thrives on. Katz and Liu (1988) similarly described the irony of even very young couples who shared interests and goals:

> The assumption was that friends knew each other too well, shared too much, were too honest — in short, there was not enough mystery between them. But if they played the stereotypical masculine and feminine game, which essentially meant they had nothing in common, they made a "perfect match." For youngsters, this formula crystallized the illusions that "opposites attract and that lovers cannot be friends." (p. 185)

Compatible couples who share values no doubt seem less exciting in media terms. And when couples share values, they usually also enjoy the approval of their family and their society. This type of relationship flies in the face of mass mediated narrative, which prefers and legitimizes the idea of the contest that is, conveniently, also typically central to infatuation, as in "the Romeo and Juliet effect" discussed in Chapter 3 (Fisher, 1992). Mass media creators far prefer to send the message that love can overcome every barrier, even death. Unfortunately, they literally have to kill off their romantic couples before the end of the narrative — or fade to black at the early stage of commitment — rather than show the more realistic usually not-so-happy endings of short-lived affairs based on the myth that all you need is love.

DIS-ILLUSIONING THIS MYTH

Above All Things, Love: *Moulin Rouge*

The theme of Baz Luhrmanm's Oscar®-nominated *Moulin Rouge* (2001) is printed on a banner hanging at the 19th century Paris nightclub and reiterated by the players throughout the film: "Truth, Freedom, Beauty, and, above all things, Love!"

In this case, the lovers fall in love at first sight and enjoy a brief whirlwind courtship. Idealistic Bohemian writer Christian (Ewan McGregor) is immediately and intensely struck by the courtesan Satine (Nicole Kidman), who dreams of becoming a legitimate actress. He speaks and sings "All You Need Is Love," which is his motif. He's practically penniless, and her livelihood depends on her customers, especially the wealthy and jealous Duke. Nevertheless they give up everything for a few moments of love. Then, like Camille, Satine falls ill and dies — so we don't see what would happen to these two people of different values and backgrounds if they were to become a day-to-day couple (including how her naïve husband would feel about his wife's "profession").

Of course, this spectacular production is a fantasy. (Luhrmann proudly acknowledges in the DVD pamphlet that the basis of this movie — as well as his *Romeo + Juliet* and *Strictly Ballroom* — is a simple myth.) Nevertheless, the glorification of the "Romeo and Juliet" effect in this depiction could be harmful to impressionable audience members.

One question a resistive reader should ask is: How can these characters espouse the first half of their motto (*"Truth, Freedom,* Beauty, and, above all things, Love!"*) with a straight face when they *lie* to each other and are *enslaved* by masters like the Duke?

A Crucial Step: Debriefing *Lady and the Tramp* (1955)

In Disney's 1955 animated classic (with Peggy Lee's outstanding songs) *Lady and the Tramp,* Tramp isn't a prostitute but a street scamp. Nevertheless, like Satine and Pretty Woman, his values and lifestyle are 180 degrees from those of his love interest. Lady is a protected, innocent, and refined lap dog. He's a tramp on the prowl who "breaks a new heart every day," according to one of my favorite songs in the movie. They meet, eat (the famous candlelight dinner where they share a meatball and a kiss), and fall in love. Because of his bad influence, she gets in trouble and is even locked up in the dog pound. But he rescues her, and they "get married" and start a family. (Does he have to change his name to match his new identity?)

The oppositional/resistive reader asks many questions. How would they raise their "children"? They have such differing views of what life is all about and how a pup should behave. What's important to one parent might seem silly to the other. Of course, Lady has already "reformed" Tramp through her good influence (Myth #7). But will he come to resent this? Will they be caught in Karpman's Drama Triangle? What will he do if he finds life as a house dog (with Lady's humans) too confining and longs for the old days on the street? Will domestic life with the pups be too tame an existence?

And what will happen when she see signs of his discontent? Will she feel inadequate if he reverts to his former behavior, despite her efforts to change him into a respectable partner and parent?

In Disney's sugar-coated presentation, none of the logical questions matter because these two dogs love each other. And love is all you need.

As with *Beauty and the Beast* and *The Little Mermaid* and *all* of Disney's fairy tales, children should be debriefed after their exposure to this irrational ideology. It's interesting that parents tend to trust Disney — primarily because there's no foul language or overt sexuality and the storylines seem so sweet. These are important factors in selecting mass media for children, but what's ironic is that most parents don't bother to interrogate the insidious messages their children are getting from these mythic and stereotypic presentations.

Dr. FUN's Realistic Romance™ Awards Nomination: Legally Blonde

In the romantic comedy *Legally Blonde* (2001), Reese Witherspoon portrays Elle Woods, a stereotypical Valley Girl/college sorority president. She's dating East Coast Blue Blood Warner Huntington III. On the very night she thinks he's going to propose, he dumps her because her life style and values don't fit his political ambitions and Harvard Law School, where he'll begin in the fall. But that cruel demonstration of the failure of Myth #9 is not the reason for my nomination. (Nominations are for positive portrayals of healthy relationships that illustrate one or more of the *Prescriptions™*.)

In an effort to win back this unworthy man, Elle transforms herself — and starts the fall semester at Harvard Law, too. She becomes a successful practicing attorney even before passing the bar, turns enemies into friends, and helps a variety of needy people. (It's a fantasy filled with self-mocking humor.) Best of all, she supercedes and dumps Warner because she realizes they truly have different values. (Hers are clearly superior to his.) Instead, she partners with a man (played by Luke Wilson) who shares her idealism and activism. He's a lawyer, too — and her true friend.

Additional Mass Media Manifestations of This Myth to *Dis*-illusion

Books

Aladdin
Love Story
Romeo & Juliet

Movies

Breakfast Club
Cocktail
Fools Rush In
Keeping the Faith
Mad Love
Notting Hill
Overboard
Pocahontas
Pretty Woman
Romeo & Juliet
Scream
Something About Mary
Titanic
West Side Story
You've Got Mail

Recorded Music

All You Need Is Love
Opposites Attract

Television

90210
Dharma & Greg
Melrose Place
Who's the Boss?

DIS-ILLUSION DIGEST

Dr. FUN's Mass Media Love Quiz Myth #9

ALL YOU REALLY NEED IS LOVE, SO IT DOESN'T MATTER IF YOU AND YOUR LOVER HAVE VERY DIFFERENT VALUES.

Opposites frequently attract — but they don't stay together very long *except* in mass media mythology. Can you image a real-life dinner party mixing the streetwalker friends of "Pretty Woman" with the friends of her Wall Street–tycoon boyfriend? Though rarely demonstrated by the mass media, shared values are what form the basis of lasting romantic relationships. A network of mutual friends also helps.

Dr. Galician's Prescription™ #9

CRAVE COMMON CORE-VALUES.

SOURCES CITED

Fisher, H. (1992). *Anatomy of love: A natural history of mating, marriage, and why we stray.* New York: Fawcett Columbine.

Karpman, S. (1968). Fairy tales and script drama analysis. *Transactional Analysis Bulletin, 7*(26), 39–43.

Katz, S. J., & Liu, A. E. (1988). *False love and other romantic illusions.* New York: Pocket Books.

Lazarus, A.A. (1985). *Marital myths: Two dozen mistaken beliefs that can ruin a marriage or make a bad one worse.* San Luis Obispo, CA: Impact.

Schwartz, P. (1994). *Peer marriage: How love between equals really works.* New York: The Free Press.

WORSHEET FOR MASS MEDIA MYTH #9

(See Chapter 6 for details of *Dr. Galician's Seven-Step* Dis-*illusioning Directions.*)

All you really need is love, so it doesn't matter if you and your lover have very different values.

R_x: CRAVE COMMON CORE-VALUES.

Title of Your Analysis & Criticism

Your Thesis

STEP 1. DETECTION (finding/identifying)

Identification (title, date, and medium, with "markers")

Entire work/specific segment

STEP 2. DESCRIPTION (illustrating/exemplifying)

Detailed description

Creator; creator's purpose

Function/purpose (entertainment/news and information/persuasion) and genre

STEP 3. DECONSTRUCTION (analyzing)

Underlying myths/stereotypes (primary/secondary)

Evidence for linking myths/stereotypes; specific examples of content (message) and form (medium) that represent embedded values

Significant omissions

Cited commentary/research

STEP 4. DIAGNOSIS (evaluating/criticizing)

Meaning and possible interpretations (preferred and oppositional)

Comparison with rational models

Possible effects (harm)

Expert citations

Judgment/evaluation

STEP 5. DESIGN (reconstructing/reframing)

Realistic reframing

Related theories and rational models

Likelihood of use

Existing reconstructions

STEP 6. DEBRIEFING (reconsidering/remedying)

Personal impact of *dis*-illusioning; comparison of personal belief before/after, including enjoyment

Personal harm from myth

STEP 7. DISSEMINATION (publishing/broadcasting)

Advocacy action plan

Timetable of specific activities (personal/public/professional)

16

DR. FUN'S MASS MEDIA LOVE QUIZ MYTH #10

The right mate "completes you" — filling your needs and making your dreams come true.

Dr. Galician's Prescription™ #10
R$_x$: CULTIVATE YOUR OWN COMPLETENESS.

Someday my Prince will come....
Some day when my dreams come true.
    — "Snow White," Frank Churchill, *Someday My Prince Will Come*

YOU ... complete me.
    — Jerry Maguire (Tom Cruise) to Dorothy (Renee Zellweger)
                                                    in *Jerry Maguire*

Here's a story of a real person[1] who — once upon a time — believed this myth and, as a result, did *not* live very happily-ever-after:

[Kate, twenty-something female university student, single]

I was so sure of this. I knew that there had to be someone just for me. We would be perfect together, and I would be so happy. I determined this from a very young age. My models were movies like *Sleepless in Seattle* and, well, almost anything with Meg Ryan as the leading lady — from *City of Angels* to *You've Got Mail*. I thought I would find the perfect guy. He would be smart, funny, handsome, everything I could want in a man.

Then I met Scott. He was nice, funny, and smart. He had a lot going for him. But because it wasn't easy or perfect, I was sure that he wasn't the "one" for me.

Here's another person's tale:

---

[1]Names have been changed to protect individuals' privacy.

[Hank, 21-year-old student, male]

I once truly believed that I would meet the perfect person who would fulfill everything I wanted in life. I pictured myself married, with an invisible force field around me that put me on a higher and deeper level of happiness. My view was like a surreal dream. One film that affected me was *The Last of the Mohicans,* based on James Fenimore Cooper's classic love story that says love will prevail. I think I was engulfed by the movie's imagery. The cinematography in the film is gorgeous and the music is sweeping and beautiful. There's a scene that absolutely captures my former belief that the right mate completes me and makes my dreams come true: Hawkeye (played by Daniel Day Lewis) and Cora (the angelic Madeleine Stowe) are gazing up at the stars together.

ADDITIONAL RESEARCH & COMMENTARY
RELATED TO THIS MASS MEDIA MYTH

Sociologist Mary Laner — an expert on dating, courtship, and marriage — suggested that the depersonalization inherent in our mass media society might lead to unrealistically high expectations and individual longings for a close relationship in which one person will satisfy every need — as in the *"Ozzie and Harriet* mythology"[2] (as cited in Blanc, 1994, p. 14). Intellectually, most of us realize that no one else can make us happy or sad, but in our heart we don't always accept that. Lazarus (1985) warned that "one of the most unfortunate errors" people make is surrendering responsibility for their own gratification and fulfillment. As he memorably phrased it:

> Mature love never transforms the other person into "emotional oxygen." A mature person's message is: "I can live with or without you. I much prefer to live with you because I love you. I hope that you feel the same way about me." (p. 87)

Male and Female University Students' Responses to This *Quiz* Item

This myth — "The right mate 'completes you' — filling your needs and making your dreams come true." — is the only myth (of the 12) with which the majority of both sexes *agree.* (Remember it's only the majority of *men* who agree with the myth that sex is easy and wonderful if your partner is really meant for you; the majority of *women* disagree with that one.) Surprisingly, it's the *men* who are *more* likely to believe this one: More than three quarters of the men agree with Myth #10, whereas only slightly more than half of the women agree. In other words, only about 25% of the men disagree with this myth, but nearly half of the women disagree.

I agree, but I can't imagine such a statement in a mass mediated script, can you? And I can't imagine turning on the radio and hearing the revised healthy lyrics (such as "I chose to love you. I must have wanted to do it then, but now I've changed my mind."), which psychologist and author Wayne Dyer (1976) suggested we substitute in place of some of the irrational yet subtly influential statements of some popular songs (such as "I can't live, if living is without you," "You make me so very happy," "You're nobody till somebody cares," and "You make me feel like a natural woman"). Dyer cautioned: "Those sweet harmless lyrics may be more damaging than you realize" (pp. 69–70), but he admitted that his revisions probably wouldn't sell.

Like Lazarus and Dyer, I believe that no one else can make you happy or complete you, and no one else can fill your needs or make your dreams come true. In fact, putting your mate in a straight jacket of unrealistic romanticized expectation

---

[2]A popular network television sit-com (1952-1966) that featured a fictionalized and idealized version of a real-life family — the Nelsons: father Ozzie, mother Harriet, and sons David and Ricky (who became a popular teen recording artist). This long-running family show was in the tradition of *Father Knows Best* and *The Donna Reed Show.* (The Nelsons were the polar opposite of another Ozzy's televised real family — *The Osbournes.*)

can actually have the opposite effect, leading to disappointment and depression. We have only to remember the tragic stories of several contemporary real-life princes and princesses whose seemingly fairytale romances ended in devastating divorce rather than the "happily-ever-afters" the media hype led us to expect.

On the other hand, while the "right mate" can't be your fairy godmother or genie in the lamp, an *appropriate* love partner can be supportive in helping you achieve your goals, which can add to your satisfaction and make your successes and joys all the more delightful and your failures and sorrows less painful.

If you feel you *need* someone to "complete" you, however, you're ironically too "needy" for a relationship. Your condition is like that of an applicant for a bank loan. Strange as it seems, lending institutions tend to give money to people who "don't need it" — that is, to people with appropriate collateral who represent "good risks" for repayment. People who desperately "need" the money are not considered good risks to pay it back.

Many people feel vaguely incomplete without a mate, longing for someone to enter their life, sweep them off their feet, and ensure that they live happily-ever-af-ter. "The End." (I myself used to feel like this.) Nowhere is this dream realized better than in Disney's *Cinderella* (1950). Even though or precisely *because* it's a cartoon ("full-length animated feature"), it presents a powerful image. To the cheering of the happy well-wishers, the prince and his bride (who is now automat-ically a princess) glide down the palace steps and into the royal coach that speeds them off into the sunset to the swells of the stirring song:

> Have faith in dreams and someday your rainbows will come shining through.
> No matter how your heart is grieving, if you'll keep on believing:
> The things that you wish will come true.

And as if *that* weren't enough, the song ends but the music swells even more (As noted in Chapter 4, music is extremely influential.) — da-da-da-DAH!! — as a book materializes out of nowhere with the page opened to "And they lived happily-ever-after." and then — da-da-da-da-DAH!!! — "The End" — da-da-da-DAH!!!!!

Little girls are conditioned to want the dream in that Disney cartoon or on that page of the *Little Golden Books* as much as little boys are later conditioned to want the dreams suggested by the "Miss September" centerfold page or "adult" movies.

"Having faith in dreams" is a nice idea. (Being a critic doesn't mean being a cynic.) But we need to do something more than "keep on believing" to make the things that we *wish* come true. As my father — a kind of folk poet — used to say: "Wishes won't wash the dishes."

But first, you have to complete yourself. *Then* you become eligible for that "bank loan." It's not that you ever become perfected or truly complete or fully "ac-tualized." Rather, you must move well beyond the poverty of the soul called "neediness." (Actually, it's more accurately termed "wantiness." We don't *need* a romantic partner; it's just that having an appropriate one is a marvelous enhance-ment — comparable to the frosting on the cake. But frosting without the cake can be pretty sickening, can't it?)

With all due respect to Plato and his hermaphroditic creatures, two incom-plete people do *not* make a whole person (in the old math or the new). Two people who are extremely needy don't really have the energy or the capacity to offer the other much of anything except grief. And someone who's already well on the road to completeness would be too healthy to be bogged down by someone who's incomplete.

When two whole people unite, they make something better than just "one plus one equals two." Great power arises from the integration and wholeness symbolized by Jung's *Syzygy* (The Divine Couple in the enchanted castle with its King and Queen). But you have to build the wholeness and integrity within and for yourself. *Then* you can share it with a well-matched, well-balanced equally integrated partner. As Katz and Liu (1988) acknowledged, it takes some work. It's not as easy as sitting around and waiting for someone else to do it for you. But doing the work is infinitely more rewarding and liberating.

Oh, and one more thing: In real life those fleeting moments idealized as the big finale of romance novels and movies don't represent "The End" by any means. They represent the *beginning.* (See the Epilogue of this book.)

Let's be honest: Using your partner as a completer, fixer, or rescuer—someone from whom you "take" or "get"—is not "romance": It's "robbery"! (And that goes for "incomplete" men like "Jerry Maguire"—to say nothing of the gold-digger in *An Officer and a Gentleman:* If she wanted to escape the assembly line, how about a night class or correspondence course?) But where's the dramatic conflict in well-adjusted, self-sufficient individuals who choose to share their already-full lives with each other? In our mass-mediated Wonderland of dreams and illusions and instant fixes, who wants to be told that we have to work to achieve our full human potential?

DIS-ILLUSIONING THIS MYTH

Codependents Day: *Jerry Maguire*

Jerry Maguire (1996) exemplifies the codependency model's dysfunction. This movie would have us believe and celebrate the myth that two incomplete individuals are "eligible" for a romantic relationship. Although the hit film struck a chord with millions of watchers, I find it depressing rather than uplifting.

Tom Cruise plays the title role, a successful bigtime sports agent whose romantic life is a failure. And then his professional life takes a nosedive.

As Dorothy, Jerry's low-status devoted accountant, Renee Zellweger incorporates many of the iconic dependent, incomplete film females discussed in previous chapters: *Serendipity*'s Sara and *Kate and Leopold*'s Kate seeking their fated other half in New York, poor unattractive *Shallow Hal*'s Rosemary waiting for someone to see her inner beauty, the struggling single mother of *As Good As It Gets,* the disrespected girlfriend in *The Mexican,* the good woman who can save the beastly guy from himself and redeem him so that she, like the needy Pretty Woman, can in turn be rescued by him. She's even like Lady, with her Tramp. (As noted earlier, Myth #10 is a culminating myth. Many of the other myths are part of the total scenario for making mass media-inspired dreams come true.)

Both Jerry and Dorothy should "cultivate their own completeness" rather relying on each other like drunks clinging to a lamppost. And Dorothy should develop her backbone. (She might start by reading *Just Ella,* my *Realistic Romance™ Award* nominee, discussed next.) When Jerry—who has deserted Dorothy on more than one occasion—finally realizes what a good woman she is, he comes back to her in the now famous scene in which she stops his apologetic speech: "You had me at hello," she pathetically tells him.

In other words, all it takes is for him to simply appear. Her desperation is painful to see — though many of the movie's viewers interpreted this dysfunctional scene as romantic.

And Jerry is equally ridiculous, with his "You complete me" nonsense. He should study Lazarus' book and learn that he can't use others as "emotional oxygen." He, too, must "cultivate his own completeness."

Dr. FUN's Realistic Romance™ Awards Nomination: *Just Ella*

Margaret Peterson Haddix' exciting novel for adolescents — *Just Ella* (1999) — is an empowering reframing of *Cinderella*.[3] The American Library Association named it a Best Book for Young Adults.

As the back cover explains:

> It's a familiar story: In spite of the obstacles put in her way by her wicked stepmother, Ella goes to the ball, sweeps Prince Charming off his feet, and is chosen to be his bride. Now she's comfortably ensconced in the palace, awaiting marriage to the man of her dreams. It's happily-ever-after time, right?
>
> Wrong! Life for Ella has become an endless round of lessons and restrictions; even worse, Prince Charming turns out to be more like Prince Boring. Why can't she talk with him the way she can with Jed, her earnest young tutor?
>
> Slowly, Ella comes to realize she doesn't want the life she fought so hard to win. But breaking her engagement proves more difficult — and dangerous — than escaping her stepmother's tyranny.

Ella's soon-to-be in-laws throw her into a dungeon and starve her to force her to come to her senses (which means stuffing herself into tight corsets and going through with the marriage) — but our plucky heroine manages to escape by using her head and relying on a scullery maid to whom she's been kind. What's refreshing in Ella's journey to escape the suffocation of the life that seemed like a perfect dream is that this independent and thoughtful young woman isn't a cardboard character: She's both strong-minded and tender. And her decisions reflect counter-mythic strategies.

She finally finds Jed, who has also left the palace to help war-ravaged refugees. Ella helps, too, and a romance blossoms, based on respect and shared values — again without the stereotypic nonsense. But they don't rush into a hasty marriage commitment. They both have work to do: Jed has a peace mission, and Ella wants to become a physician. They'll take it slow, and they'll continue to be good supportive friends as well as self-sufficient romantic partners.

I especially like Ella's response to Jed's detailing of the "story going around the palace" about how she got to the ball thanks to her "fairy godmother." In this first-person narrative she tells the reader her reaction to hearing this rumor: "I was laughing so hard tears were streaming down my face. 'Some ... someone ... actually ... believes that?' I finally sputtered between giggles" (p. 66).

Later, when Ella tells Jed her true story and asks him to stop the rumors, he explains: "People would rather believe in fairy godmothers and ...and ...well, divine intervention, if you will — than to think that you took charge of your own destiny" (p. 93).

---

[3]*Just Ella's* publisher, Aladdin/Simon & Schuster, also published the collection *A Wolf at the Door and Other Retold Fairy Tales*, in which "Cinder Elephant" (my Chapter 11 nomination) appears.

These young people offer young readers excellent and entertaining lessons in "cultivating your own completeness."

Additional Mass Media Manifestations of This Myth to *Dis*-illusion

Books

Cinderella
Most romance novels
Sleeping Beauty
Snow White
   and the Seven Dwarfs

Newspapers

Most reporting of marriages
   of princes and princesses
   and other media celebrities

Magazines

Cosmo
Teenzines

Movies

Cinderella
City of Angels
Last of the Mohicans
An Officer & a Gentleman
Only You
Pretty Woman
Sleeping Beauty
Sleepless in Seattle
Snow White
   and the Seven Dwarfs
The Wedding Planner
When Harry Met Sally
You've Got Mail!

Recorded Music

All of My Life
Because You Love Me
How Can I Live Without You
I Can Love You Like That
You Light Up My Life

Television

90210
Dawson's Creek
I Dream of Jeanie
Mad About You
Ozzie & Harriet

DIS-ILLUSION DIGEST

Dr. FUN's Mass Media Love Quiz Myth #10

THE RIGHT MATE "COMPLETES YOU" —
FILLING YOUR NEEDS AND MAKING YOUR DREAMS COME TRUE.

"Love" songs are prime culprits for cultivating this "Snow White" syndrome. Remember, her big Disney solo was "Someday My Prince Will Come"; meantime, she remained totally un*self*-empowered (literally unconscious) until he did arrive on the scene. Using your partner as a completer, fixer, or rescuer (someone from whom you "take" or "get") is not *romance* — it's *robbery!* And that goes for "incomplete" needy men like Jerry Maguire. But where's the dramatic conflict in well-adjusted, self-sufficient individuals who choose to share their already-full lives?

Dr. Galician's Prescription™ #10

CULTIVATE YOUR OWN COMPLETENESS.

SOURCES CITED

Blanc, T. (1994, Spring/Summer). Marriage mythology. *ASU Research,* pp. 13–15.

Dyer, W. W. (1976). *Your erroneous zones.* New York: Avon Books.

Katz, S. J., & Liu, A. E. (1988). *False love and other romantic illusions.* New York: Pocket Books.

Lazarus, A. A. (1985). *Marital myths: Two dozen mistaken beliefs that can ruin a marriage or make a bad one worse.* San Luis Obispo, CA: Impact.

WORKSHEET FOR MASS MEDIA MYTH #10

(See Chapter 6 for details of *Dr. Galician's Seven-Step* Dis-*illusioning Directions*.)

The right mate "completes you" — filling your needs and making your dreams come true.

R$_x$: CULTIVATE your own COMPLETENESS.

Title of Your Analysis & Criticism

Your Thesis

STEP I. DETECTION (finding/identifying)

Identification (title, date, and medium, with "markers")

Entire work/specific segment

STEP 2. DESCRIPTION (illustrating/exemplifying)

Detailed description

Creator; creator's purpose

Function/purpose (entertainment/news and information/persuasion) and genre

STEP 3. DECONSTRUCTION (analyzing)

Underlying myths/stereotypes (primary/secondary)

Evidence for linking myths/stereotypes; specific examples of content (message) and form (medium) that represent embedded values

Significant omissions

Cited commentary/research

STEP 4. DIAGNOSIS (evaluating/criticizing)

Meaning and possible interpretations (preferred and oppositional)

Comparison with rational models

Possible effects (harm)

Expert citations

Judgment/evaluation

STEP 5. DESIGN (reconstructing/reframing)

Realistic reframing

Related theories and rational models

Likelihood of use

Existing reconstructions

STEP 6. DEBRIEFING (reconsidering/remedying)

Personal impact of *dis*-illusioning; comparison of personal belief before/after, including enjoyment

Personal harm from myth

STEP 7. DISSEMINATION (publishing/broadcasting)

Advocacy action plan

Timetable of specific activities (personal/public/professional)

17

DR. FUN'S MASS MEDIA LOVE QUIZ MYTH #11

In real life, actors and actresses are often very much like the romantic characters they portray.

Dr. Galician's Prescription™ #11
R$_x$: (DE)CONSTRUCT CELEBRITIES.

The problem, dear Brutus, is not in our stars but in ourselves.
— "Mark Antony," William Shakespeare, *Julius Caesar*

I loved that she was really herself!
— Comment of a fan, who had never met her idol,
gushing about the "genuineness" of Julia Roberts'
Academy Awards® acceptance speech (March 2001)

Here's a story of a real person[1] who — once upon a time — believed this myth and, as a result, did *not* live very happily-ever-after.

[Martha, 19-year-old female student]

No matter how much I know, intellectually, that actors are just that — people who act a part — emotionally I still expect actors and their characters to have some similarity. That's why I'm always shocked when I hear of the arrest of a famous actor who portrays good guys. Likewise I hold the same irrational expectations of actors who portray romantic characters. Take, for example, the shy Englishman persona of Hugh Grant. As a younger teen, I was infatuated with him and his charmingly shy, gentle screen characterizations. Imagine my shock when I discovered he'd been arrested with a prostitute in Hollywood — and this at a time when gorgeous Elizabeth Hurley was his girlfriend! Even though I realize he's only reading lines that someone else has written, I felt disappointed and betrayed because of the image I'd built up of this actor whom I'd associated with his fictional roles.

---

[1]Names have been changed to protect individuals' privacy.

Here's a different true story:

[Greta, a sixth-grade girl in Scandinavia]

When I was 12, my best friends were Karin and Lina. We adored American movies like *Top Gun, Cocktail,* and *Days of Thunder* — for one reason: Tom Cruise! We must have watched *Cocktail* about 50 times. Anything to see his great white smile, over and over again. It all started out as fun. We laughed and joked about knowing him and being the girl in the movie. After a while, though, the discussions about "Mr. Flanagan" (the charming Tom Cruise bartender character) got a little rough. Karin and Lina each started referring to him as her boyfriend. Each one got mad when the other would say it. Crazy as it sounds, they came to believe that he was their boyfriend. They stopped talking to each other over it — and I was caught in the middle.

ADDITIONAL RESEARCH & COMMENTARY
RELATED TO THIS MASS MEDIA MYTH

Although *you* might not confuse actors and actresses with their roles, many men and women are less than satisfied with their real-life romantic partners who aren't like their idealized images of celebrities they think they know personally. For example, after the 2001 Academy Awards®, I was amazed to hear a Julia Roberts fan inanely gush about how "real" the actress was in her somewhat unorthodox acceptance speech — as if this fan knew the "real" Julia. Of course, "fan" is short for "fanatic" — but it's still ridiculous that millions of people who have never met their celebrity icons nevertheless irrationally believe that they are intimately acquainted.

> **Male and Female University Students' Responses to This *Quiz* Item**
>
> Nearly *all* men and woman disagree that actors and actresses are often very much like the romantic characters they portray. However, around 3% of both sexes *agree* with this myth.

McLuhan predicted that as the world became a smaller and smaller global village because of the mass media's instant communication we'd be more and more interested in the personal lives of our "neighbors" — even though it was none of our business. And today the tabloids and fanzines and "E"-type channels and talk shows literally extend our eyes and ears (and noses!) into the private lives of the only too human men and women — and now even children who become national idols, like Britney Spears and Leonardo DiCaprio — whom we've elevated to the status of modern-day heroes and heroines to lead our culture like the half-god characters of ancient myth.

For some fans, this means merely idolizing these superstars. For others, it means imitating them as well. (See Fraser and Brown's comparisons of heroes, celebrities, and role models in Box 17-1 on the next page.) Either way, it's an obsession for the millions of readers and viewers who support the extensive (and lucrative) gossip media. What's sad is that nearly all the "facts" that these media consumers believe to be true are based on illusion. Even celebrities' "officially sanctioned web sites" are primarily media-created narratives.

The home of the ancient Greek gods and goddesses was Mt. Olympus. Today's modern media mythological figures reside in the Hollywood Hills. But not much else seems to have changed.

Box 17-1. Media, Celebrities, and Social Influence

In the research journal article "Media, Celebrities, and Social Influence," Fraser and Brown (2002, p. 187) compared heroes, celebrities, and role models. Some of the differences they noted are:

Distinguishing characteristic

Heroes: achievement
Celebrities: image or trademark
Role models: their influence

Creator

Heroes: self
Celebrities: the media
Role models: psychological need

Basis of admiration

Heroes: character attributes
Celebrities: name recognition
Role models: achievement, name, or character

Source of status

Heroes: interpersonal relationships
Celebrities: media coverage
Role models: none (they provide desired status to others)

Means of generating reputation

Heroes: actions
Celebrities: pseudo-events
Role models: followers

Value

Heroes: intrinsic and lasting
Celebrities: short term (fades)
Role models: endures

It's one thing to appreciate talented artists for their professional work, but it's quite another to confuse reality with fiction. It's actually the ultimate *dis*-service to these stars, who are idealized and thus objectified and dehumanized not only by the unfeeling corporate interests that benefit from their popularity but also by the so-called loving worshipers who — lacking any genuine intimacy with their favorites — are engaged in what we can only describe as infatuated or possibly fatuous (foolish) relationships (to extrapolate from Sternberg's model).

Wouldn't you say that these fans are in need of *dis*-illusioning?

DIS-ILLUSIONING THIS MYTH[2]

A Method to Her Madness? *Nurse Betty*

The movie *Nurse Betty* (2000) is a delightful multi-layered send-up of Myth #11. Renee Zellweger (in a Golden Globe-Award-winning performance) portrays Betty Sizemore, a diner waitress with a crush on Dr. David Ravell (Greg Kinnear), the central character of her favorite soap opera, *A Reason to Live*. After witnessing her sleazy husband's murder by two hitmen, the sweet woman goes into shock and suddenly believes that she is Nurse Betty, who left the good doctor at the altar several seasons ago. To rectify this error, she dashes to Los Angeles and gets the part in the soap because everyone thinks she's the greatest method actress around. She can't discriminate between the actor who plays Ravell and the character of Ravell.

---

[2]The seven-step process must be slightly adapted to apply to Myth #11, as we are examining fan behavior relative to celebrities rather than specific manifestations across all media.

Betty is suffering from a traumatic experience that has left her mind out of whack, but many fans of actors and actresses experience an almost identical confusion.

Just Like Bogey & Bacall: *Play It Again, Sam*

Another movie character who believes this myth is Allen Felix, played by Woody Allen in the 1972 comedy *Play It Again, Sam,* which also satirizes the myths it paradoxically reveres. Allen Felix is such a failure at romance that he has come to imagine and rely on the presence of long-dead movie idol Humphrey Bogart for advice about women. In fact, the movie opens with Allen — a San Francisco film critic — watching the concluding scene of *Casablanca*[3] and trying to imitate his mentor. The advice Allen gets when he asks Bogey a question reflects the star's most famous screen personas, but dorky Allen is unable to follow the advice.

Perfect Couples — Until the Divorce

I understand the phenomenon of fandom. When I was only 7 years old, I saw the movie *Houdini* (1953), the first teaming of Janet Leigh and Tony Curtis (big stars in their day, now perhaps better known as the parents of Jamie Lee Curtis), who had been married only a few years then. I immediately felt that when I grew up I wanted a marriage like these actors had. They were a magical couple. Of course, I knew only what I saw on the screen and read in the movie magazines. I also relished seeing them together in *The Black Shield of Falworth* (1954) and *The Vikings* (1958). I even wrote an essay about wanting to be like them when I got married. When they divorced in 1962, I was shocked. To my limited view, they had appeared to be the perfect couple.

Until recently, millions of fans worldwide thought the same of Tom Cruise and Nicole Kidman. But actors and actresses are just actors and actresses, and their personal lives are not like their screen characters' lives.

Official Celebrity Websites & Online Shrines

Official celebrity websites are usually creations of publicists or studios. What you read there is not necessarily factual. Most people understand this — but others believe every word. Even less reliable are the wave of "online shrines"or fan-created sites honoring their creator's idols. One of my students who searched for Tom Cruise sites found thousands of them. Many offered Mr. Cruise advice about his impending divorce from Nicole Kidman, and others offered themselves as his next wife. For example, a posting on an internet discussion board pleaded:

> Tom, it's a bit obvious you still love Nicole and she still loves you.
> She said that recently, so please get back together with her.
> You were the best couple.
> Wait ...you were supposed to marry me.

Do you think these fans imagine that the stars read these postings?

---

[3]The American Film Institute (AFI) recently named this 1942 film — starring Bogart and Ingrid Bergman as ill-fated lovers — the most romantic American movie.

Role vs. Real

Although it's obvious that actors and actresses are *not* their roles but rather real people, many fans have mistaken their romantic characters for their personal identities. Millions of women fantasized about hunky Rock Hudson, who was in real life a homosexual. Sex goddess Raquel Welch often complained about sitting home alone on date nights. When Hugh Grant was arrested for soliciting a prostitute on the streets of Los Angeles while in a committed relationship with Elizabeth Hurley, fans were shocked to learn that he wasn't the reserved character he played in their favorite movies and that even the gossip about his romantic life covered in celebrity magazines and television shows wasn't necessarily true. And Meg Ryan, who portrays such angelic romantic characters, shocked her fans by carrying on an adulterous affair and subsequently divorcing her husband (and losing boyfriend Russell Crowe).

The mass media make it seem as if we know these performers — actors, actresses, recording artists, and other celebrities. Fans who really appreciated their favorites would value their work and respect their privacy. And self-actualized individuals wouldn't mindlessly ape them.

Additional Mass Media Manifestations of This Myth to *Dis*-illusion

Books

"Tell-all" biographies and autobiographies

Newspapers

Tabloids (*Enquirer, Star,* etc.)

Magazines

EW
Fanzines
People

Movies

Hugh Grant movies
Meg Ryan movies
Julia Roberts movies
Rock Hudson movies

Television

E channel, etc.
"Reality" shows
Talk shows

Internet

Celebrity sites
Online "shrines"

DIS-ILLUSION DIGEST

Dr. FUN's Mass Media Love Quiz Myth #11

**IN REAL LIFE, ACTORS AND ACTRESSES ARE OFTEN
VERY MUCH LIKE THE ROMANTIC CHARACTERS THEY PORTRAY.**

Many men and women are less than satisfied with their real-life romantic
partners because they aren't like their idealized image of a celebrity they
think they know. Obsessive fan behavior — reinforced by the thriving
sensationalistic gossip media — not only promotes unrealistic real-life
expectations but also ultimately and ironically dehumanizes the very
icons these devotees irrationally purport to cherish.

Dr. Galician's Prescription™ #11

(DE)CONSTRUCT CELEBRITIES.

SOURCES CITED

Fraser, B. P., & Brown, W. J. (2002). Media, celebrities, and social influence. *Mass Media &
Society, 5* (2), 187.

McLuhan, M. (1964). *Understanding media: The extensions of man.* New York: McGraw-Hill.

Shakespeare, W. (n.d.). *Julius Caesar.* In W. G. Clark & W. A. Wright (Eds.), The complete
works of William Shakespeare: Vol. II (pp. 571–596). Garden City, NY: Nelson
Doubleday.

WORKSHEET FOR MASS MEDIA MYTH #11

(See Chapter 6 for details of *Dr. Galician's Seven-Step* Dis-*illusioning Directions*.)

In real life, actors and actresses are often very much like the romantic characters they portray.

R$_x$: (De)CONSTRUCT CELEBRITIES.

Title of Your Analysis & Criticism

Your Thesis

STEP 1. DETECTION (finding/identifying)

Identification (title, date, and medium, with "markers")

Entire work/specific segment

STEP 2. DESCRIPTION (illustrating/exemplifying)

Detailed description

Creator; creator's purpose

Function/purpose (entertainment/news and information/persuasion) and genre

STEP 3. DECONSTRUCTION (analyzing)

Underlying myths/stereotypes (primary/secondary)

Evidence for linking myths/stereotypes; specific examples of content (message) and form (medium) that represent embedded values

Significant omissions

Cited commentary/research

STEP 4. DIAGNOSIS (evaluating/criticizing)

Meaning and possible interpretations (preferred and oppositional)

Comparison with rational models

Possible effects (harm)

Expert citations

Judgment/evaluation

STEP 5. DESIGN (reconstructing/reframing)

Realistic reframing

Related theories and rational models

Likelihood of use

Existing reconstructions

STEP 6. DEBRIEFING (reconsidering/remedying)

Personal impact of *dis*-illusioning; comparison of personal belief before/after, including enjoyment

Personal harm from myth

STEP 7. DISSEMINATION (publishing/broadcasting)

Advocacy action plan

Timetable of specific activities (personal/public/professional)

18

DR. FUN'S MASS MEDIA LOVE QUIZ MYTH #12

Since mass media portrayals of romance aren't "real," they don't really affect you.

Dr. Galician's Prescription™ #12
R_x: CALCULATE THE VERY REAL CONSEQUENCES OF UNREAL MEDIA.

...[T]he myths of love generally determine our individual behavior, the apparent accidents of our encounters, and the choices we imagine we are making freely.
— Denis de Rougemont, "The Rising Tide of Eros," *Sex in America*

It's a difficult task to find anything in the media that has much to teach us about the realities of love.
— Robert J. Sternberg, *Cupid's Arrow*

Here's a story of a real person[1] who — once upon a time — believed this myth and, as a result, did *not* live very happily-ever-after.

[Suzy, 8-year-old girl]

A perfect boyfriend should be rich and give his girlfriend nice clothes. When his girlfriend is in trouble, he must help her. Even if the girlfriend doesn't like his kiss, she soon will because the girl and boy will fall in love. [How did Suzy know these things?] Because Belle and Ariel's boyfriends did these things...

Here's another true story:

[Tucker, 21-year-old male university student]

Three years ago when I first came to school I would have told you that television doesn't affect me. I believe that one of the most difficult things to do in our society is to admit what a negative influence TV can be. I am now a confessed television addict. I've watched it since I was a child. I'd see all the romances, especially on the soaps. I thought it'd be pretty exciting to have a relationship as dynamic as those people on TV. I didn't realize the influence until my fiancee and I began planning

---

[1]Names have been changed to protect individuals' privacy.

219

our real wedding. The more I talked about what I wanted, I realized I was trying to imitate a fictitious ceremony from TV or from *The Father of the Bride,* where everything is so perfect! In our real wedding, we had to pay for everything. And some of our ideas just couldn't be worked out.

I'm grateful that I realize how powerful the mass media can be in influencing me, but I think it's important to realize that most people aren't aware of the effects. They believe they can go about their lives and choose what's going to influence them.

And one more:

[Denise, 21-year-old female university student]

I've always been into romantic movies, songs, and novels. Some people say those movies, songs, and novels don't influence people one bit, but I must disagree. I know that when I watch a movie like *Titanic* or TV show like *Dawson's Creek,* I wish my real boyfriend would be like Jack and rescue me or show up and say just the right thing at the right time. The mass media puts all these ideas into our head about what a guy should be or do, and then that's what I expect. It's caused problems in my relationship because my boyfriend isn't like the media characters. He's real — not a knight-in-shining-armor.

ADDITIONAL RESEARCH & COMMENTARY RELATED TO THIS MASS MEDIA MYTH

There's a lot of evidence to support the third-person effects theory. As "Tucker" commented, most people think they personally are not that affected by the mass media. But the research suggests otherwise.

> **Male and Female University Students' Responses to This *Quiz* Item**
>
> Nearly *all* men and women disagree that mass media portrayals of romance have no effect on us because they're not real. In other words, most people acknowledge that the mass media *do* affect us. Within the small percentage of respondents who don't believe that these portrayals affect us, the great majority are consistently men.

In my studies of Baby Boomers and Generation Xers, I found that frequent consumers of movies (action as well as romantic) and men's and women's fashion and fitness magazines tend to have more unrealistic and stereotypical expectations about coupleship, and, correspondingly, less satisfaction in their own real romantic relationships. This finding was also partially supported for television (soaps, comedies, and movies) and music videos.

In this book, I've shared just some of the testimony of experts and the criticism of commentators who believe that the mass media influence our thoughts and feelings about sex, love, and romance and, ultimately, our actions. Many argue that the media represent one of several social forces that create or at least reinforce dysfunctional unrealistic beliefs about coupleship that can lead to unhappiness and harm; others assert that the mass media are the primary socializers.

Very few models of realistic and rational ("healthy"), nondependent, self-responsible egalitarian coupleship can be found in the popular culture. We have much work to do.

Of course, attempting to completely change the mass media is clearly too formidable a task. At any rate, they may serve a cathartic or escapist function for some consumers. We can still enjoy even romanticized portrayals in the mass media, but we must do so with our illusion detectors firmly in place.

Media literacy offers constructive avenues for *dis*-illusioning these major mass media myths about sex, love, and romance and for *dis*-illusioning ourselves so that we can increase our chances of enjoying more productive and satisfying real-life relationships that we build on a rational healthy basis rather than on the potentially damaging and dangerous illusions the mass media perpetuate.

DIS-ILLUSIONING THIS MYTH

Myth #12 is perhaps the most damaging myth of all: If we're unaware of the influence of the other 11 myths, we're more likely to fall under their power. As Rosie O'Donnell tells Meg Ryan in *Sleepless in Seattle:* "You want to be in love in a movie."

Because this final myth is actually a statement *about* all the myths, we won't *dis*-illusion any specific mass media manifestations, and I won't offer any additional suggested titles that contain relevant portrayals of sex, love, and romance. Those in the preceding 11 chapters should serve as stimuli for your continuing analysis and criticism of unrealistic depictions. (At this point in your study, your *dis*-illusionings should focus not on one sole myth but rather on all of the interrelated major mass media myths that you detect within a mass media portrayal.) You've also read many cases studies of the effects of these portrayals on real people. I encourage you to conduct your own cases — and to read research about the effects of the mass media.

Now it's time for you to become a full-time media literacy activist by following the *Seven-Step* Dis-*illusioning Directions* — going beyond Steps 1–4 that form your analysis and criticism and "taking the extra three steps" (5–7) that make all the difference. The Epilogue that concludes this book offers you some final motivation.

Dis-illusioning these mass media myths shouldn't be about spoiling your enjoyment but rather about questioning your enjoyment of what's not healthy. Why did millions of women and girls gush over the unrealistic romantic couple in *Titanic* — and why did so many of them watch it dozens of times? Why do millions of men and boys fantasize over centerfolds who are as unreal as comic book characters? Why do young adults of both sexes feel that the characters portrayed by million-dollar-an-episode television stars on shows like *Friends* are actual people? And why do millions of fans obsess over and idolize performers they don't know?

How can we get real?

One recommendation is offered by popular singer Alanis Morissette in her innovative music video *Precious Illusions* (2002), which echoes the themes of this book. It's a great example of a *dis*-illusioning of several Mass Media Myths, and it's my final *Dr. FUN's Realistic Romance™ Awards* Nomination.

Dr. FUN's Realistic Romance™ Awards Nomination: *Precious Illusions*

The music video rendition of Alanis Morissette's *Precious Illusions* (2002) from her *Under Rug Swept* album is presented primarily in split screen, offering a side-by-side comparison of the mythic and the real versions of a romantic relationship. On one side we see a knight-in-shining-armor sending notes written in script with quill pens to a dainty version of a medieval Morissette. On the other side, we get the realistic portrayal of a 21st century Morissette. Her boyfriend rides a motorcycle rather than a horse, and the notes come via email. This couple is "interdependent" — caring, open, and sharing, but not clinging.

This smart and talented woman doesn't have to jump off a bridge like poor Kate in search of a Leopold from the distant mythic past. She now mocks her earlier dreams of being rescued or completed by a man. She's decided not to be a victim of illusions. She acknowledges that it's not easy: Parting with her "precious illusions," she sings, "is like parting with invisible best friends" or "a childhood best friend." But, her hauntingly honest lyrics explain, it's the difference between "survival and bliss."

DIS-ILLUSION DIGEST

Dr. FUN's Mass Media Love Quiz Myth #12

SINCE MASS MEDIA PORTRAYALS OF ROMANCE AREN'T "REAL," THEY DON'T REALLY AFFECT YOU.

Though we might not be aware of the all-pervasive media culture, we subconsciously incorporate its messages and myths into our own lives. My studies of Baby Boomers and Generation Xers have found that frequent consumers of movies and fashion and fitness magazines tend to have more unrealistic and stereotypical expectations about coupleship, and, correspondingly, less satisfaction in their own real romantic relationships. Through media literacy strategies and skills, we can become more aware and active, thereby increasing our own chances of satisfying and successful real-life close relationships.

Dr. Galician's Prescription™ #12

CALCULATE THE VERY REAL CONSEQUENCES OF UNREAL MEDIA.

SOURCES CITED

de Rougemont, D. (1964). "The rising tide of Eros." In H.A. Grunwald (Ed.), *Sex in America* (pp. 291–311). New York: Bantam Books.

Galician, M.-L. (1995, October). *The romanticization of love in the mass media: A comparison of the relationship among unrealistic romantic expectations, ideal role models, heterosexual coupleship satisfaction, and mass media usage of Baby Boomers and Generation Xers.* Paper presented at the annual meeting of The Organization for the Study of Communication, Language, and Gender, Minneapolis/St. Paul, MN.

Galician, M.-L. (1997, February). *The romanticization of love in the mass media: The relationship of mass communication media usage, unrealistic romantic expectations, coupleship dissatisfactions of Baby Boomer and Generation X males and females.* Paper presented at the annual meeting of the Western States Communication Association, Monterey Bay, CA.

Sternberg, R. J. (1998). *Cupid's arrow: The course of love through time.* New York: Cambridge University Press.

EPILOGUE

DON'T STOP!
"The End Is Where We Start From"

What we call the beginning is often the end
And to make an end is to make a beginning.
The end is where we start from.

— T.S. Eliot, "Little Gidding," _Four Quartets_

At the very beginning of this book, I asked you to _stop_ and take my _Dr. FUN's Mass Media Love Quiz._ Now that you've come to the end of the book, I'm asking you _not to stop_. This is _not_ "The End" (though I wish you a genuine "happily-ever-after").

At the end of so many books that we read for courses that we take, we study for the final exam and then quickly forget everything. I hope that won't be the case for you.

I hope that you understand why and how the "Romanticization of Love in the Mass Media" can hurt you, and I hope that everything you've learned about _dis_-illusioning the myths and stereotypes of the mass media's portrayals of sex, love, and romance will be used by you in your real life — to make your life more real. I hope that you'll continue your analysis and criticism of unrealistic portrayals — personally, publicly, and professionally. As I've said all along: _We can still enjoy the romanticized mass media. We just don't have to be seduced by them._

Most mass media portrayals of sex, love, and romance shape or reinforce unrealistic expectations that most of us can't dismiss completely. They make us dissatisfied with our real partners as well as with ourselves. So it's just plain common sense to become aware and change our unhealthy views.

It's foolish to use unrealistic mass media portrayals as models for your own thoughts, feelings, or actions. It's much healthier and smarter to make _yourself_ the hero or heroine of your own real-life love story.

I can personally vouch for that.

As I type this last page of this book that I wrote for you, it's a fitting moment to invite _you_ to do what I finally did several years ago: "Get real about romance."

When I did, my own life changed dramatically and delightfully. I'm living a nonillusional _"Happily-Ever-After"_ story. Even in my most romantically inspired dreams when I was under the influence of those mass media myths and stereotypes, I never imaged how wonderful, satisfying, and joyful a _realistic romance_ could be.

Realistic romance is possible for anyone who opposes the myths and stereo-types in *Dr. FUN's Mass Media Love Quiz* with the "antidotes" from *Dr. Galician's Prescriptions™ for Getting Real About Romance*. (These are provided once again on the facing page.)

These guidelines have worked for me and countless others — and I know they can work for *YOU*. In your continuing course in Life, no one will grade you but you yourself.

> *We shall not cease from exploration*
> *And the end of all our exploring*
> *Will be to arrive where we started*
> *And know the place for the first time.*
>   — T.S. Eliot, "Little Gidding," *Four Quartets*

Major Mass Media Myths
& Corresponding Prescriptions™ for Healthy Coupleship

> Numbered items = *Dr. FUN's Mass Media Love Quiz©*
> Rx = *Dr. Galician's Prescriptions™ for Getting Real About Romance*

PARTNER IS PREDESTINED ...

   1. Your perfect partner is cosmically predestined, so nothing/nobody can ultimately separate you.

      Rx: CONSIDER COUNTLESS CANDIDATES.

RIGHT AWAY, YOU KNOW ...

   2. There's such a thing as "love at first sight."

      Rx: CONSULT your CALENDAR and COUNT CAREFULLY.

EXPRESSION NOT NECESSARY ...

   3. Your true soul mate should KNOW what you're thinking or feeling (without your having to tell).

      Rx: COMMUNICATE COURAGEOUSLY.

SEXUAL PERFECTION ...

   4. If your partner is truly meant for you, sex is easy and wonderful.

      Rx: CONCENTRATE on COMMITMENT and CONSTANCY.

CENTERFOLDS PREFERRED ...

   5. To attract and keep a man, a woman should look like a model or a centerfold.

      Rx: CHERISH COMPLETENESS in COMPANIONS (not just the COVER).

ROLE OF GENDER (OR "REAL MEN") ...

   6. The man should NOT be shorter, weaker, younger, poorer, or less successful than the woman.

      Rx: CREATE COEQUALITY; COOPERATE.

INTO A PRINCE (FROM BEAST) ...

   7. The love of a good and faithful true woman can change a man from a "beast" into a "prince."

      Rx: CEASE CORRECTING and CONTROLLING; you CAN'T CHANGE others (only yourself!).

PUGILISM = PASSION ...

   8. Bickering and fighting a lot mean that a man and a woman really love each other passionately.

      Rx: COURTESY COUNTS; CONSTANT CONFLICTS CREATE CHAOS.

TOTALLY OPPOSITE VALUES ...

   9. All you really need is love, so it doesn't matter if you and your lover have very different values.

      Rx: CRAVE COMMON CORE-VALUES.

INCOMPLETE WITHOUT MATE ...

   10. The right mate "completes you" — filling your needs and making your dreams come true.

      Rx: CULTIVATE your own COMPLETENESS.

OFTEN, ACTORS = ROLES ...

   11. In real life, actors and actresses are often very much like the romantic characters they portray.

      Rx: (DE)CONSTRUCT CELEBRITIES.

NOT REAL/NO EFFECT ...

   12. Since mass media portrayals of romance aren't "real," they don't really affect you.

      Rx: CALCULATE the very real CONSEQUENCES of unreal media.

APPENDIX A

Sample Completed Worksheet

SAMPLE COMPLETED WORKSHEET FOR MASS MEDIA MYTH #7

(See *Chapter 6* for details of *Dr. Galician's Seven-Step Dis-illusioning Directions*.)

The love of a good and faithful true woman can change a man from a "beast" into a "prince."

R$_x$: CEASE CORRECTING and CONTROLLING; you CAN'T CHANGE others (only yourself).

Title of Your Analysis & Criticism
Analysis & Criticism of the Portrayal of Mass Media Myth #7 (The love of a good and faithful true woman can change a man from a "beast" into a "prince.) in the 1997 Movie "As Good As It Gets"

Your Thesis   Legitimizes and glorifies Myth #7 — as well as #6, #9, #10.
Understanding good woman (harried single mother) turns mean obsessive-compulsive man into loving adequate romantic partner (#7). Completely different values (#9). He's twice her age and rescues her financially (#6). Unrealistic happy ending implies that without a man, the woman is incomplete and that even a pathologically disturbed and mean man with virtually no redeeming qualities can make this vulnerable woman's dreams come true (#10). Clever dialog and great acting, but underlying messages contradict models of rational healthy coupleship. Preferred reading should be carefully examined, strongly resisted, and actively opposed.

STEP 1. DETECTION (finding/identifying)

Identification (title, date, and medium, with "markers")
"As Good As It Gets" (1997) movie — available on VHS and DVD

Entire work/specific segment   Entire movie

STEP 2. DESCRIPTION (illustrating/exemplifying)

Detailed description   Plot basics and ending; describe "better man" scene: Melvin Udall (racist, misogynist, homophobic, obsessive-compulsive but commercially successful pulp novelist). Resents neighbor Simon Nye = homosexual artist with cute dog. Eats at same restaurant daily, waited upon by Carol Connelly, struggling single mother of a seriously asthmatic child. Melvin has to TCO dog when Simon is hospitalized. Carol leaves job to TCO of son; upsets M's routine so he TCO of the boy (doctor and bills). M, C, and S drive together to Baltimore, where C forces M to give her a compliment (the BM scene). Back at home, M suddenly goes back on drug therapy and courts C. They become a couple. (Mutual rescue)

Creator; creator's purpose
James L. Brooks = producer/director/co-author; Make money/entertain audience with a "feel-good" movie

Function/purpose (entertainment/news and information/persuasion) and genre
Primary = entertainment — romantic comedy genre

STEP 3. DECONSTRUCTION (analyzing)

Underlying myths/stereotypes (primary/secondary)   Primary: #7; secondary = #6, #9, #10

Evidence for linking myths/stereotypes; specific examples of content (message) and form (medium) that represent embedded values
(#7) After nearly killing the dog and voicing homophobia (opening scenes), Melvin changes and becomes dog's best friend and even homosexual neighbor's protector and roommate — as well as rescuer of Carol's sick child — all under Carol's "influence." In "Better Man" scene he actually paraphrases the myth (98 minutes into movie), reinforced by long lingering closeup and "mystical" music. (#6) His apt. = luxurious; she lives with mom, unattractive place. He = famous novelist; she = waitress. M = twice C's age. (#9) He's homophobic and racist and suffers from OCD; she's kind and generous and seems healthy. (#10) Final rescue scene (last 15 minutes; 125 in) = M at C's home to "claim" her and rescue her; even the mother is thrilled. Music reinforces, as does cutting to happy, approving mother.

Significant omissions
Disc. of seriousness of Melvin's untreated OCD and improbability of sudden change. How would a child fit into his life? We don't see their actual life together as a couple and with the child (and the mother). Where are any friends of Carol? What about her overprotectiveness of her child? Would she be interested if he weren't rich (maybe a poor waiter?)? What are M's selling points in C's eyes (other than money)? Also: Dog would be dead after Melvin shoves it down incinerator. Consequences of behaviors are not shown.

Cited commentary/research   John Harte (film.com); reviews at RottenTomatoes.com (?)

STEP 4. DIAGNOSIS (evaluating/criticizing)

Meaning and possible interpretations (preferred and oppositional)
Preferred = be kind and good, and even the worst people will change for better and become good rom. Partner (easy to fix others, even the mean and mentally ill); mean/ill person just need good partner to snap out of it. Any man is better than none. Age/class/$ differences don't matter. Different values are fine.

Oppositional = no motivation shown for changes; pairing is unlikely and high-risk; rescuers and rescuees should first get themselves healthy: Melvin needs professional long-term help and demo of behavioral change over time. Carol isn't really the paragon the pref. rdg. shows: Low self-esteem, no girlfriends, too protective of son, needs job with med. plan for son, should re-pay Melvin. Also: mental illness is not a laughing matter this movie makes it out to be. Dog would be dead when shoved down incinerator by M. Consequences of actions should be shown.

Comparison with rational models
Lazarus : rescue = toxic; rescuer = emot. weakling. Also Karpman (drama triangle); Schwartz (peer couples); Gottman (neg/pos interactions)

Possible effects (harm)
Thinking we can change others; being codependent; being abused in return or feeling inadequate

Expert citations
(Check Chapter 3 and other reviewers.)

Judgment/evaluation
Pretense of realism is deceptive. Mocking of mental illness is crass. This couple is high-risk, and both are unhealthy. This movie is overly sentimental. Good acting and some funny bits, but it's amazing it was so popular.

STEP 5. DESIGN (reconstructing/reframing)

Realistic reframing
Carol doesn't even get personally involved with M (other than helping him get professional attention) and shouldn't go to Baltimore with him! (He's a stranger. He could kill her!) Do anything other than take his money. Rather than falling for the sappy compliment, she should tell him to make himself better because she's not a fairy godmother or Beauty to his Beast. She works on her own issues and holds out for more appropriate romantic partner. Meantime, interacts with friends of both sexes more.

Related theories and rational models
Lazarus : rescue = toxic; rescuer = emot. weakling. Also Karpman (drama triangle); Schwartz (peer couples); Gottman (neg/pos interactions). Even Brooks: "Defies all logic."

Likelihood of use
Slim to none!

Existing reconstructions
Rare. Martin Lawrence's former girlfriend in movie "Blue Streak" kicks him out when he claims he's changed.

STEP 6. DEBRIEFING (reconsidering/remedying)

Personal impact of *dis*-illusioning; comparison of personal belief before/after, including enjoyment
Reinforced my awareness of futility and danger of being codependent. Already aware of myth before viewing movie. It's seductive to enjoy seeing people change for the better. I like that part. But I don't like the lack of genuine motivation. Also = a feel-good to see lonely people "find" someone, but these two = a recipe for disaster. Because of the good acting by major and minor characters (and wonderful dog!), I still have mixed feelings watching it.

Personal harm from myth
Tried to change alcoholic boyfriend. It didn't work. Depressing situation until I finally got out of the relationship.

STEP 7. DISSEMINATION (publishing/broadcasting)

Advocacy action plan
Media literacy promotion (writing, teaching, speaking); Ongoing

Timetable of specific activities (personal/public/professional)
Prof/Pub = Teach course; do presentations at conventions and for groups; write articles (newspaper and magazine); post web info on my site; complete tradebook

Pers = Discuss issues with friends; employ Rxs in my own marriage.

APPENDIX B

Sample Analysis & Criticism

An Analysis & Criticism of the Portrayal of Mass Media Myth #7
(The love of a good and faithful true woman
can change a man from a "beast" into a "prince.")
in the 1997 Movie *As Good As It Gets*

Thesis

As Good As It Gets (1997) legitimizes and glorifies Mass Media Myth #7, suggesting that all it takes is an understanding good woman (and a cute dog) to turn a mean obsessive-compulsive man into a loving adequate romantic partner for a harried single mother who has completely different values from the man (Myth #9) who is twice her age and rescues her financially (Myth #6). Further, the movie's logic-defying unrealistic happy ending promotes Myth #10, implying that without a man, the woman is incomplete and that even a pathologically disturbed and mean man with virtually no redeeming qualities (until the last hour of the movie) can make this vulnerable woman's dreams come true. While the clever dialog is entertaining and the acting is award-winning, the underlying messages, which contradict models of rational healthy coupleship in the social psychology literature (to say nothing of mental health models of O-C disorder), should be carefully examined, strongly resisted, and actively opposed.

Step 1: Detection

Identification

The entire 1997 Movie *As Good As It Gets* is the subject of this analysis and criticism. The movie is available on VHS and DVD.

Step 2: Description

Detailed Description

Jack Nicholson portrays a mean, obsessive-compulsive but commercially successful pulp novelist, Melvin Udall. Greg Kinnear plays painter Simon Nye, who lives across the hall from Melvin in a New York City apartment building with his cute but neurotic dog and endures Melvin's gay-bashing. (Melvin's also a racist and misogynist.) Helen Hunt plays Carol Connelly, a struggling single mother of a seriously asthmatic child. Vulnerable on the inside (and failing in her search for a decent boyfriend), she's tough on the outside, dealing daily with Melvin when he comes for breakfast at the restaurant where she's a waitress.

When Simon gets mugged and hospitalized, Melvin is forced to take care of the dog, with which he somehow bonds even though he originally hated it and tried to kill it. And when Carol leaves her job to take of her son, Melvin's compulsive routine is jeopardized, so he arranges for (and pays for) the boy to get first-rate medical care. Then Melvin and Carol — who are beginning to show signs of unrealized romantic attraction — drive Simon to Baltimore so he can ask his parents for financial aid. Finally, Carol forces Melvin to give her a compliment. He tells her she makes him "want to be a better man," and the "Beauty and the Beast" fairy tale moves to its inevitable conclusion, suggesting a "happy ending" in which Melvin makes an instant remarkable recovery and this couple become more committed to each other as a romantic couple, each "rescuing" the other.

Creator; Creator's Purpose

From his commentary on the DVD version of this movie, producer/director and co-author James L. Brooks' purpose seems to be to create a romantic comedy that will entertain the audience by making us laugh and "feel good" — as well as to produce a box office success.

Function/Purpose and Genre

The primary function is entertainment (romantic comedy).

Step 3: Deconstruction

Underlying Myths/Stereotypes

The primary myth illustrated is #7 (The love of a good and faithful true woman can change a man from a "beast" into a "prince."). Other myths portrayed in this movie include #6 (The man should NOT be shorter, weaker, younger, poorer, or less successful than the woman.), #9 (All you really need is love, so it doesn't matter if you and your lover have very different values.), and #10 (The right mate "completes you" — filling your needs and making your dreams come true.).

Evidence for Linking Myths/Stereotypes;
Specific Examples of Content and Form that Represents Embedded Values

This movie exemplifies every one of the elements of Myth #6 except physical strength, which is not demonstrated by either character. Both characters look the age of the actors portraying them: Nicholson (born in 1937 [Craddock, 2001, p. 1540]) is 26 years older then Hunt (born in 1963 [Craddock, 2001, p. 1464]) — a more likely candidate for playing her father (or as a romantic interest for her *mother*); nevertheless, it is Melvin who insultingly introduces *Carol's* no longer youthful age into the conversation. Melvin lives in a luxurious Manhattan highrise; Carol lives with her mom in a dreary apartment in a row house. He's a famous novelist; she's a waitress in a neighborhood eatery. Although he's not tall, he's taller than she is.

Of the many examples that could be described to illustrate how this movie perpetuates and reinforces the other myths, perhaps the most illustrative and important occur in two key scenes: the compliment scene (appx. 98 minutes into the film) and the final rescue scene at the end (beginning at about 125 minutes — i.e., in the last 13 minutes of the film).

Melvin specifically states a paraphrase of Myth #7 in the scene (approximately 98 minutes into the 138-minute DVD version) — at their table-for-two in an upscale Baltimore restaurant. Carol has demanded a compliment, and Melvin complies:

MELVIN

My compliment is that when you came to my house that time and told me how you'd never — well, you were there, you know … the next morning I started taking these pills.

CAROL

I don't quite know how that's a compliment for me.

MELVIN

You make me want to be a better man.

CAROL

That's maybe the best compliment of my life.

MELVIN

Then I've really overshot here 'cause I was aiming at just enough to keep you from walking out.

Right after Melvin pops his unexpectedly effective compliment, the camera zooms in very slowly on Carol for a reaction close-up. This makes time stand still, signaling to the audience that this is important and meaningful. Further, dramatic music underscores the moment — manipulating our emotions very subtly. In fact, the music is nearly identical to the transformation music in the Disney cartoon version of *Beauty and the Beast*, with celestial chimes and ascending lilts.

Of course, the mutual rescue theme has also been explicitly articulated (albeit satirically) near the beginning of the movie (at appx. 35 minutes), when Melvin is seated at his computer with his new friend (the dog who is now living with him) and writing dialog for his new book. We hear it through his voiceover: "He had made the girl happy. And what a girl! 'You saved my life,' she said." This is Melvin's fantasy as much as Carol's. Thus, the ideology expressed in this movie is that it's O.K. to be a rescuer if you are also a rescuee.

Melvin does indeed seem to have suddenly become a better person. Not only has he been taking care of Simon's dog and Helen's son's medical bills but also he's offering part of his apartment to the now homeless Simon. Back again in New York, he telephones Carol, who tells him that she doesn't know whether he's being "cute or crazy"; "I know I should stay away from you because you're not ready... ." Clearly, they still don't truly share values or lifestyles (Myth #9). Melvin is still suffering from OCD, a very serious and difficult-to-cure mental illness. Throughout the movie (until Melvin's sudden change), Carol has been shown to be kind and thoughtful, while Melvin has been shown to be selfish and mean.

Undaunted, at the end of the movie he rushes to her house in the middle of the night to rescue her from her dreary existence (Myth #10). In this other illustrative scene (in the walk-up apartment where Carol lives with her mother and son, who now is, of course, in much better health thanks to Melvin's intervention), Melvin stumbles up the stairs and says, "I had to see you." At that, there's a cut to the mother, who is standing nearby and watching. Smiling broadly, she breathes a deep sigh of happiness and puts her hand over her heart, like a character in an Italian opera. This corny but effective narrative device influences and reinforces how we are supposed to feel: Thrilled for Carol that Melvin has come to claim her.

This embedded value is further insinuated by the following ironic subtext. Carol pleads: "Why can't I just have a normal boyfriend — . . . who doesn't go nuts on me?" The mother (representing the font of wisdom) replies: "Everybody wants that, dear. It doesn't exist."

In other words, this is *as good as it gets*.

Significant Omissions

What's left out of this movie is important to consider: Would Carol have been the slightest bit interested in Melvin if he'd been a poor struggling fellow waiter? (Melvin's rescue of Carol appears to be primarily a financial one.) What does Melvin have to offer beyond mere financial security?

And how is Carol going to deal with her over-protectiveness of her son? If the relationship grows in to a long-term commitment, how would Melvin deal with having not only Simon and his dog in the apartment but also Carol and her child (and possibly her mother)? Does Carol have any friends?

We're not shown any truly devastating consequences of Melvin's behaviors. (For example, wouldn't the poor dog he cruelly threw down the *incinerator* have been *incinerated?*) And what about the seriousness of his untreated OCD and the improbability of his sudden change due to the goodness of Carol (and the cuteness of the dog)?

Other than the dinner in Baltimore (which was not that successful as a date) and the rescue scene at the end of the movie, we're not shown this couple *as* couple.

Step 4: Diagnosis

Meaning and Possible Interpretations (Preferred and Oppositional)

The preferred (dominant) reading of this text is that if we're just kind and good to even the meanest of people with lifelong hateful prejudices and serious mental illnesses, we can make more of a change (for the better, of course!) than the medical profession can. This movie also implies that the mentally ill could and would easily change their behavior and instantly become sane and happy sane if only the right person(s) administered this kindness. (The film makes it clear that Melvin has consciously discontinued treatment from his psychiatrist for a long time, and he refuses to resume treatment simply because the doctor won't fit Melvin in the minute he decides to come back.)

Moreover, the text encourages us to believe we can "fix" others pretty easily, so it shouldn't be something we would avoid doing. We ourselves might even benefit materially from our good deed, as Carol did when Melvin took charge of her son's medical care. And the beastly person will then be a better romantic partner.

Further, the writer has a disappointing view of male-female relationships: The stage direction in the script excerpt that accompanies the DVD version of the film offensively explains Carol's reaction to Melvin's "compliment": "Carol never expected the kind of praise which would so slip under her guard. She stumbles a bit — flattered, momentarily moved and his for the taking."

In addition, the preferred reading is that age and class differences don't matter at all, nor do differences in behaviors, values, and lifestyles. Finally, once having rescued each other, these two unfortunate individuals are now much better off because they have each other and, by definition, "love."

The oppositional (resistive) reading refuses to be conned by the unrealistic and dangerous messages inherent in this text (despite its comic and entertaining presentation with its excellent cast of talented performers) — primarily the too quick, too sketchily motivated major change in both lead characters as well as their unlikely pairing despite their vast age and class differences as well as their totally different values, behaviors, and lifestyles. An oppositional reading recognizes that their "rescuing" of each other at the end — she changes him and makes him become a better man who cares for others and won't have to be alone anymore; he helps her son conquer his illness (or at least control it enough to play soccer and lead a normal life) and offers the hope that she might eventually move out of her mother's cramped quarters and live in her own (Melvin's) luxurious apartment (though it might be just as cramped now that Simon is living there!) and once again have a man at her side — is not the best course for real people. Codependent individuals must first take care of themselves and become more eligible for a romantic relationship. An oppositional reading acknowledges that people do not just snap out serious mental disorders just because "someone cares." And mental illness is not a laughing matter.

Finally, the oppositional reading resists the notion that Carol is a paragon of virtue or a completely sympathetic character to be modeled. The oppositional reader recognizes her low self-esteem and asks questions. Why is she so overly protective of her son? Will she transfer these behaviors to Melvin (and Simon)? Why is she without any friends? Why does she irrationally allow one bad date (who runs off at the first sign of her ill son's spit-up) to convince her there's no one decent out there so she'd better latch onto Melvin after all? We cannot mindlessly accept that love conquers all, so we cannot rejoice for Carol or Melvin at then end.

Comparison with Rational Models

Most rational models indicate that one can't change a romantic partner into a "better person" and that trying to do so is counterproductive. Lazarus (1985) explained:

> Marriages based on the rescue fantasies of one or both partners are invariably exceedingly complex, but he end results are often predictable. To satisfy the rescuer's desire for power, approval, or control, the recipient must continue to be (or appear to be) needy. These relationships seldom stand the strain of readjustment to an equal footing. Frequently, the rescuer turns out to be far more emotionally indigent than the person being rescued. (p. 129)

He advised that because we can't change others, we should carefully select those who don't need much changing. And he cautioned: "… leave rescuing to lifeguards, firefighters, and emergency medical teams" (p. 129).

In addition to their rescuing fantasies, Carol and Melvin have exchanged more negative interactions than positive ones, which also suggests relational dissatisfaction and failure (Gottman, 1994; 1999). Their different values also represent an indicator of failure, as shown by most of the research. Clearly, they are not a peer couple (Schwartz, 1994). What they have in common are their irrational reactions to the real world.

Ironically, on the director's cut of the DVD, Brooks himself admits (at appx. 67:00) that this coupleship "defies all logic." Only the acting makes it work, he adds.

Potential Effects (Harm)

Believing in such a myth is dangerous for anyone who wants to be the fixer of Melvin-type characters or a rescuer of Carol-type people. At the extreme, people like Melvin could be dangerous — like the real-life man who broke the nose of his "girlfriend" who thought she could change him, as described by Galician (2002, p. 196). Another harmful effect is that a real person like Carol who could *not* change someone like Melvin might feel guilty or inadequate, even though it's highly unlikely that such change could take place in real life. Of course, people who obsess about fixing and rescuing others are themselves "co-dependent," another unhealthy behavior. The Karpman Drama Triangle (1968) — victim, rescuer, persecutor — predicts continuous cyclic role reversal for such individuals until they discontinue this dysfunctional practice.

Judgment/Evaluation

Like the millions of moviegoers who enjoyed this movie as well as the cinema groups that awarded it their top prizes, I found the movie engaging and entertaining. Just because the movie is unrealistic doesn't mean it's not enjoyable. However, what's disconcerting about this movie is that — unlike an unrealistic science fiction movie that we would not use as a model of real-life expectation — this movie encourages too many unhealthy mythically based possibilities for real relationships.

In that way, it operates much like the more recent Academy Award-winning film, *A Beautiful Mind*, whose subtext is also that a beautiful and good woman can change even a seriously mentally ill man into a decent partner — despite the facts that were the basis of that heavily fictionalized "bio-pic." We all know that mental illness is not a laughing matter, but because Brooks frames this film as a comedy, we laugh anyway.

I'm also concerned about the way the film pretends to acknowledge "reality," particularly in the mother's above-noted comment that Carol just isn't "realistic" in her desire for someone who isn't crazy. While this is comedic as enacted, it's also insidious in that it suggests that we should accept crazy behavior as normal and that we should expect nothing better. After all, that's "as good as it gets." Such a subtext merely serves to reinforce the fantasy of the portrayal, which for all the reasons stated above is not a healthy message — no matter how entertaining it might be for the moment.

Step 5: Design

Realistic Reframing

When Melvin gives her the "compliment," here's the dialogue I'd prefer:

CAROL

Why, Melvin — that's just about the biggest crock of - - - - I've ever heard! Sorry — but *I'M* only interested in a partner who wants to be a better man for his own sake, not because *I'M* there as the enforcer and punisher. If you ever get back into serious therapy and make some serious changes in your life that you can demonstrate for more than just one weekend or a few weeks of walking a dog, I'll certainly be there to support you. Perhaps we'll even have the basis of a healthy relationship. Meantime, I need to work on my relationship with my son — and with myself. And then I need to find some more appropriate dating partners who share my values and lifestyle.

I'd like Carol to internalize that message. In fact, I'd like Carol to refuse to go to Baltimore with Melvin. That's just too personal — especially with a stranger in New York City who not only *could* be dangerous but also actually *is* mentally unbalanced with a serious disorder (in addition to his racism, homophobia, and misogyny). I wish she'd have the guts and self-respect to get another job (any job!) rather than debasing herself by allowing Melvin to manipulate her with money. Carol should determine a re-payment plan of some sort (or secure a job with a better medical plan; alternately, she could be more assertive at the HMO), and she should allow her willing mother to care for the boy more often so she could get out and meet more appropriate potential romantic partners. (Her mother hints at how smothering Carol is, which she herself acknowledges.) She should find some girlfriends as well so she can experience a real life, which is not just about having a man. She should not accept that the realistic opposite of an idealized romantic partner is an insane one who will have to do because he's better than nothing. She should hold out for a more appropriate dating partner.

For his part, Melvin should return to his physician and seek professional help. If he shows genuine commitment, his friends — including Carol — could and should support him, though it will no doubt be a long journey.

Likelihood of Use

Unfortunately (but realistically), I rate the likelihood of Hollywood's use of my reframing of Carol's dialog above as "Slim to none."

Existing Reconstructions

The only such reconstruction that I can recall occurs in the Martin Lawrence diamond heist comedy, *The Blue Streak*. However, it's not relative to the main plot but rather just a scene very early in the film, when Lawrence's character returns after two years in prison to try to con his former girlfriend, who refuses to be fooled and promptly (and wisely) sends him packing.

Step 6: Debriefing

Personal Impact of *Dis*-illusioning;
Comparison of Personal Belief Before/After (Change/Reinforce)

I finally learned several years ago about the futility of trying to effect major changes in others, so my *dis*-illusioning of this film merely reinforced my oppositional reading. However, before I finally came to this realization, other similar films did influence and reinforce my belief in my ability to change someone's bad behavior by being good and kind. I also believed in that someone would come along and fill my needs and make my dreams come true.

Personal Harm from Myth

Until I began my study of these unrealistic portrayals and their influence, I truly believed that I could change others. Even though I knew little about the disease of alcoholism, I even thought I could "cure" it in a man I was dating. When I couldn't, I thought it was my fault that I couldn't make him "see the light" and change his self-destructive patterns. After all, in the movies, the true heroines *were* able to do this — usually just by being such a shining example. Finally, I myself "saw the light"! I learned that I'd probably never change his behavior: Only he could do that. I finally ended our relationship because I could see that he wasn't ready to change. But even then, for a while at least, I questioned what *I* could have done better so that I could have "fixed" him and transformed him into someone who would be more in line with what I wanted. It was a most depressing episode in my life.

Step 7: Dissemination

Advocacy Action Plan

Because I believe passionately in the danger of blindly accepting the myths subconsciously disseminated by the mass media — even in seemingly light-hearted "romantic comedies" like *As Good As It Gets* — I've committed myself to an action plan of media literacy promotion that is ongoing, including teaching the Sex, Love, & Romance in the Mass Media course that I created at ASU and revising this textbook, offering *Realistic Romance™* seminars and workshops, and completing my related tradebook. I also make regular appearances as a speaker at national conferences as well as for local group, and I serve as a resource for other teachers and media professionals.

Timetable of Specific Activities (Personal/Public/Professional)

For me, the personal is professional and the professional is personal, as the early feminists claimed. And for me, what's important personally and professionally should be shared with the public. Specific activities that I will undertake this year include teaching my class in all three semesters (Fall, Spring, and Summer), revising the textbook for an academic publisher before the end of the year, addressing several conventions in the Fall (including a workshop on creating and teaching a course like mine), and developing a 2003–2004 sabbatical project centered on my continuing research.

References

Brooks, J. L. (Producer & Director). (1997). *As good as it gets* [DVD]. (Available from Columbia TriStar Home Video, Culver City, CA.).

Craddock, J. (Ed.). (2001). *VideoHound®'s golden movie retreiver 2001: The complete guide to movies on videocassette and dvd.* New York: Thompson Learning.

Galician, M-L. (2002). *Sex, love, & romance in the mass media: Analysis & criticism of unrealistic portrayals & their influence.* Mahwah, NJ: Lawrence Erlbaum Associates.

Gottman, J. (1999). *The seven principles for making marriage work.* New York: Crown.

Karpman, S. (1968). Fairy tales and script drama analysis. *Transactional Analysis Bulletin, 7* (26), 39-43.

Lazarus, A. A. (1985). *Marital myths: Two dozen mistaken beliefs that can ruin a marriage or make a bad one worse.* San Luis Obispo, CA: Impact.

Schwartz, P. (1994). *Peer marriage: How love between equals really works.* New York: The Free Press.

INDEX